C/929.820942

FALMOUTH
Tel. 314901

WITHDRAWN

NF

Hatchments in
Britain; Cornwall,
Devon, Dorset,
Gloucestershire,
Hampshire, Isle of
Wight and Somerset
0850336511

C/929.820942

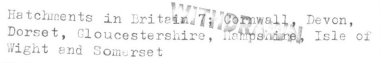

Hatchments in Britain 7; Cornwall, Devon,
Dorset, Gloucestershire, Hampshire, Isle of
Wight and Somerset

CORNWALL COUNTY COUNCIL
LIBRARIES AND ARTS DEPARTMENT

HATCHMENTS IN BRITAIN

7

Cornwall, Devon, Dorset, Gloucestershire, Hampshire, Isle of Wight and Somerset

7

Cornwall, Devon, Dorset, Gloucestershire, Hampshire, Isle of Wight and Somerset

Edited by

PETER SUMMERS, F.S.A.
and
JOHN E. TITTERTON

PHILLIMORE

1988

Published by
PHILLIMORE & CO. LTD.
Shopwyke Hall, Chichester, Sussex

ISBN 0 85033 651 1

Thanks are due to the Manifold Trust,
whose support enabled this book to be published

Printed and bound in Great Britain by
OXFORD UNIVERSITY PRESS

CONTENTS

ILLUSTRATIONS

GENERAL INTRODUCTION

Hatchments are a familiar sight to all those who visit our parish churches. They are not only decorative, but of great interest to the herald, genealogist and local historian. It is therefore surprising that — apart from local surveys in a few counties mostly in recent years — no attempt has yet been made to record them on a national scale. This series will, it is hoped, remedy the deficiency; it is proposed to publish separate volumes covering all English counties as well as Wales, Scotland and Ireland.

It is probable that no volume will be complete. Previously unrecorded hatchments will turn up from time to time; many have already been found in obscure places such as locked cupboards and ringing chambers. There are likely to be some inaccuracies, for hatchments are often hung high up in dark corners, and the colours may have faded or be darkened with age and grime. Identification is a problem if the arms do not appear anywhere in print: and even if the arms are identified, pedigrees of the family may not always be available. But enough has been done to make publication worth while; the margin to the pages will perhaps allow for pencilled amendments and notes.

Since I began the survey in 1952 many hatchments, probably evicted at the time of Victorian restorations, have been replaced in the churches when they came. On the other hand, during the same period just as many hatchments have been destroyed. An excuse often made by incumbents is that they are too far gone to repair, or that the cost of restoration is too great. Neither reason is valid. If any incumbent, or anyone who has the responsibility for the care of hatchments which need attention, will write to me, I shall be happy to tell him how the hatchments may be simply and satisfactorily restored at a minimal cost. It is hoped that the publication of this survey will help to draw attention to the importance of these heraldic records.

The diamond-shaped hatchment, which originated in the Low Countries, is a debased form of the medieval achievement — the shield, helm, and other accoutrements carried at the funeral of a noble or knight. In this country it was customary for the hatchment to be hung outside the house during the period of mourning, and thereafter be placed in the church. This practice, begun in the early 17th century, is by no means entirely obsolete, for about 80 examples have so far been recorded for the present century.

Closely allied to the diamond hatchment, and contemporary with the earlier examples, are rectangular wooden panels bearing coats of arms. As some of these bear no inscriptions and a black/white or white/black background, and as some otherwise typical hatchments bear anything from initials and a date to a long inscription beginning 'Near here lies buried . . .', it will be appreciated that it is not always easy to draw a firm line between the true hatchment and the memorial panel. Any transitional types will therefore also be listed, but armorial boards which are clearly intended as simple memorials will receive only a brief note.

With hatchments the background is of unique significance, making it possible to tell at a glance whether it is for a bachelor or spinster, husband or wife, widower or widow. These different forms all appear on the plate immediately following this introduction.

Royal Arms can easily be mistaken for hatchments, especially in the West Country where they are frequently of diamond shape and with a black background. But such examples often bear a date, which proves that they were not intended as hatchments. Royal hatchments, however, do exist, and any examples known will be included.

All hatchments are in the parish church unless otherwise stated, but by no means are they all in churches; many are in secular buildings and these, if they have no links with the parish in which they are now found, are listed at the end of the text. All hatchments recorded since the survey began are listed, including those which are now missing.

As with the previous volumes much work has been done in the past by many friends; their records have proved invaluable and greatly lessened the amount of research needed. As for those now responsible for each county who have checked and added to all these early records, I am most grateful for their care and efficiency. For the last two volumes I was greatly helped by John Titterton as Assistant Editor. For the remainder of the series he is Co-Editor.

The illustrations on the following two pages are the work of the late Mr. G. A. Harrison and will provide a valuable 'key' for those unfamiliar with the complexity of hatchment backgrounds.

One last, but important note. Every copy sold of this book helps a child in the Third World; for I have irrevocably assigned all royalties on the entire series to a charity, The Ockenden Venture.

PETER SUMMERS
Paddocks, Reading Road, Wallingford

1. MARRIED MAN
2. MARRIED WOMAN
3. BACHELOR
4. WIDOW
5. WIDOWER
6. SPINSTER

1, 2, 3 and 4—
   FOR A MAN
   SURVIVING
   TWO WIVES

5. FOR A BISHOP

6. FOR A PEER OF
    THE REALM

ABBREVIATIONS

B.P.	= Burke's *Peerage, Baronetage and Knightage*
B.L.G.	= Burke's *Landed Gentry*
B.E.P.	= Burke's *Extinct and Dormant Peerages*
B.E.B.	= Burke's *Extinct and Dormant Baronetcies*
V.C.H.	= *Victoria County History*
D.N.B.	= *Dictionary of National Biography*
M.I.	= Monumental Inscription
P.R.	= Parish Register
M.O.	= *Musgrave's Obituary*
G.M.	= *Gentleman's Magazine*
Gen. Mag.	= *Genealogists' Magazine*
M.G. & H.	= *Miscellanea Genealogica et Heraldica*
C.R.O.	= Cornwall Record Office
Mormon	
I.G.I.	= Mormon International Genealogical Index

NOTE

Blazons throughout are exactly as noted at the time of recording, not as they ought to be.

CORNWALL

by

Tom Barfett

Treslothian: For Edward Payne Pendarves, 1853
(*Photograph by Mr. John Miles*)

INTRODUCTION

Cornwall has few hatchments compared with some other counties. It is probable that there were more but some have disappeared from churches and others do not ever seem to have been in a church. To this day one is kept in a house and another was discovered in a barn.

The quarterings of some of these hatchments indicate alliances with families outside Cornwall and this in spite of difficulties involved in travelling in the 18th century. It took five days by post chaise and considerable expenses to get a boy back to Eton at the beginning of the term. Presumably the season in Bath enabled many families to strike up acquaintances with each other.

Only one church in Cornwall has a number of hatchments. This is Madron which boasts eight. Sometimes hatchments of the same family are to be found in widely separated places. That of Sir Humphry Davy, the inventor of the miners' safety lamp, and Fellow of the Royal Society, is to be found in the Geological Museum in Penzance, whereas his wife's is in a Gloucestershire church.

I would wish to express my gratitude to all who have co-operated so generously in this work and thank particularly Major-General E. M. Hall, Lieutenant-Colonel Sir Colin Cole, Garter Principal King of Arms, Miss E. A. Johnstone and Mr. Michael Galsworthy, Miss Damaris Tremayne, Lord Teviot, Mr. M. C. V. Stephens, Mrs. Donald Bray, and Mrs. D. Nicholls.

Tom Barfett,
57 Falmouth Road, Truro,
Cornwall

CROWAN
1. All black background (should be dexter background black)
Ermine on a cross gules five bezants, the Badge of Ulster (St Aubyn), impaling, Argent on a bend cotised gules three pairs of wings conjoined in lure or (Wingfield)
Crest: A falcon rising proper   Mantling: Gules and argent
Motto: In coelo quies
For Sir John St Aubyn, 4th Bt., M.P. for Cornwall, who m. Miss Wingfield, and d. 12 Oct. 1772. His widow remarried in 1782, John Baker.   (B.E.B.; M.I.)

FOWEY
1. All black background
Sable a cross or between in the first quarter a Cornish chough argent beaked and legged or, in the second a text T argent and in the third and fourth a crescent argent (Rashleigh), impaling, Or a fess chequy argent and azure in chief a rose gules, over all a bend engrailed gules (Stuart)
No crest   Mantling: Sable and argent   Motto: Mors janua vitae
For William Rashleigh, of Menabilly, who m. 1843, Catherine (d. 8 Nov. 1872), eldest dau. of Robert Walter, 11th Lord Blantyre, and d. 31 Oct. 1871.   (B.L.G. 1937 ed.)
(In view of background perhaps used subsequently for his widow)

LANDULPH
1. All black background
Azure three garbs or (Reed), impaling, Or a cross engrailed per pale gules and sable (Brookes)
Crest: A hand or holding ears of corn proper   Mantling: Gules and argent
For the Rev. John Reed, who m. Thomasine, dau. of the Rev. Job Brookes, Rector of Landulph, 1683-1720, and d. 1736.   (per Rector)

LANHYDROCK
1. Dexter background black
Azure a lion rampant or (Agar)   In pretence: Qly of six, 1st and 6th, Per pale argent and azure a saltire counterchanged a canton ermine (Hunt), 2nd, Azure three estoiles and a chief wavy or (Robartes), 3rd, Azure on a chevron argent three molets sable (Roberts), 4th, Azure billetty or a lion rampant or (Brune), 5th, Argent a griffin segreant sable (Bold)
Crest: A demi-lion rampant or   Mantling: Gules and argent
Motto: Resurgam

For Charles Bagenal Agar, who m. 1804, Anna Maria, only dau. and heir of Thomas Hunt, of Mollington Hall, Cheshire, and d. 16 June 1811.   (B.P. 1875 ed.)

LANREATH

1. Dexter background black

Sable on a cross quarter pierced argent four eagles displayed sable, a crescent argent on a crescent gules for difference (Buller), impaling, Qly azure and gules an antique temple argent, in the first quarter an eagle displayed or in the second quarter a stag passant or (Templer)
Crest: A Saracen's head couped at the shoulders proper   Mantling: Gules and argent   Motto: Aquila non capit muscas
For the Rev. Richard Buller, Rector of Lanreath, who m. Anne, dau. of James Templer, of Stover, and d.s.p. July 1826.   She d. 13 Mar. 1866.   (B.L.G. 1937 ed.)

LELANT

1. All black background

Qly, 1st and 4th, Azure six molets, three, two and one argent (Praed), 2nd, Per pale indented sable and ermine on a chevron gules five crosses formy or (Mackworth), 3rd, Gules a bend between two martlets or (Slaney)
In pretence: Qly, 1st and 4th, Argent on a chevron sable three covered cups or (Backwell), 2nd and 3rd, Azure a saltire argent
(Tyringham)   Crest: From a ducal coronet or a unicorn's head argent maned and horned or   Mantling: Gules and argent   Motto: Resurgam
For William Mackworth Praed, M.P. for St Ives 1781-1806, who m. 1778, Elizabeth Tyringham, dau. of Barnaby Backwell, and d. 9 Oct. 1833, aged 83.   (B.L.G. 1937 ed.; G.M.)

MADRON

1. Dexter background black

Gules three mailed arms embowed fesswise in pale proper (Armstrong)   In pretence: Paly of six or and azure per fess counterchanged (Gurnell)
Crest: A mailed arm embowed fesswise proper   Mantling: Gules and argent   Motto: In coelo quies   Winged skull in base
For Major John Armstrong, who m. 1806, Mary Anne, dau. and co-heir of Jonathan Gurnell, and d. May 1835.   (B.L.G. 1937 ed.)

2. All black background

On a lozenge surmounted by a cherub's head
Sable a cross engrailed and in dexter chief a molet or, on the cross a crescent azure for difference (Peyton)   In pretence: Gules a chevron between three boars statant or (Trewile)
Motto: In caelo quies   Skull in base

For Susanna, who m. Admiral John Peyton, and d. 11 Feb. 1836.
(Lake's Parochial History)

3. All black background
On a lozenge   Ermine on a bend sable two cubit arms issuing from
clouds the hands rending a horseshoe proper (Borlase)   In pretence:
Azure a falcon rising between three molets or (Pendarves)   Crest: A
wolf passant reguardant argent struck in the shoulder with an arrow
which it holds in its mouth proper   Motto: Disce mori
moriturae   Skull in base
For the Rev. Walter Borlase, Vicar of Madron, who m. Margaret, dau.
and heir of the Rev. Henry Pendarves, and d. 26 Apr. 1776.
(B.L.G. 1937 ed.)

4. Dexter background black
Azure three pheons argent (Nicholls), impaling, Gules three eagles
displayed between two bendlets or (Usticke)
Crest: A gloved cubit arm in fess holding a crossbow proper
Mantling: Gules and argent   Motto: Mors janua vitae
For William Nicholls, of Trereife, who m. Mary, dau. of William
Usticke, of Botallack, and d. 9 May 1814.   (B.L.G. 2nd ed.; family)

5. All black background
Qly, 1st and 4th, Qly gules and azure on a bend or three boars passant
azure (Le Grice), 2nd and 3rd, Per chevron or and azure three molets
counterchanged (Day), impaling, Gules on a bend cotised argent three
eagles displayed gules (Usticke)
Crest: A boar passant azure collared or   Mantling: Gules and
argent   Motto: Mors janua vitae
For the Rev. C. V. Le Grice, who m. Mary, dau. of William Usticke, of
Botallack, and relict of William Nicholls, of Trereife (No. 4), and d. 24
Dec. 1858.   (B.L.G. 2nd ed.; M.I.)

6. All black background
Qly, 1st and 4th, Argent three pheons azure (Nicholls), 2nd and 3rd,
Gules a doubleheaded eagle displayed between three fleurs-de-lys or
(Godolphin)
Crest, mantling and motto: As 4.
Probably the hatchment of John Godolphin Nicholls, who d. unm.
1815.   (B.L.G. 2nd ed.)

7. Sinister background black
Sable a chevron or ermined sable between three spearheads proper
embrued gules, the Badge of Ulster (Price), impaling, Gules three
cinquefoils argent (Lambart)
Motto: In caelo quies   Shield suspended from bow, and with a
cherub's head at each top angle of shield

For Elizabeth, dau. of Charles Lambart, of Beau Parc, co. Meath, who
m. 1795, Sir Rose Price, 1st Bt., and d. 2 Dec. 1826.   (B.P. 1965
ed.)

8. All black background
Arms: As 7, but sexfoils on Lambart coat
Crest: A dragon's head erased proper   Mantling: Gules and
argent   Motto: In coelo quies   Winged skull in base
For Sir Rose Price, 1st Bt., who d. 29 Sept. 1834.   (B.P. 1965 ed.)

MYLOR
1. All black background
On a lozenge surmounted by a coronet of a baroness
Qly, 1st and 6th, Argent a chevron between three spindles sable
(Trefusis), 2nd, Or on a fess dancetty between three billets azure each
charged with a lion rampant or three bezants (Rolle), 3rd, Argent on a
chief azure two molets or (Clinton), 4th, Qly or and gules (Say), 5th,
Azure an eagle displayed argent (Cotton), impaling, Per pale argent and
or to the dexter a lion's head erased proper and to the sinister a castle
gules (Gaulis)
Motto: Tout vient de Dieu   Supporters: Two greyhounds argent
gorged and lined or   Skull below
For Albertina Marianna, dau. of John Abraham Rodolph Gaulis of
Lausanne, and widow of Robert, 17th Baron Clinton; she d. 7 Feb.
1798.   (B.P. 1963 ed.)

2. All black background
Qly of eight, 1st, Gules three dexter arms conjoined at the shoulders or
fists clenched proper (Tremayne), 2nd, Or a chevron between three
escallops azure (Ermy), 3rd, Gules three round buckles argent
(Trenchard), 4th, Purpure three eagles displayed or (Dodscombe), 5th,
Sable three chevronels ermine (Wise), 6th, Argent three falcons sable
(   ), 7th, Gules a chevron per chevron embattled argent and azure
between three martlets proper (   ), 8th, Sable a fess between three
escallops argent (   )
Crest: Two arms embowed holding in the hands a human head erased
proper   Mantling: Gules and argent   Winged skull below
Probably for John Hearle Tremayne who m. Caroline Matilda Lemon,
and d. 27 Aug. 1851.   (Tremayne family)

PAUL
1. Dexter background black
Paly of six argent and gules on a chief azure a lion passant guardant or
(Langford), impaling, Per pale argent and or a fess nebuly between
three lions' heads erased gules in each mouth a spearhead sable
(Dansey)

Motto: In coelo quies   Shield surmounted by a gilt urn, and two
palm branches flank base of shield
Inscribed on frame: Edward Langford of Trungle, Gent, 1781.
For Edward Langford, of Trungle, who m. Elizabeth, dau. of Frederick
Dansey, of Plymouth Dock, and d. Sept. 1781.   (B.L.G. 2nd ed.;
inscr. on frame)

PELYNT, Trelawne Manor
1. All black background
Argent on a chevron sable the Badge of Ulster (Trelawny), impaling,
Argent
All within a decorative border or and gules
Crest: A wolf statant proper   Mantling: Gules   Motto: Sermoni
consona Facta   In base: Requiescat in pace 1834
Probably for the Rev. Sir Harry Trelawny, 7th Bt., who m. Anne, dau.
of the Rev. James Brown, and d. 24 Feb. 1834.   (B.P. 1963 ed.)

PENZANCE, Geological Museum
1. All brown background
Sable a chevron engrailed or ermined sable between in chief two
annulets or and in base a flame proper encompassed by a chain sable
issuant from a civic wreath or (Davy)
Crest: From a civic wreath or an elephant's head sable, ears or, tusks
argent, the trunk attached by a line to a ducal coronet around the neck
or   Mantling: Gules and argent   Motto: Igne constricto vita
secura
For Sir Humphry Davy, Bt., who m. 1812, Jane, dau. and co-heiress of
Charles Kerr, and d.s.p. at Geneva, 1829. She d. Sept.
1855.   (B.E.B.)
(The hatchment of Sir Humphry's widow is at Newnham, Glos.)

PROBUS, Trewithen House
1. Dexter background black
Argent on a saltire sable five fleurs-de-lys argent (Hawkins), impaling,
Argent two bars gules a bordure engrailed sable (Sibthorpe)
Crest: A demi-falcon wings elevated proper collared and charged with
two bendlets gules   Mantling: Sable and or   Motto: Servare
modum
For John Hawkins, of Bignor and Trewithen, who m. 1801, Mary Hester,
dau. of Colonel Humphrey Sibthorpe, and d. 4 July 1841.   (B.L.G.
2nd ed.; Family and Estate Archives)

ST ANTHONY-IN-ROSELAND

1. Dexter background black

Azure two bars and in chief a chevron or (Spry)   In pretence:
Argent two swords in saltire proper hilts and pommels or, in chief a
bunch of grapes stalked and leaved proper (Thomas)
Crest: A dove standing on a serpent nowed proper   Mantling: Azure
and or   Motto: Esperance en Dieu
For Admiral Thomas Spry, who m. 1796, Anna Maria, sister and sole
heiress of Samuel Thomas, of Tregolls, Cornwall, and d. 27 Nov.
1828.   (Burke's Commoners, Vol. 4, pp. 695-6)

2. Identical to No. 1.

ST CLEER

1. All black background

On a decorative lozenge   Argent a fess dancetty between three
eagles displayed gules (Connock), impaling, Or a fess between three
crescents sable (Hodges)
For Mary, dau. of Ambrose Hodge, of Stoke Damerel, who m. Nicholas
Connock, and d. 18 Dec. 1804, aged 82.   (Treworgey Manor
Archives)

ST ERNEY

1. Dexter background black

Argent a chevron between three garbs sable (Blake), impaling, Azure a
saltire argent between four martlets or (Smith)
Crest: On a chapeau gules and ermine a martlet argent   Date below
shield: 1770
For Richard Blake, who d. 1770.   (Jewer)

ST EWE

1. All black background

Qly, 1st and 10th, Gules three dexter arms conjoined at the shoulders
and flexed in triangle or, in dexter chief a crescent or for difference
(Tremayne), 2nd, Or a chevron between three escallops azure (Ermy),
3rd, Gules three bezants each bearing a chevron sable (Trenchard), 4th,
Purpure three eagles displayed argent (Dodscombe), 5th, Sable three
chevronels ermine (Wise), 6th, Argent a cross sable (Downing), 7th,
Argent on a fess azure three escallops argent (Pye), 8th, Gules a fess and
a canton ermine (Dart), 9th, Or three lions passant in pale sable
(Carew)   In pretence: Qly, 1st and 4th, Azure a chevron ermine
between three oak garlands or (Clotworthy), 2nd and 3rd, Azure a cross
or between in chief a dove and the letter T argent, in base two crescents
argent (Rashleigh)   In pretence: Qly, 1st and 4th, Argent on a
saltire azure five fleurs-de-lys or (Hawkins), 2nd and 3rd, Argent three
fleurs-de-lys gules in chief a label azure (Scobell)

Crest: Two arms embowed holding in the hands a head
proper   Mantling: Gules and ermine   Motto: Honor et honestas
For John Tremayne, son of Lewis Tremayne and Mary Clotworty, who
m. Grace, dau. and co-heir of Henry Hawkins, of St Austell, and d. 16
Feb. 1756.   (B.L.G. 5th ed.; College of Arms)

2. Sinister background black
Tremayne   In pretence: Qly, 1st and 4th, Argent a fess gules
between three shovellers proper (Hearle), 2nd and 3rd, Azure three
billets argent each charged with an annulet sable (Paynter)
Motto: Honor et honestas   Cherub's head above shield
For Harriet, dau. of John Hearle, who m. 1767, the Rev. Henry Hawkins
Tremayne, and d.   (B.L.G. 1937 ed.)

3. All black background
Sable a chevron between three pheons argent (Archer), impaling, Or
three bars wavy gules (Basset)
Crest: A quiver of arrows, fesswise proper, above it a pheon
or   Motto: Resurgam
For Swete Nicholas Archer, of Trelaske, who m. Anne Basset, and
d.s.p.   (Burke's Commoners, Vol. 1.)

ST GERMANS
1. All black background
Qly, 1st and 4th, Argent a fess gules between two bars gemel wavy
azure (Eliot), 2nd and 3rd, Sable on a fess between three molets or three
cross crosslets gules (Craggs), impaling, Argent a chevron between three
estoiles sable (Mordaunt)
Earl's coronet   Crest: An elephant's head couped argent doubly
collared gules   Motto: Mors janua vitae   Supporters: Two
eagles reguardant proper each charged with an ermine spot
For William, 2nd Earl of St Germans, who m. 4thly, 1814, Susan,
youngest dau. of Sir John Mordaunt, 7th Bt., and d. 19 Jan.
1845.   (B.P. 1949 ed.)

ST MAWGAN-IN-PYDAR
1. All black background
Argent a fess chequy gules and vert between three griffins' heads erased
vert each encircled with a coronet or (Willyams), impaling, Argent on a
fess sable between three trefoils slipped vert an eagle displayed or, a
bordure engrailed gules bezanty (Champion)
Crest: On a ducal coronet or a falcon proper   Motto: In coelo quies
For James Willyams, who m. 1770, Anne, dau. of William Champion, of
Warmley, Glos., and d. 10 Feb. 1828.   (B.L.G. 1939 ed.)

ST MELLION, Pentillie Castle
1. All black background
Qly, 1st and 4th, Or a saltire sable (Coryton), 2nd and 3rd, Or a cross
patonce gules in chief three griffins' heads erased sable (Tillie),
impaling, Qly, 1st and 4th, Barry of eight or and gules over all a cross
flory sable (Gower), 2nd and 3rd, Azure three laurel leaves or (Leveson)
Crest: A lion passant gules   Mantling: Gules and or   Motto: In
coelo quies
For John Tillie Coryton, of Pentillie Castle, St Mellion, who m. 1803,
Elizabeth, 2nd dau. of Adm. the Hon. John Leveson-Gower, and d. Sept.
1843.   (B.L.G. 1937 ed.)

ST TUDY
1. Dexter background black
Argent a chevron azure between seven dragons' heads erect erased, four
and three vert, with cross crosslets issuing from their mouths (Michell),
impaling, Gules on a bend argent three trefoils slipped vert (Hervey)
Crest: An arm embowed in armour in the hand a sword
proper   Mantling: Gules and argent   Motto: Resurgam
For Matthew Michell, of St Tudy, who m. Louisa Hervey, and d. 28
Aug. 1817.   (M.I.)

2. All black background
On a lozenge   Per chevron argent and azure three garbs
counterchanged (Sarel), impaling, Hervey
For Louisa, relict of Matthew Michell (No. 1), who m. 2nd, Mr. Sarel,
and d. 7 Sept. 1847.   (M.I.)

TRESLOTHAN
1. All black background
Qly of twelve, 1st, qly i. & iv. Sable a falcon rising between three
molets or (Pendarves), ii. & iii. Gules a chevron between three lions
rampant or (Wynne), 2nd, Argent a garb between three saltires gules, in
a chief a shed (Stackhouse), 3rd, Argent a greyhound courant sable
between three Cornish choughs proper within a bordure engrailed gules
charged with eight crosses formy or and as many bezants (Williams),
4th, qly i. & iv. Or three roundels gules, a crescent for difference
(Courtenay), ii. & iii. Or a lion rampant azure (Redvers), 5th, Barry
lozengy or and azure (Bellomont), 6th, Gules two lions passant or a
bend sinister azure (Acton), 7th, Azure a stag's head argent (Trethurfe),
8th, Ermine on a cross gules five bezants (St Aubyn), 9th, as 4th, 10th,
Argent on a bend cotised sable three annulets argent (Dawnay), 11th,
Argent three bars gules in chief a wolf passant argent (Reskymer), 12th,
Sable a falcon rising between three molets or (Pendarves)   In
pretence: Qly, 1st and 4th, Azure a quatrefoil pierced within an orle of
estoiles or, a canton ermine (Trist), 2nd, Azure three garbs or (Browse),

3rd, Sable a doubleheaded eagle or within a bordure engrailed argent (Hoare)

Crests: A demi-bear ermine and a lion rampant or   Mantling: Gules and argent   Motto: Nec timeo nec tumeo

For Edward Wynne Pendarves, who m. 1804, Tryphena, 3rd dau. and heiress of the Rev. Browse Trist, of Bowden, Devon, and d. 26 June 1853.   (B.L.G.; C.R.O.; College of arms; parish records)

DEVON

by

Peter Summers

Brixham 1: For John, 1st Baron Churston, 1871
(*Photograph by Mr. D. Oates*)

INTRODUCTION

A total of 86 hatchments has been recorded in the county. The great majority date from the 19th century; only one has been recorded for the 17th century and none for the 20th. They are well distributed, the largest number in any church being five, at both Fremington and Gittisham. At Powderham there are four, for the 9th Earl of Devon, the 10th Earl and his wife, and the wife of the 11th Earl. The four Poltimore hatchments are all for the Bampfylde family; the one for Sir Coplestone Bampfylde, the 2nd baronet, bears the unusually large number of 29 quarterings. It also has the distinction of being the only 17th-century hatchment in the county.

Only one hatchment recorded since the Survey began is now noted as missing, the 19th-century hatchment for Philip Stowey at Exminster.

Few of those commemorated achieved fame. Henry Addington, Viscount Sidmouth, whose hatchment is at Upottery, was Prime Minister from 1801 to 1804. The Rev. John Swete, Prebendary of Exeter, whose hatchment is at Kenton, was a well-known Devon antiquary; the son of Nicholas Tripe of Ashburton, he understandably changed his name to the more attractive one of Swete. The hatchments at both Woodbury and Yarcombe display two historic coats, the arms of Sir Francis Drake, and those of George Augustus Eliott, General Lord Heathfield, bearing as an Augmentation the arms of Gibraltar.

All the hatchments recorded are in churches. Some still remain unidentified, others with the arms identified lack the genealogical details. Two, in particular, have defied full identification despite much research; the one at Ipplepen, with an unknown coat impaling the arms of Furse, and the hatchment at Modbury, which bears a quarterly coat impaling the arms of Hele.

Most of the hatchments were originally recorded by myself and many friends to whom I am most grateful. More recently

much checking has taken place mainly by the late Ken
Armitstead; my thanks are also due to various helpers, especially to Mr. Richard Jones of Milborne Port, and Mr.
David Oates of Exeter, whose colour photographs of many of
the hatchments have been of great assistance, and who have
also been most helpful in checking blazons and in identification.

A few rectangular armorial boards have also been recorded,
at Oldridge, Plymouth St Andrew and Totnes; it is hoped
that these and others will be dealt with in a supplementary
volume when the hatchment series is completed.

Peter Summers
Paddocks, Reading Road,
Wallingford, Oxon.

ALWINGTON

1. Dexter background black

Qly, 1st and 4th, Gules a chevron ermine between three pinecones or (Pine), 2nd and 3rd, Azure crusilly or three bezants (Coffin)
Crests: Dexter, A pine tree proper cones or   Sinister, A martlet azure charged on the breast with two bezants, a molet argent for difference   Mantling: Gules and argent   Motto: Resurgam   Frame decorated with skulls and crossbones
Probably for the Rev. John Thomas Pine-Coffin, Rector of Alwington, who m. 1st, Frances, dau. of William Speke of Jordans, and 2nd, 1848, Charlotte, dau. of Samuel Chandler, of Bath, and d. 31 Jan. 1861. Or for the Rev. John Pine-Coffin, who m. 1765, Grace (d. 1830), dau. of James Rowe, of Alverdiscott, and d. 29 Apr. 1824.   (B.L.G. 5th ed.; Alumni Cantab.)

BICTON

1. Sinister background black

Or on a fess dancetty between three billets azure each charged with a lion rampant or three bezants (Rolle)   In pretence: Argent three bulls' heads cabossed sable armed or (Walrond)
Baroness's coronet   Motto: Resurgam   Supporters: Two leopards reguardant gules bezanty ducally crowned or   Cherub's head above and skull below   Frame decorated with skulls and crossbones
For Judith Maria, dau. and heir of Henry Walrond, of Bovey, who m. 1778, as his 1st wife, John, 1st Baron Rolle, and d. 1 Oct. 1820.   (B.E.P.)

BIDEFORD

1. All black background

Qly, 1st, Per fess embattled argent and sable three bucks' antlers fixed to the scalp counterchanged (Buck), 2nd, Azure three pears or (Stucley), 3rd, Per pale azure and gules three Danish axes or (Dennis), 4th, Or a lion rampant sable, on a chief indented sable three molets or (Pawley)
Crest: A lion rampant or between a buck's antlers fixed to the scalp sable, bearing over his shoulder a Danish axe sable   Mantling: Gules and ermine   Motto: Bellement et hardiment
For Lewis Buck, who d.s.p. 5 June 1781.   (Vivian's Visitation of Devon)

19

2. Dexter background black
Qly, 1st, Buck, 2nd, Stucley, 3rd Azure three Danish axes or (Dennis),
4th, Pawley, impaling, Azure a fess argent between three pears or
(Orchard)
Crest: As 1.   Mantling: Gules and argent   Motto: In coelo
quies   Skull below
For George Buck, of Affeton, who m. Anne, dau. of Paul Orchard, of
Hartland Abbey, and d. 26 Jan. 1794.   (Source, as 1.)

BLACKAWTON
1. All black background
Or on a fess invecked sable a rose between two roundels argent, in chief
a greyhound courant sable (Hayne)
Crest: A tortoise argent, thereon an eagle proper, winged argent, on its
breast a rose and on each wing a crescent argent   Mantling: Gules
and argent   Motto: In coelo salus   Skull in base
Frame decorated with skulls and crossbones
For Charles Hayne of Fuge House, who d. unm. 1821.   (B.L.G. 6th
ed.)

BRANSCOMBE
1. All black background
Qly, 1st and 4th, Per bend sinister dovetailed or and azure a lion
rampant double queued argent (Stuckey), 2nd and 3rd, Argent two bars
between three cinquefoils sable (Bartlett)
Crest: A demi-lion rampant double queued argent   Mantling: Gules
and argent   Motto: Fortitudine et fidelitate
For John Stuckey, of Weston, who d. 26 Jan. 1810, aged 91.   (M.I.)

BRIXHAM
1. All black background
Qly, 1st and 4th, Sable on a cross argent quarter-pierced sable four
eagles displayed sable (Buller), 2nd and 3rd, Argent a chevron between
three water-bougets gules (Yarde), over all the Badge of Ulster,
impaling two coats per fess, in chief, Qly, 1st and 4th, Lozengy ermine
and sable a canton gules (Patten), 2nd and 3rd, Sable a wolf rampant
and in chief three estoiles or (Wilson), and in base, Sable three demi-
lions rampant argent (Newman)
Baron's coronet   Crest: A Saracen's head couped proper   Motto:
Aquila non capit muscas   Supporters: Dexter, An ostrich proper in
the beak a horseshoe or   Sinister, An eagle sable
For John, 1st Baron Churston, who m. 1st, 1823, Elizabeth (d. 20 Feb.
1857), dau. of Thomas Wilson-Patten, of Bank Hall, Lancs., and 2nd,
1861, Caroline, dau. of Sir Robert William Newman, Bt., and d. 4 Sept.
1871.   (B.P. 1965 ed.)

2. All black background
On a lozenge surmounted by a cherub's head
Azure three wyverns' heads erased within a bordure or (Cutler),
impaling, Per pale sable and argent a chevron between three
greyhounds' heads erased and collared all counter-changed (   )
Motto: Resurgam
Possibly for Sarah, who m. John Cutler, of Upton, and d. 24 June
1824.   (M.I.)

BRIXTON
1. All black background
Per pale azure and gules three saltires couped argent (Lane)   In
pretence: Argent on a bend cotised sable a lion passant argent (Tothill)
Crest: From a crescent argent two griffins' heads addorsed azure and
gules   Mantling: Gules and argent   Motto: Celeriter
For Thomas Lane, who m. Penelope, only dau. and heir of Thomas
Tothill, of Bagtor, and d. 4 Oct. 1817, aged 75.   (B.L.G. 2nd ed.;
P.R.)

CHARDSTOCK
1. Dexter and top sinister background black
Argent a fess wavy between three bows stringed paleways gules
(Bowditch), impaling, Argent a chevron between three garbs sable
(Blake)
Crest: A sheaf of five arrows points downwards or headed and banded
gules   Mantling: Gules and argent ending in tassels or   No
motto   Skulls and crossbones on frame
Unidentified

COLYTON
1. All black background
Qly embattled or and ermine an eagle displayed sable (Piper)
Crest: A cubit arm encircled by a wreath of laurel proper grasping a
boar's head fessways sable   Mantling: Azure and or   Motto:
Feroci fortior
For General Robert Sloper Piper, who d. 1873.   (Church guide)

DARTMOUTH, St Petrox
1. Sinister background black
Qly, 1st and 4th, Argent the trunk of a tree raguly couped and
eradicated in bend proper (Holdsworth), 2nd and 3rd, Argent three
battleaxes sable (Gibbs), impaling, Sable a lion passant argent (Taylor)
Cherub's head above and skull below   Frame decorated with skulls
and crossbones
For Rebecca, dau. of Joseph Taylor, of Denbury, who m. 1755, as his 1st
wife, Arthur Holdsworth, of Widdicombe, Governor of Dartmouth
Castle, and d. May 1757.   (B.L.G. 1937 ed.)

2. Dexter and top sinister background black

Qly, as 1., impaling two coats per fess, in chief Taylor, and in base,
Argent a lion's head erased between three crescents sable (Newcombe)
Crest: In front of a wreath argent and sable a tilting spear erect point
upwards behind two others in saltire proper   Motto: In coelo
quies   Skull in base   Frame decorated with skulls and
crossbones
For Arthur Holdsworth, who m. 1st, Rebecca, dau. of Joseph Taylor,
and 2nd, Hannah (Newcombe), and d. 1777.   (B.L.G. 1937 ed.)

DARTMOUTH, St Saviour
1. Sinister background black
Or a fess sable between three wolves' heads erased proper (Seale),
impaling, Or on a fess engrailed three roundels argent, in chief a
greyhound courant sable (Hayne)
Mantling: Gules and argent   Motto: In coelo salus   Cherub's
head above and skull below
For Sarah, dau. of Charles Hayne, of Lupton, who m. John Seale, of
Mount Boone, and d. 4 Nov. 1815.   (B.P. 1965 ed.)

2. All black background
Qly, 1st and 4th, Or a fess vert between three wolves' heads erased
sable (Seale), 2nd and 3rd, Ermine on a bend sable three fleurs-de-lys
argent (   ), impaling, Argent on a fess sable three roundels argent,
in chief a greyhound courant sable (Hayne)
Crest: From a ducal coronet or a unicorn's head argent   Mantling:
Gules and argent   Motto: In coelo salus
For John Seale, who m. Sarah, dau. of Charles Hayne, of Lupton and
Fuge House, and d. 23 May 1824, aged 71.   (B.P. 1965 ed.)

3. Dexter background black
Qly, 1st and 4th, Or on a fess invecked sable a rose between two
roundels argent, in chief a greyhound courant sable (Hayne), 2nd and
3rd, Or a fess vert between three wolves' heads erased sable (Seale),
impaling, Qly, 1st and 4th, Argent a chevron gules between three
plummets or (Jennings), 2nd and 3rd, Sable a chevron argent between
three fleurs-de-lys or (   )
Crest: An eagle with wings displayed seizing a tortoise proper each wing
charged with a roundel argent and the breast with a rose
argent   Mantling: Gules and argent   Motto: In coelo salus
For Charles Seale-Hayne, of Fuge House, Dartmouth, who m. 1832,
Louisa, dau. of Richard Jennings, of Portland Place, and d. 31 Oct.
1842.   (B.P. 1965 ed.)

4. Dexter background black
Qly, 1st and 4th, Or two bars vert between three wolves' heads erased
sable, in fess point a mural coronet gules (Seale), 2nd and 3rd, Or on a

fess sable a rose between two roundels argent, in chief a greyhound courant sable (Hayne), over all the Badge of Ulster, impaling, Sable ermined argent a trefoil slipped or between three round buckles tongues pendent argent (Jodrell)
Crest: From a mural coronet or a wolf's head argent, the neck encircled with a wreath of oak leaves vert   Mantling and motto: As 3.
For Sir Henry Seale, 1st Bt., who m. 1805, Paulina Elizabeth, dau. of Sir Paul Jodrell, and d. 29 Nov. 1844.   (B.P. 1965 ed.)

DITTISHAM
1. All black background
Argent on a chevron between three dolphins naiant embowed sable a crescent argent (Kendall)
Crest: A lion passant gules   Mantling: Gules and argent
Frame decorated with skulls and crossbones
For Nicholas Narracott Kendall, d. of fever, bur. 28 Jan.
1800.   (P.R.)
(A brass plate below the hatchment is inscribed: This hatchment was restored by Messrs. Frost & Reed Ltd. of Bristol in May 1972 having been commissioned to do so by Frank Kendall Narracott his sons and grandsons)

EXMINSTER
1. Dexter background black
Gules a chevron engrailed between three boars' heads couped argent (Stowey), impaling, Per pale indented argent and azure (Hickman)
Crest: On a chapeau gules and ermine a boar passant
argent   Mantling: Gules and argent   Motto: Resurgam
For Philip Stowey, of Kenbury House, J.P., D.L., who d. 3 Sept. 1804.
His widow, Martha, d. 21 Dec. 1846.   (M.I.)
(This hatchment, recorded in 1958, is now missing)

FREMINGTON
1. Dexter background black
Qly of six, 1st and 6th, Or two chevrons between three fleurs-de-lys gules (Barbor), 2nd, Chequy sable and argent a fess gules (Acland), 3rd, Or on a fess sable a lion passant guardant argent (Hussey), 4th, Barry of eight gules and or (Poyntz), 5th, Per pale gules and sable a lion rampant between eight cross crosslets fitchy argent (Hutchinson), impaling, Ermine a lion rampant sable a canton chequy or and gules (Jeffreys)
Crest: From a ducal coronet or a bull's head gules.   Mantling:
Gules and argent   Motto: Resurgam   Frame decorated with skulls and crossbones
For George Barbor, who m. as his 2nd wife, Jane, eldest dau. of Gebriel Jeffreys, of Swansea, and d. 24 Mar. 1817. She d. 16 Mar.
1843.   (M.I.)

2. Dexter background black

Qly of six, 1st and 6th, Barbor, 2nd, Chequy or and gules a fess gules (Acland), 3rd, Argent on a fess sable a lion passant guardant argent (Hussey), 4th, Poyntz, 5th, Hutchinson
Crest: From a ducal coronet or a bull's head proper armed argent   Mantling: Or and argent   Motto: Resurgam   Frame decorated with skulls and crossbones
For William Barbor, who m. Letitia Marshall, and was bur. 12 July 1800. She was bur. 11 Jan. 1815.   (Devonshire Association, Vol. 38)

3. Sinister background black

Qly of six, 1st and 6th, Barbor, with field argent, 2nd, Acland, as 1., 3rd, Or on a fess azure a lion passant guardant or (Hussey), 4th, Barry of eight azure and or (Poyntz), 5th, Hutchinson, but lion rampant or Cherub's head above and skull and crossbones in base
Probably for Mary, née Yeo, 1st wife of No. 1, who was bur. 19 Mar. 1804.   (Source, as 2.)

4. Dexter background black

Qly, 1st and 4th, Argent a chevron between three ducks azure (Yeo), 2nd and 3rd, Sable six martlets, three, two and one argent (Arundell)
Crest: A peacock proper   Motto: In coelo quiesco
Probably for William Arundell Yeo, of Fremington, who m. Eliza, dau. of Dr. Charles Edward Bernard Clifton, and d. 20 Apr. 1862.   (M.I.)

5. All black background

Yeo arms only, but ducks beaked and legged gules
Crest: As 4.   Mantling: Azure and argent   Motto: As 4.
Probably for William Arundell Yeo, who d. at Ostend, 9 Sept. 1880.   (M.I.)

GITTISHAM
1. Dexter background black

Argent a lion rampant within a mascle sable, the Badge of Ulster (Putt), impaling, to dexter, Gules a demi-horse argent hoofed and maned or issuing out of water in base barry wavy of six argent and azure (Trevelyan), and to sinister, Sable a lion rampant between two flaunches or (Prestwood)
Crest: A lion's gamb sable holding an arrow or barbed and feathered argent   Mantling: Gules and argent   Frame decorated with skull and crossbones
For Sir Thomas Putt, 2nd Bt., who m. 1st, Margaret, dau. of Sir George Trevelyan, Bt., and 2nd,   and d.s.p. 5 May 1721.   (B.E.B.)

2. All black background
Argent a lion rampant within a mascle sable (Putt)
Crest and mantling: As 1.   Motto: Resurgam
Probably for the Rev. Thomas Putt, of Gittisham, who was bur. 26 July
1832.   (MS pedigree at Society of Genealogists)

3. Dexter background black
Argent a lion rampant within a mascle sable (Putt), impaling, Azure a
griffin segreant or a bordure engrailed ermine (Walker)
Crest and mantling: As 1.   Motto: Lex est non poena
perire   Frame decoratd with crossbones
For the Rev. William Putt, who m. Mary Walker, and d. 21 Feb. 1797.
She was bur. 19 Oct. 1808.   (Source, as 2.)

4. Dexter background black
Qly, 1st and 4th, Argent a lion rampant within a mascle sable (Putt),
2nd and 3rd, Or four chevronels gules (Every)   In pretence: Per
pale or and sable (Searle)
Crest: As 1.   Mantling: Gules and argent   Skull in
base   Frame decorated with skulls and crossbones
For Raymond Putt, who m. Anne, dau. of John Searle and d. Mar. 1751.
She d. 26 Jan. 1770.   (Source, as 2.)

5. Dexter background black
Argent a lion rampant within a mascle sable (Putt), impaling, Azure
three bars wavy argent (Samford)
Crest and mantling: As 1.   No helm   Frame decorated with
skulls and crossbones
Possibly for Raymond Putt, who d. 8 July 1812. His widow d.
1814.   (Source, as 2.; G.M.)

HACCOMBE
1. Dexter background black
Or three lions passant in pale sable, in chief the Badge of Ulster
(Carew)   In pretence: Azure an eagle displayed within a bordure
argent (Palk)
Crest: A mainmast the roundtop set off with palisadoes or, a demi-lion
issuant sable   Motto: Nil conscire sibi   Supporters: Two
antelopes gules armed and unguled or   All on a mantle gules and
ermine, tasselled or
For Sir Henry Carew, 7th Bt., who m. 1806, Elizabeth, only dau. of
Walter Palk, of Marley, and d. 31 Oct. 1830.   (B.P. 1965 ed.)

2. All black background
Carew, as 1., impaling, Azure a lion passant argent and in chief a label
of three points azure (Taylor)
Crest, motto and supporters: As 1.

For Sir Walter Palk Carew, 8th Bt., who m. 1837, Anne Frances, eldest
dau. of Major-Gen. Taylor, of Ogwell House, and d. 27 Jan.
1874.   (B.P. 1965 ed.)

HALWELL
1. Sinister background black
Azure a lion rampant crowned or (   )
No helm, crest, mantling or motto
Unidentified
(This small hatchment hangs immediately below a tablet in memory of
Ann (d. 9 Jan. 1847), widow of Majr-Gen. John Hilley Symons)

HARBERTON
1. All black background
On a cartouche surrounded by gold decoration
Azure a quatrefoil within an orle of seven estoiles or, a canton ermine
(Trist), impaling, Argent on a chevron engrailed sable between three
Cornish choughs proper three chessrooks argent (Rooke)
Crest: On a mount vert an osprey holding in its beak a fish
proper   Mantling: Gules and argent   Motto: Nec triste nec
trepide   Below the motto the dates 1741 and 1754
Frame decorated with skulls, crossbones and hourglasses
Despite dates, probably for Elizabeth, dau. of George Rooke, of Totnes,
who m. Nicholas Trist of Harberton (d. 29 July 1711), and d. 17 Nov.
1751.   (M.I. at Totnes)

IPPLEPEN
1. All black background
Or a two-towered castle with two flags flying supported by a lion
rampant to the sinister gules (   ), impaling, Gules a chevron
embattled counter-embattled between three pairs of halberds in saltire
or (Furse)
No crest   Mantling: Gules and argent   Motto: (hidden by
frame)
Unidentified

KENTON
1. All black background (should be dexter background black)
Gules two chevrons between in chief two molets and in base a rose
argent seeded or (Swete), impaling, Gules a lion rampant between ten
crescents argent (Beaumont)
Crest: A pierced molet or between two gillyflowers proper
Mantling: Gules and argent   Motto: In Christo est mea
spes   Double frame; narrow inner, decorated with skulls and
crossbones, wide outer covered with black crape

For the Rev. John Swete, Prebendary of Exeter, who m. Charlotte
Beaumont, and d. 23 Oct. 1821, aged 69. She d. 10 Dec. 1831, aged
66.   (D.N.B.; M.I.)

2. All black background
Argent a fess embattled between two escallops sable (Newcombe),
impaling, Argent a bend gules gutty argent between two choughs proper,
a chief chequy or and sable (Pleydell)
Crest: On a mural coronet or an eagle wings elevated and inverted
sable   Mantling: Sable, or and argent   Motto: Resurgam
For John Newcombe, of Starcross, who m. Harriet, dau. of Jonathan
Morton Pleydell, and d. 1 Mar. 1846.   (B.L.G. 5th ed.; M.I.)

3. Dexter background black
Gules a chevron embattled counter-embattled argent between three pairs
of halberts in saltire or headed argent (Furse), impaling, Or a millrind
sable, on a chief gules three antelopes' heads erased or (Marshall)
Crest: A tower or   No mantling or motto
For Philip Furse, who m. 1819, Elizabeth Marshall, and d.
(Mormon I.G.I.)

MODBURY
1. Sinister background black
Qly, 1st and 4th, Argent an eagle displayed with two heads azure
charged on the breast with an escutcheon, gules a bend lozengy ermine
(   ), 2nd and 3rd, Qly argent and azure in the first and fourth
quarters a lion rampant gules armed and langued azure (Pollexfen),
impaling, Gules a bend lozengy ermine (Hele)
Crest: An eagle displayed azure   Mantling: Gules and
argent   Motto: Deo adjuvante vincam   Skull in base
Unidentified

NEWTON ST CYRES
1. Dexter background black
Sable a chevron vairy or and sable between three griffins' heads erased
or a label for difference (Quicke), impaling, Or a fess embattled between
two escallops gules (Nutcombe)
Crest: A demi-antelope argent, armed or maned gules collared sable
and chained or   Mantling: Gules and argent   Motto: Petit
ardua virtus   Frame decorated with skulls and crossbones
For John Quicke, who m. 1720, Rebecca, dau. and heir of Richard
Nutcombe, and d. 1729.   (B.L.G. 5th ed.)

2. Dexter background black
Sable a chevron vairy or and sable between three griffins' heads erased
or (Quicke)   In pretence: Ermine a chevron azure (Coster)

Crest: A demi-antelope collared and chained or   Mantling and
motto: As 1.   Skull and crossbones below
For John Quicke, who m. 1759, Jane, dau. and heir of Thomas Coster,
and d. 1776.   (B.L.G. 1937 ed.; M.I.)

3. Dexter background black
Quicke, as 2., impaling, Azure three garbs or (Cumming)
Crest: A demi-antelope argent, maned gules collared and lined
or   Mantling and motto: As 1.
For John Quicke, who m. 1780, Emilia, dau. of Alexander Cumming,
and d. 12 June 1830; or for John Quicke, who m. 1814, Frances
Catherine, dau. of Thomas Cumming, of Bathampton, Somerset, and d.
9 Sept. 1859.   (B.L.G. 1937 ed.)

4. Dexter background black
Qly, 1st and 4th, Quicke, as 2., 2nd and 3rd, Ermine a chevron per pale
argent and sable (?Coster), impaling, Cumming
Crest: A demi-antelope argent, armed, ducally gorged and chained
or   Mantling and motto: As 1.   Cherub's head at each top
angle of shield and skull in base
For John Quicke, d. 12 June 1830, or for John Quicke, d. 9 Sept. 1859
(see 3.)
(There is much variation in the crest on these hatchments, but it has
been blazoned as a demi-antelope throughout, as it is presumably
intended as such)

PAIGNTON
1. All black background
Sable a stag's head cabossed between two flaunches argent, in chief a
crescent argent for difference (Parker), impaling, Azure a fox statant on
grass proper in chief a sun in splendour or (Ourry)
Crest: A cubit arm erect vested azure cuffed argent the hand holding a
stag's antler proper   Mantling: Gules and argent   Motto: In
coelo salus   Skull below
Frame decorated with skulls and crossbones
For Montagu Edmund Parker, of Whiteway, who m. 1775, Charity, dau.
of Adm. Paul Ourry, and d. Jan. 1813.   (B.P. 1963 ed.)

PLYMOUTH, St Andrew
1. Dexter background black
Per pale or and sable a chevron between three greyhounds' heads erased
counterchanged (?Olive), impaling, Ermine an anchor azure between
three escallops gules, on a chief azure a naval crown or (Parker)
Crest: A greyhound's head erased proper   Mantling: Gules and
argent   Motto: Resurgam
For Lionel Olive, who m. Elizabeth Charlotte, dau. of Sir William
George Parker, 2nd Bt., and d. 1865.   (Guide to church)

2. All black background
On a lozenge   Arms: As 1.
For Elizabeth Charlotte, widow of Lionel Olive, who d. 1867. (Guide to
church)

PLYMSTOCK
1. Dexter background black
Sable three crescents argent (Harris), impaling, Sable two bars and in
chief three molets or, a molet for difference (Freke)
Crest: An eagle displayed or   Mantling: Gules and
argent   Motto: In coelo quies   Cherub's head on frame
For Christopher Harris, who m. 1755, Susannah Freke and
d.   (M.Lic.)

2. All black background
On a lozenge   Arms: As 1.   Skull in base
For Susannah, widow of No. 1 and d.   (as 1.)

3. Dexter background black
Qly, 1st and 4th, Argent a bend between ten billets gules (Bulteel), 2nd
and 3rd, Argent a chevron engrailed gules between three ravens proper
(Crocker), impaling, Harris
Crest: From a ducal coronet or a pair of wings displayed argent billetty
gules   Mantling: Gules and argent   Motto: Loyaulte passe par
tout   Date below: 1815
For Major Thomas Hillersdon Bulteel, of Bellevue House, who m. 1791,
Miss Harris, dau. of Christopher Harris of Bellvue House, and d.
1815.   (G.M.; M.I.)

POLTIMORE
1. Dexter background black
Qly of thirty, 1st, Or on a bend gules three molets argent, in dexter
chief the Badge of Ulster (Bampfylde), 2nd, Or a maunch gules
(Hastings), 3rd, Argent a lion rampant sable (Huxham), 4th, Argent on
a fess sable three cross crosslets or a bordure azure charged with twelve
bezants (Faber), 5th, Gules on a chevron or three eagles displayed sable
(Cobham), 6th, Argent on a chevron sable between three roundels gules
three bezants (Bolhay), 7th, Argent a bend gules between three lions'
heads erased and ducally crowned sable (Pederton), 8th, Gules crusilly
argent a lion or (Pauncefoot), 9th, Argent fretty gules over all a fess
azure (Cann), 10th, Argent an annulet between three escallops gules
(Tourney), 11th, Argent two chevrons gules a label of three points azure
(St Maur), 12th, Gules a saltire vairy sable and argent (Willington),
13th, Gules ten bezants, four, three, two and one, a canton ermine
(Zouch), 14th, Gules seven mascles, three, three and one or (Quincy),
15th, Gules a cinquefoil pierced ermine (Leicester), 16th, Gules a pale
or (Grandmeisnil), 17th, Sable a lion rampant between eight cinquefoils

argent (Clifton), 18th, Argent a human heart within a double tressure flory counter-flory gules (David, Prince of Scotland), 19th, Argent a lion rampant azure (Galloway), 20th, Azure three garbs or (Peverall), 21st, Azure a boar's head erased erect argent (Lupus, Earl of Chester), 22nd, Azure six lions rampant or (Longespee), 23rd, Or crusilly a lion rampant azure (Lovell), 24th, Argent a bend sable a label of three points gules (St Lo), 25th, Azure a cross flory argent (Paveley), 26th, Argent three lions rampant sable (Cheverell), 27th, Gules three escallops within a bordure indented argent (De-Erleigh), 28th, Azure a chevron between three swans argent (Charlton), 29th, Or three piles azure (Brian), 30th, Azure a double-headed eagle displayed argent charged with a coronet or (Leofric, Earl of Mercia), impaling, Azure semy-de-lys or a lion rampant argent (Pole)
Crest: A lion's head erased sable ducally crowned or   Mantling: Gules and argent   Frame originally decorated with skulls and crossbones – now plain black
For Sir Coplestone Bampfylde, 2nd Bt., who m. 1st, Margaret Bulkeley, and 2nd, Jane, dau. of Sir Courtenay Pole, Bt., and d. 9 Feb. 1691.   (B.P. 1949 ed.; L. C. Bampfylde.)

2. Dexter background black
Or on a bend gules three molets argent a label gules for difference (Bampfylde), impaling, Chequy or and azure a fess gules (Clifford)
Crest and mantling: As 1.   Frame originally decorated with skulls and crossbones – now plain black
For Hugh Bampfylde, eldest son of Sir Coplestone Bampfylde, 2nd Bt., who m. Mary, dau. of Hugh Clifford, and d.   (Source, as 1.)

3. Dexter background black
Or on a bend gules three molets argent (Bampfylde), impaling, Sable on a cross quarterpierced argent four eagles displayed sable (Buller)
Baron's coronet   Crest: A lion's head erased sable ducally crowned or   Motto: Delectare in Domino   Supporters: Two lions reguardant sable ducally crowned gules collared or, from the collars pendent shields of the arms of Bampfylde   All on a mantle gules and argent
For George Warwick, 1st Baron Poltimore, who m. 2nd, 1836, Caroline, eldest dau. of Lt.-Gen. Frederick Buller, of Pelynt and Lanreath, Cornwall, and d. 19 Dec. 1858.   (Source, as 1.)

4. All black background
On a lozenge surmounted by a baroness's coronet
Qly of eight, 1st, Or on a bend gules three molets argent (Bampfylde), 2nd, Argent two chevrons gules a label of three points azure (St Maur), 3rd, Or a maunch gules (Hastings), 4th, Argent a lion rampant sable (Huxham), 5th, Chequy or and azure a fess gules (Clifford), 6th, Argent on a fess sable three cross crosslets or a bordure azure (Faber), 7th,

Gules a lion passant guardant between six cross crosslets argent
(Pauncefoot), 8th, Or a lion rampant between six cross crosslets azure
(Lovel), in chief the Badge of Ulster, impaling, Sable on a cross quarter-
pierced argent four eagles displayed sable, in dexter chief from a ducal
coronet or an arm embowed holding a trident proper (Buller)
Supporters: As 3., but collared gemel or
For Caroline, widow of George Warwick, 1st Baron Poltimore, who d. 29
May 1863.   (Source, as 1.)

POWDERHAM
1. All black background
Qly, 1st and 4th, Or three roundels gules (Courtenay), 2nd, Or a lion
rampant azure (Redvers), 3rd, Azure three fleurs-de-lys or (   )
Earl's coronet   Crest: A dolphin embowed proper   Mantling:
Gules and ermine   Motto: Ubi lapsus quid feci   Supporters:
Two boars argent, bristled, tusked and unguled or
For William, 9th Earl of Devon, who d. unm. 26 May 1835.   (B.P.
1965 ed.)

2. Sinister background black
Qly, 1st and 4th, Or three roundels gules a label of three points gules
(Courtenay), 2nd and 3rd, Or a lion rampant sable (Redvers), impaling,
Qly, 1st and 4th, Sable on a bend or between two horses' heads erased
argent three fleurs-de-lys sable (Pepys), 2nd and 3rd, Argent on a bend
azure three round buckles or (Leslie)
Countess's coronet   Supporters: As 1.
For Harriet Leslie, dau. of Sir Lucas Pepys, Bt., who m. 1804, as his 1st
wife, William, 10th Earl of Devon, and d. 16 Dec. 1839.   (B.P. 1965
ed.)

3. Dexter and top sinister background black
Qly, 1st and 4th, Or three roundels gules a label of three points azure
(Courtenay), 2nd and 3rd, Or a lion rampant azure (Redvers), impaling
three coats, in chief per pale and per fess, in dexter chief, Pepys, but
fleurs-de-lys azure, in sinister chief, Leslie, in base, Argent three
catherine wheels sable (Scott)
Earl's coronet   Crests: Dexter, A dolphin embowed
argent   Sinister, From a ducal coronet or a plume of seven feathers
argent   Motto: Quod verum tutum   Supporters: As 1.   All
on a mantle gules and argent
For William, 10th Earl of Devon, who m. 1st, 1804, Harriet Leslie, dau.
of Sir Lucas Pepys, Bt., and 2nd, 1849, Elizabeth Ruth (d. 17 Mar.
1914), dau. of the Rev. John Middleton Scott, and d. 19 Mar.
1859.   (B.P. 1965 ed.)

4. Sinister background black

Qly, 1st and 4th, qly i. & iv. Courtenay as 2., ii. & iii. Redvers as 3., 2nd and 3rd, qly i. Gules on a bend between six cross crosslets fitchy argent the Augmentation of Flodden (Howard), ii. Gules three lions passant guardant in pale or in chief a label of three points argent (Brotherton), iii. Chequy or azure (Warren), iv. Gules a lion rampant argent (Mowbray), impaling, Azure a bend engrailed argent cotised or (Fortescue)

Countess's coronet   Crests, and supporters: As 3.   Motto: As 1.

For Elizabeth, dau. of Hugh, 1st Earl Fortescue, who m. 1830, William Reginald, 11th Earl of Devon, and d. 27 Jan. 1867.   (B.P. 1965 ed.)

ST BUDEAUX

1. Sinister background black

Qly, 1st and 4th, Qly or and argent a lion passant guardant per pale azure and gules (Gennys), 2nd and 3rd, Argnt a falcon sable bezanty in the beak a sprig of myrtle proper (Henn)   In pretence: Gennys

Mantling: Gules and argent   Motto: Mors janua vitae

For Mary, only child and heir of John Gennys, of Whitleigh, who m. 1801, Edmund Henn, of Paradise, co. Clare (who assumed the additional name and arms of Gennys), and d. 24 Apr. 1824.   (B.L.G. 1937 ed.)

2. Dexter background black

Qly, as 1., impaling, Qly, 1st and 4th, Argent a chevron gules, in base a lion couchant sable, on a chief azure three fleurs-de-lys or (Croad), 2nd and 3rd, Argent a lion rampant gules a chief ermine (   )

Crests (on dexter side only): Dexter, An eagle displayed per pale azure and gules   Sinister, a hen pheasant proper   Motto: Deus est pures   Frame inscribed 1869

For Edmund Henn-Gennys, who m. 1836, Ann Chapell, only child and heir of John Croad, and d. 6 June 1869.   (B.L.G. 1937 ed.)

SAMPFORD SPINEY

1. All black background

Argent three griffins' heads sable langued gules between nine crosses formy gules (Hall), impaling, Argent on a chief gules two molets pierced or (St John)

Crest: A griffin's head sable langued gules   Mantling: Gules and argent   Motto: In coelo quies

For Humphrey Hall, who m. Jane, dau. of John, 10th Baron St John, and d. 25 Sept. 1801.   (B.P. 1875 ed; G.M.)

2. Dexter background black

Argent three bulls' heads cabossed sable armed or (Walrond)   In pretence: Hall

Crest: From a mural coronet (indecipherable)   Mantling: Gules and
argent   Motto: Resurgam
For Lt.-Col. Maine Swete Walrond, who m. 2nd, 1803, Elizabeth, dau.
and co-heir of Humphrey Hall, of Manadon, and d. 1817.   (B.L.G.
1937 ed.)

TAMERTON FOLIOT
1. All black background
Argent a bend engrailed sable (Radcliffe), impaling, Or a chevron azure
(Bastard)
Crest: From a mural coronet argent a bull's head sable armed and
crined or   Mantling: Gules and argent   Date below shield 1752
For Walter Radcliffe, of Warleigh, who m. 1721, Admonition, dau. of
William Bastard, of Garston, Devon, and d. 16 Nov. 1752. She d. 3 Sept.
1758.   (B.L.G. 5th ed.; Mr. Walter Radcliffe)

2. All black background
Argent a bend engrailed sable, on a canton argent a horse's head couped
sable (Radcliffe)
Crest and mantling: As 1.   Motto: Ceteris major qui melior
For Walter Radcliffe, of Warleigh, who d. 9 Apr. 1803.   (Sources, as
1.)

TAWSTOCK
1. All black background
Qly, 1st, Sable a fess between three pole-axes helved gules (Wrey), 2nd,
Argent a cross engrailed gules between four water bougets sable
(Bourchier), 3rd, France modern quartering England (Woodstock), 4th,
Azure on a bend argent cotised or between six lions rampant or three
molets gules (Bohun), over all the Badge of Ulster
Crest: A man's head in profile proper with a cap gules encircled with a
crown or   Mantling: Gules and argent   Motto: Resurgam
For either John or Christopher Wrey, sons of Sir Bourchier Wrey, 5th
Bt.   (The Heraldry of Tawstock church; B.P. 1963 ed.)

2. Sinister background black
Wrey, with Badge of Ulster, impaling, Per bend sinister ermine and
sable ermined argent a lion rampant or (Edwards)
Crest and mantling: As 1.   Motto: Bon temps viendre   Skulls
and crossbones on frame
For Mary, dau. of John Edwards, who m. as his 1st wife, Sir Bourchier
Wrey, 6th Bt., and d.s.p. 3 Sept. 1751.   (Sources, as 1).

3. Dexter background black
Qly, as 1., with Badge of Ulster, but Woodstock has a bordure
argent   In pretence: Argent a chevron gules between three dragons'

34

heads erect and couped vert, in the mouth of each a cross crosslet fitchy gules (Thresher)
Crest and mantling: As 1.   Motto: Le bon temps viendra
For Sir Bouchier Wrey, 6th Bt., who m. 2nd, Ellen, dau. of John Thresher, and d. 13 April 1784.   (Sources, as 1.)

4. Sinister background black
Wrey, with Badge of Ulster   In pretence: Argent a bend sable ermined argent between two lions rampant sable (Osborne)
No helm, crest or mantling, but gilt scrollwork above and flanking shield   Motto: In coelo quies
For Anne, dau. of John Osborne, 2nd wife of Sir Bourchier Wrey, 7th Bt., d. 26 Jan. 1813.   (Sources, as 1.)

TEIGNMOUTH, St James
1. All black background
Qly, !st, Vert six molets pierced, three, two and one argent (Praed), 2nd, Per pale indented sable and ermine, on a chevron or five roundels gules (Mackworth), 3rd, Gules a bend or between three martlets argent (Slaney), 4th, Ermine on a chief gules three lozenges or (   ), impaling, Argent three chevronels gules over all a lion rampant sable (Winthrop)
Crest: From a ducal coronet or a unicorn's head argent maned and armed or   Mantling: Gules and argent   Motto: Resurgam
For William Mackworth-Praed, of Bitton Court, who m. 1795, Elizabeth, dau. of Benjamin Winthrop, and d. 24 Feb. 1835.   (B.L.G. 1937 ed.)

2. Dexter background black
Qly, 1st and 4th, Sable a chevron or between three escallops argent (Michell), 2nd and 3rd, Or a talbot's head erased proper (   )
Crest: An arm in armour embowed proper holding a sword argent hilted or   Mantling: Gules and argent   Motto: Resurgam
For Henry Chichley Michell, who m. Catherine Ann, and d. 29 July 1806.   (M.I.)

TOPSHAM
1. All black background
Sable a chevron ermine between three castles argent (Spicer)   In pretence: Sable a stag's head cabossed between two flaunches or (Parker)
Crest: From a mural coronet or a cubit arm vested azure the hand holding a bomb fired proper   Mantling: Gules and argent   Motto: Fortissimus qui se   Skull in base
John Spicer, of Weer, who m. Elizabeth, dau. of Francis Parker, of Blagdon, and d.   (B.P. 1963 ed.)

2. All black background

Sable a chevron between in chief two escallops and in base a boar's
head couped argent langued gules (Travers)
Crest: A boar's head erased or   Mantling: Gules and
argent   Motto: Resurgam
For George Francis Travers, of H.E.I. Co., d. 7 Dec. 1851, aged
75.   (M.I.)

3. All black background

Argent a bear rampant sable muzzled or (Barnard)
Mantling: Gules and argent   Motto: In coelo quies
Probably for John Barnard, bur. 16 Feb. 1788, aged 20   (P.R.)

UPOTTERY

1. All black background

Per pale ermine and sable ermined argent, on a chevron five lozenges
all counterchanged, between three fleurs-de-lys or
(Addington)   Two escutcheons of pretence: Dexter, Azure three
demi-lions rampant or (Hammond)   Sinister, Argent an anchor
sable between three lions' heads erased gules, on a chief azure a
portcullis chained and ringed or (Scott)
Viscount's coronet   Crest: A cat-a-mountain sejant guardant proper
bezanty its dexter paw resting on a shield, Azure a mace in pale
surmounted with a regal crown or a bordure engrailed
argent   Motto: Libertas sub rege pio   Supporters: Dexter, A
stag sable ermined argent attired or collared with a chain pendent from
which is a key or   Sinister, As dexter but stag ermine   All on a
mantle gules and ermine
For Henry, 1st Viscount Sidmouth, Prime Minister 1801-4, who m. 1st,
1781, Ursula Mary, dau. and co-heir of Leonard Hammond, and 2nd,
1823, Marianne, dau. and heir of William Lord Stowell, and d. 15 Feb.
1844.   (B.P. 1965 ed.)

2. Dexter background black

Addington, impaling, Argent on a bend sable three griffins' heads erased
argent (Young)
Viscount's coronet   Crest, motto and supporters: As 1.
For William Leonard, 2nd Viscount Sidmouth, who m. 1820, Mary, dau.
of the Rev. John Young, and d. 25 Mar. 1864.   (B.P. 1965 ed.)

WASHFIELD
1. Dexter background black

Azure a chevron engrailed ermine, on a chief argent two stags' heads
cabossed gules (Nibbs), impaling, Gules a duck proper   Crest: A
stag's head cabossed gules pierced between the antlers with an arrow in
pale proper   Mantling: Gules and argent   Motto: Ego
surgam   Skull below

Probably for James Langford Nibbs, of Beauchamp Hall, who m.
Elizabeth, and d. 1795.   (M.I. under hatchment)

2. All black background
Qly, 1st and 4th, Argent a double-headed eagle displayed sable
(Worth), 2nd and 3rd, Gules two bars and in chief an eagle displayed
or, over all a bend vair (Lee)
Crest: A mailed fist erect proper grasping an eagle's leg erased
or   Mantling: Gules and argent   Motto: In coelo
quies   Skull and crossbones on frame
For John Francis Worth, son of John Worth and Jane Mary, née Lee of
Woodbury; he m. Lucy (surname unknown) and bur. 14 June
1878.   (M.I.; Mormon I.G.I., P.R.)

WEARE GIFFORD
1. All black background
On a lozenge   Azure a bend engrailed argent plain cotised or
(Fortescue) impaling, Vert on a cross argent five roundels gules
(Grenville)
Countess's coronet   Supporters: Two greyhounds argent collared
gules lined or
For Hester, dau. of the Rt. Hon. George Grenville, who m. 1782, Hugh,
1st Earl Fortescue, and d. 13 Nov. 1847.   (B.P. 1965 ed.)

WESTLEIGH
1. Dexter background black
Azure a hare salient or collared gules from which pendent a buglehorn
sable (Clevland), impaling, Chequy or and gules a chief vair
(Chichester)
Crest: A cubit arm vested azure cuffed argent the hand proper holding a
dagger in bend sinister argent hilted or   Mantling: Azure and
argent   Mottoes: (above crest) Fortuna audaces juvat   (below
shield) The righteous shall be had in everlasting remembrance
For Augustus Clevland, of Tapley, who m. 1830, Margaret Caroline,
dau. of Col. Chichester, of Arlington Court, and d. 5 July 1849, aged
68.   (M.I.)

2. All black background
Clevland arms only
Crest: As 1., with motto above, Fortuna audaces juvat   Mantling:
Azure and argent   Motto: His sun is gone down while it yet was day
Probably for Archibald Clevland, who d. 6 Nov. 1854.   (M.I.)

3. All black background
Or three bars gules (Berry), impaling, Per chevron azure and argent in
chief two falcons rising or (Stevens)

Crest: A griffin's head erased per pale or and gules   Mantling:
Gules and argent   Motto: Integer vitae sceleris que
purus   Skull in base
For Thomas Berry, who m. Honour Stevens and bur. 8 Feb.
1784.   (P.R.)

4. Sinister background black
A blank, impaling, Berry
Crest: A griffin's head erased gules   Mantling: Gules and
argent   A cherub's head at each top corner of shield, and skull
below
Possibly for Jane, elder dau. of Thomas Berry, who m. Robert Boatfield,
and d. 16 June 1756.   (M.I.)

WOLFORD Chapel
1. Dexter background black
Argent a lion rampant sable ermined argent collared or (Gwillim),
impaling, Or a fess chequy argent and azure a bordure ermine (Steward)
Crest: An arm embowed in armour the hand grasping a scimitar
proper   Mantling: Gules and argent   Motto: Mors janua vitae
For Thomas Gwillim, who m. 1726, Elizabeth, dau. of Nicholas
Steward, of Pateshall, and d. 10 Nov. 17--   (Devon & Cornwall
Notes and Queries, Vol. 21, p. 74)

2. All black background
On a lozenge surrounded by decorative scrollwork   Arms: As
1.   Cherub's head below
For Elizabeth, widow of Thomas Gwillim, who d. 13 July
1767.   (Source, as 1.)

3. All black background
Azure a fess wavy ermine between in chief two estoiles of six points and
in base a cannon fesswise or (Simcoe)   In pretence: Argent a lion
rampant sable collared or (Gwillim)
Mantling: Gules and argent, ending in gilt tassels
For John Graves Simcoe, who m. 1782, Elizabeth Posthuma, dau. of
Lieut.-Col. Thomas Gwillim, and d. 26 Oct. 1806; or for his widow who
d. 17 Jan. 1850.   (Source, as 1.)

WOODBURY
1. All black background
Qly, 1st and 4th, Sable a fess wavy between the two pole-stars argent
(Drake), 2nd, Gules on a bend or a baton proper, on a chief the arms of
Gibraltar, Azure between two pillars a castle argent, the words 'Plus
Ultra' inscribed under (Eliott), 3rd, Argent three bars and a canton
gules (Fuller), impaling, Qly, 1st and 4th, Argent a greyhound statant
proper collared or, on a chief azure three fleurs-de-lys or (Halford), 2nd

and 3rd, Per fess embattled gules and or three gates counterchanged, in
chief a cinquefoil or for difference (Yates), the Badge of Ulster over
impalement line
Crests: Centre, A ship under ruff, drawn round a terrestrial globe with a
cable rope by a hand out of the clouds, and on a scroll the words,
Auxilio divino   Dexter, A cubit arm in armour grasping a cutlass in
bend proper the wrist charged with a key in pale or   Sinister, From
a ducal coronet gules a lion's head argent   Mottoes: Centre,
Resurgam   Dexter, Fortiter et recte   Sinister, Sic parvis
magna   Broad frame covered with black crape
For Sir Thomas Trayton Fuller-Eliott-Drake, 1st Bt., who m. 1819,
Eleanor, only dau. of James Halford, of Laleham, and d. 6 June
1870.   (B.P. 1875 ed)
(Lady Fuller-Eliott-Drake's hatchment is at Yarcombe)

YARCOMBE
1. Sinister background black
Arms: As Woodbury 1., but Yates coat per fess embattled gules and or
ermined sable; and Badge of Ulster over all on dexter
Shield surrounded with gilt scrollwork and surmounted by two cherubs'
heads
For Eleanor, only dau. of James Halford, of Laleham, who m. 1819, Sir
Thomas Trayton Fuller-Eliott-Drake, 1st Bt., and d. 18 Sept.
1841.   (B.P. 1875 ed.)
(Husband's hatchment is at Woodbury)

2. All black background
Qly, 1st and 4th, Eliott, 2nd and 3rd, Drake
Baron's coronet   Crest: A cubit arm in armour the mailed hand
grasping a scimitar proper the wrist charged with a key
sable   Motto: Fortiter et recte   Supporters: Dexter, A ram
argent collared with a wreath of laurel proper   Sinister, A goat
argent collared as dexter
For Francis August, 2nd Baron Heathfield, who d.s.p.
1813.   (B.E.P.)

DORSET

by

John E. Titterton

East Lulworth Castle Chapel 5: For Edward Weld, 1755
(*Photograph courtesy of John Stark and Partners*)

INTRODUCTION

Dorset has 72 hatchments recorded since the survey started in 1952. At first sight there may seem nothing unusual or remarkable about the collection. There are no national heroes and only three members of the aristocracy. Closer examination reveals that 12 are pre-1700 with a further eight belonging to the period 1700-25. The reasons for the survival of this high proportion of earlier hatchments are uncertain, but no doubt they will contribute to the study of the development of hatchments in the final volume in the series.

The most remarkable collection, probably unique in this country, is the set of five at Marnhull where all are 17th century with no two for members of the same family. Each has some point of interest and at least three do not conform to accepted normal practice. There are, or were, three good family collections. The five recorded at Forde Abbey for the Prideaux and Gwyn families were in bad condition in 1972, and have since been destroyed. Five out of six recorded for the Weld family survive in their private chapel at Lulworth Castle and there are five for the Goodden family at Over Compton.

A further Dorset family well represented is the Strangways. There is one at Melbury Sampford House for Thomas Strangways d. 1713, and two for his descendants, the 3rd and 4th Earls of Ilchester, in the tower at Abbotsbury. A fourth Strangways hatchment is one of those at Marnhull, although the connection with the main family is uncertain. It is unusual in that the impaled Strangways arms on an all black background are surmounted by 'M.A.S.', with the date 1663 in base. The only Strangways death recorded that year is that of Mary Ann Strangways, i.e. M.A.S., the seven year old daughter of a John Strangways.

The three hatchments to members of the Drax family have had a chequered career. The current whereabouts of two is uncertain and the third is now at Morden although it was originally recorded at Charborough.

Both the earliest and latest hatchments have inscriptions on their frames and are for men with military connections. At Marnhull the hatchment for Lieutenant Filliol is dated 1631, while at Thorncombe there is the hatchment of Captain John Arthur Bragge who fought in the Crimean War.

As with many counties in the series this is the result of the efforts of several people who made the original recordings in the 1950s. Special thanks are due to Mr. R. Saunders who checked most of the blazons in 1974.

John E. Titterton
7 Cecil Aldin Drive, Tilehurst,
Reading, Berks.

ABBOTSBURY

1. All black background

Qly, 1st and 4th, Ermine on a chevron azure three foxes' heads erased or, on a canton azure a fleur-de-lys or (Fox), 2nd, Azure two lions passant paly of six argent and gules (Strangways), 3rd, Sable three talbots passant argent (Horner), impaling, Qly of six, 1st, Azure three molets argent within a double tressure flory or (Murray), 2nd, Gules three legs conjoined proper knees and spurs or (Isle of Man), 3rd, Argent on a bend azure three stags' heads cabossed or (Stanley), 4th, Gules two lions passant argent (Strange), 5th, Azure two pales or (Athole), 6th, Or a fess chequy azure and argent (Stewart)

Earl's coronet   Crest: On a chapeau azure and ermine a fox sejant or   Motto: Faire sans dire   Supporters: Two foxes, the dexter ermine fretty or, collared dovetailed azure bearing three fleurs-de-lys or, the sinister proper collared as dexter

For Henry Stephen, 3rd Earl of Ilchester, who m. 1812, Caroline Leonora, dau. of the Rt. Hon. and Rt. Rev. Lord George Murray, Bishop of St Davids, and d. 3 Jan. 1858.   (B.P. 1949 ed.)

2. Dexter background black

Qly, 1st and 4th, Fox, 2nd, Strangways, 3rd, Horner, impaling, Argent a chevron between three garbs gules (Sheffield)

Earl's coronet   Crest, motto and supporters: As 1.

For William Thomas Horner, 4th Earl of Ilchester, who m. 1857, Sophia Penelope, 2nd dau. of Sir Robert Sheffield, 4th Bt., and d.s.p. 10 Jan. 1865.   (B.P. 1949 ed.)

ALMER

1. Sinister background black

Qly of six, 1st, Chequy or and azure, on a chief gules three ostrich feathers in plume issuant or (Drax), 2nd, Gules three escallops argent a bordure engrailed argent (Erle), 3rd, Or two bars azure each charged with a barrulet dancetty argent a chief indented azure (Sawbridge), 4th, Or semy of cross crosslets fitchy gules three crescents gules (Sawbridge), 5th, Or ermined sable a cross tau surmounted by a crescent or (Wanley), 6th, Gules on a bend or ermined sable three leopards' heads azure (Stephenson)   In pretence: Qly, 1st, Chequy or and azure, on a chief gules three ostrich feathers in plume issuant or (Drax), 2nd and 3rd, Gules three escallops and a bordure engrailed argent (Erle), 4th, Azure a garb or (Grosvenor)

No crest or mantling   Shield surmounted by two cherubs' heads,
also one on either side   Motto: Mort en droit
For Jane Frances, 1st wife of John Samuel Wanley Sawbridge-Erle-Drax,
who d. 29 Dec. 1853.   (B.L.G. 5th ed.)
(Recorded in 1952 this hatchment is now missing)

BINGHAMS MELCOMBE
1. All black background
Qly, 1st, Azure a bend cotised between six crosses formy or (Bingham),
2nd, Ermine a lion rampant gules crowned or (Turbeville), 3rd, Azure
three arrows points downwards or (Chaldecott), 4th, Per bend or and
sable a bend lozengy per bend gules and argent between six fleurs-de-lys
counterchanged (Potenger)   In pretence: Per pale argent and gules a
griffin segreant counterchanged a bordure engrailed or
(Ridout)   Also impaling, Argent on a pile sable three eagles' heads
erased argent (Halsey)
Crest: An eagle rising from a rock proper   Mantling: Gules and
argent   Motto: Spes mea Christus
For Richard Bingham, who m. 1st, 1766, Sophia, dau. of Charles
Halsey, and 2nd, 1775, Elizabeth, dau. of John Ridout, of Dean's Lease,
and d. 7 Apr. 1824.   (B.L.G. 1937 ed.; M.I.)

BLANDFORD
1. All black background
On a lozenge surmounted by a cherub's head
Argent on a bend sable cotised gules three lozenges ermine (Ryves)
Unidentified

BRIDPORT
1. Dexter background black
Or three bulls' heads cabossed sable (Bull), impaling, Barry wavy of
ten argent and sable a chevron argent gutty sable between three
seahorses or (Tucker)
Crest: A bull's head couped sable   Mantling: Gules and argent
For Samuel Bull, of the South Sea House, London, who d. 1777, aged
77.   (M.I.)
(This hatchment was in poor condition when recorded in 1953, and has
since disappeared)

CRANBORNE
1. Dexter and top sinister background black
Two shields   Dexter, within the Garter, Qly, 1st and 4th, Barry of
ten argent and azure six escutcheons sable each charged with a lion
rampant argent, a crescent for difference (Cecil), 2nd and 3rd, Argent on
a pale sable a conger's head or (Gascoyne)   Sinister, Qly as dexter,
impaling two coats per fess, in chief, Gascoyne, and in base, Qly, 1st

and 4th, Argent a fess dancetty sable (West), 2nd and 3rd, Qly or and
gules a bend vair (Sackville)
Marquess's coronet   Crests: Dexter, Six arrows in saltire bound with
a belt proper   Sinister, From a ducal coronet or a conger's head
proper   Motto: Sero sed serio   Supporters: Two lions ermine
For James, 2nd Marquess of Salisbury, K.G., who m. 1st, 1821, Frances
Mary, dau. of Bamber Gascoyne, of Childwall Hall, Lancs, and 2nd,
1847, Mary Catherine, dau. of George, 5th Earl De La Warr, and d. 12
Apr. 1868.   (B.P. 1949 ed.)

2. Dexter background black
Argent six roundels and a chief embattled sable (Brouncker), impaling,
Paly of six argent and sable on a bend gules three martlets or (Burdett)
Crest: An arm in armour embowed, the gauntleted hand holding a
sword proper   Mantling: Gules and argent   Motto: Duty
For Richard Brouncker, who m. 2nd, 1836, Catherine Jane, dau. of Capt.
George Burdett, R.N., of Longtown House, co. Kildare, and d.
1862.   (B.L.G. 1937 ed.)
(This hatchment was formerly in Boveridge church)

DORCHESTER
1. All black background
Argent a greyhound courant in fess sable between three choughs proper,
within a bordure engrailed gules charged with crosses formy or and
bezants alternately (Williams)   In pretence: Or a fessy dancetty
sable ( )
Crest: A cubit arm habited sable charged with a cross formy or, the
hand proper holding an oak branch vert fructed or   Motto: In coelo
quies   Frame decorated with skull and crossbones
For Sydenham Williams, of Herrington, who m. Agnes, dau. of Nicholas
Forward, of Moor House, Devon, and d. 1757.   (B.L.G. 1937 ed.)

2. All black background
On a lozenge   Argent three battering rams in pale proper headed
and garnished azure (Bertie)   In pretence: Per saltire azure and or a
lion rampant counterchanged (Gould)
Countess's coronet   Motto: Mors mihi vita   Supporters: Dexter,
A grey friar habited proper with cross formy and rosary pendent from his
girdle   Sinister, A savage wreathed about the temples and loins with
leaves proper   Each supporter charged with a fret or   Frame
decorated with skulls, crossbones and an hour glass
For Mary, widow of General Charles Churchill, and dau. of James
Gould, of Dorchester, who m. as his second wife, Montagu, 2nd Earl of
Abingdon, and d. 10 Jan. 1757.   (B.P. 1949 d.)

FOLKE

1. All black background
Barry wavy of six argent and azure, on a chief gules three bezants
(Henning)
Crest: A seahorse per pale argent and or holding a
bezant   Mantling: Gules and argent   Motto: Undis undiq
ditant   Above the crest the date, 1658
For Dorothy, dau. of Richard Henning, of Poxwell House, who m.
Edward Moleyns of West Hall, Sherborne, and d. 17 Jun
1658.   (Per Mrs. Thomas)

2. Dexter background black
Azure a lion passant or a chief or ermined sable (Kent), impaling, Azure
five lozenges conjoined in fess a canton argent (Chafe)
Crest: A talbot's head erased or ermined sable a fetterlock about the
neck azure   Mantling: Gules and argent   Motto: Mors janua
vitae
For Charles Kent, who m. 1700, Susanna, dau. of Thomas Chafe, of
Westhall, Dorset, and d. 14 Apr. 1716, aged 49. She d. 16 Feb. 1718,
aged 53.   (M.I.)

FORDE ABBEY

1. Dexter background black
Qly, 1st and 4th, Argent a chevron sable a label of three points gules
(Prideaux), 2nd and 3rd, Or four chevronels gules (Ivory), impaling,
Argent a chevron between three pierced molets gules (Fraunceis)
Crest: A man's head in profile couped at the shoulders proper, wearing a
chapeau gules and argent   Mantling: Gules and argent
For Edmund Prideaux, who m. Amy, dau. and co-heir of John Fraunceis,
of Combe Flory, and d. 1702.   (B.L.G. 2nd ed.; M.O.)

2. All black background
On a lozenge   Arms: As 1.
For Amy, widow of Edmund Prideaux. She d.   (B.L.G. 2nd
ed.)

3. All black background
Per pale azure and gules three lions rampant argent (Gwyn)   In
pretence, and impaling, Qly, 1st and 4th, Prideaux, 2nd and 3rd,
Fraunceis
Crest: A lion rampant argent langued gules   Mantling: Gules and
argent   Cherub's head in base   Frame decorated with skull and
crossbones
For Francis Gwyn, of Lansanor, who m. 1690, Margaret, only dau. and
heiress of Edmund Prideaux, and d. 1734.   (B.L.G. 2nd ed.)

4. Sinister background black
Qly, 1st and 4th, Gwyn, 2nd and 3rd, qly i. & iv. Prideaux, ii. & iii.
Fraunceis, impaling, Azure a fess chequy argent and azure between three
bezants (Pitt)
Crest: A lion rampant argent   Mantling: Gules and
argent   Motto: Expectes et sustineas
For Lora, dau. of Geo. Pitt, of Stratfield Saye, who m. Francis Gwyn,
and d.   (B.E.P.)

5. All black background
Prideaux arms only
Crest and mantling: As 1.   Motto: In morte quies
Probably for Francis Prideaux, son of No. 1., who d. 14 Feb.
1677.   (Hutchins Dorset; M.I.)
(These hatchments were destroyed because they were in poor condition)

GILLINGHAM
1. All black background
On a lozenge within ornamental scrollwork
Qly, 1st and 4th, Argent a chevron between three storks sable (Dirdoe),
2nd and 3rd, Gules three crosses botonny in bend or (White)   In
pretence: White
For Francis Dirdoe (or one of her nine sisters), daughters and co-heirs of
Henry Dirdoe, by his wife, Dorothy, dau. and heiress of Roger White of
Sherborne. Frances d. 18 Jan. 1733.   (M.I.s)

HAMPRESTON
1. Dexter background black
Argent four barrulets between ten martlets, three, two, two, two and one
azure (Greathed), impaling, Gules a fess embattled ermine between
three crescents argent (   )
Crest: A stag's head erased proper, in its mouth an arrow in bend barb
downwards or   Mantling: Gules and argent   Motto:
Resurgam   Frame decorated with skulls, crossbones and an
hourglass
For Edward Greathed, of Uddens House, who m. Jane, and d. 18 Jan.
1803, aged 60.   (M.I. with arms in relief)

IWERNE MINSTER
1. Dexter background black
Qly, 1st and 4th, Sable in chief three talbots' heads couped argent
(Bower), 2nd and 3rd, qly i. & iv. Per fess indented gules and or in chief
three trefoils slipped or (   ), ii. & iii. Argent a chevron and in dexter
chief a trefoil slipped sable (Foote), impaling, Sable a fess between three
mascles argent (Whitaker)
Crests: Dexter, A talbot's head couped sable   Sinister, A cubit arm
vested gules cuffed or the hand proper holding three trefoils slipped

vert   Mantling: Gules and ermine   Motto: Hope well and have
well
For Thomas Bowyer Bower, of Iwerne House, who m. 1792, Harriett,
dau. of Walter Whitaker, Recorder of Shaftesbury, and d. 21 Sept.
1840.   (B.L.G. 1937 ed.)

2. Dexter background black
Qly, 1st and 4th, Sable a cinquefoil ermine and in chief three talbots'
heads couped argent (Bower), 2nd and 3rd, qly i. & iv. Or on a chief
indented gules three trefoils slipped or (   ), ii. & iii. Gules a
chevron ermine and in dexter chief a trefoil slipped argent (Foote),
impaling, Argent on a chevron sable cotised gules between three molets
gules three leopards' faces or (Creed)
Crests: Dexter, A talbot's head couped argent   Sinister, A cubit arm
vested or cuffed argent holding three trefoils slipped
argent   Mantling and motto: As 1.
For Thomas Bowyer Bower, of Iwerne House, who m. 1828, Eliza, only
dau. of William Creed, of Ballygrennan Castle, co. Limerick, and d. 8
Sept. 1868.   (Source, as 1.)

3. Dexter 3/4 background black
Two shields   Dexter, Sable in chief three talbots' heads couped or
(Bower), impaling two coats per fess, in chief, Argent a chevron between
three trefoils slipped sable (   ), and in base, Or on a chief indented
gules three trefoils slipped or (   )   Sinister, Qly, 1st and 4th,
Sable three talbots' heads couped, two and one or (Bower), 2nd and 3rd,
Or on a chief indented gules three trefoils slipped or (   ), impaling,
Azure a fess argent (   )
Crest: A talbot's head couped sable   Mantling: Gules and
argent   Motto: Mors janua vitae
Frame decorated with cherub's head and skull and crossbones
Unidentified

EAST LULWORTH, Castle chapel
1. All black background
On a lozenge   Qly, 1st and 4th, Azure a fess nebuly between three
crescents ermine (Weld), 2nd, Azure three lions rampant and a chief or
(Boton), 3rd, Argent three chevrons sable each charged with a bezant
(Fitzhugh), impaling, Vert fretty or (Whitmore)
Inscribed on frame: Sir John Weld, Knight, 1647.
Despite inscription, presumably for Frances, dau. of William Whitmore,
who m. Sir John Weld, of Arnolds Court, Middlesex, and d. 1656. He d.
1622.   (B.L.G. 1937 ed.)
(This hatchment was recorded in 1953, but has since disappeared)

2. Sinister background black, dexter grey
Weld, impaling, Sable a bend or between six fountains proper
(Stourton)   Cherub's head above
Inscribed on frame: Sir John Weld, Knight Banneret, 1674.
For Sir John Weld, of Compton Bassett, Wilts, who m. 1648, Mary, dau.
of William, Lord Stourton, and d. 12 July 1674. In view of the
background probably first used for his wife, who d. 1650.   (Source,
as 1.)

3. All black background
Qly of 12, 1st, Weld, 2nd, Vert a bend ermine (Philpot), 3rd, Vert a
cross engailed ermine (Whetnall), 4th, Azure three eagles displayed
between eight cross crosslets or (   ), 5th, Argent a fess gules
between three wolves passant proper (   ), 6th, Azure three lions
rampant or a chief argent (Boton), 7th, Or a griffin segreant sable
(   ), 8th, Or a lion rampant sable (   ), 9th, Gules a chevron
between three esquires' helmets argent (   ), 10th, Ermine on a chief
gules three martlets or (Fitzhugh), 11th, Argent three chevronels sable
each charged with a bezant (   ), 12th, Argent on a chief azure two
Catherine wheels argent (Wheler), impaling, Per fess sable and or a
pale counterchanged and three trefoils slipped or (Simeon)
Crest: From a ducal coronet or a demi-wyvern sable collared, chained
and gutty or   Mantling: Gules and argent   Motto: Nil sine
numine   Inscribed on frame: Humphrey Weld, Esq. 1722.
For Humphrey Weld, of Lulworth Castle, who m. 1701, Margaret, only
dau. of Sir James Simeon, Bt., of Chilworth, and d. 1722.   (Source,
as 1.)

4. All black background
Weld, impaling, Per pale azure and gules three lions rampant argent
(Vaughan)   Cherub's head above and winged skull below
Inscribed on frame: Edward Weld, Esq. 1761.
For Edward Weld, of Lulworth Castle, who m. 2nd, 1740, Mary
Theresa, dau. of John Vaughan, of Courtfield, and d. 8 Dec.
1761.   (Source, as 1.)

5. Dexter 2/3 background black
Qly, 1st and 4th, Weld, 2nd, qly i. & iv. Argent a lion rampant
guardant vert (   ), ii. & iii. Vert an eagle displayed argent (   ),
3rd, Qly or and gules a bordure engrailed sable charged with escallops
argent (Heveningham), impaling, two coats per pale, dexter, Gules a
bend or between two escallops argent (Petre), and sinister, Sable three
roses argent (Smyth)
Crest: From a ducal coronet or a demi-wyvern sable langued gules
collared or   Mantling: Gules and argent   Motto: Nil sine
numine
Inscribed on frame: Edward Weld, 1775.

For Edward Weld, of Lulworth, who m. 1st, 1763, Juliana, dau. of
Robert, Lord Petre, and 2nd, 1775, Mary Anne, dau. of Walter Smythe,
of Brambridge, Hants, and d. 1775.   (Source, as 1.)

6. Dexter background black

Qly, 1st, Weld, 2nd and 3rd, as 5., 4th, Per fess or and sable a pale
counterchanged and three trefoils slipped or (Simeon), impaling, Argent
on a bend azure three stags' heads cabossed or (Stanley)
Crest: From a ducal coronet or a demi-wyvern sable ermined or,
collared and chained or   Mantling: Gules and argent   Motto:
Nil sine numine
Inscribed on frame: Thomas Weld Esq. 1810.
For Thomas Weld, of Lulworth Castle, who m. 1772, Mary, eldest dau.
of Sir John Stanley Massey Stanley, Bt., of Hooton, and d.
1810.   (Source, as 1.)

St Andrew
1. Dexter background black

Qly, 1st and 4th, Azure a fess or, in chief a bear's head couped proper
muzzled argent (Baring), 2nd and 3rd, Gules a cross formy fitchy or
between three fishes hauriant argent and an orle of seven cross crosslets
fitchy or (Herring), over all a martlet for difference, impaling, Gules a
chevron between three molets or (   )
Crest: A molet or ermined sable between two wings elevated
proper   Mantling: Gules and argent   Motto:
Resurgam   Cherub's head on either side of shield
Unidentified

LYDLINCH
1. Dexter background black

Azure three sinister gauntlets or (Fane), impaling, Per chevron gules
and azure, in chief two demi-lions rampant and in base a key in pale or
(Flint)
Crest: From a ducal coronet or a bull's head argent pied sable armed or
charged on the neck with a rose proper   Mantling: Gules and
argent   Motto: Ne vile fano
For Rear Admiral Francis William Fane, R.N., of Bath, who m. 1824,
Anne, dau. of William Flint, and d. 28 Mar. 1844.   (B.L.G. 5th ed.;
M.I.)

2. Dexter background black

Qly, 1st and 4th, Azure a cross moline or (Brune), 2nd and 3rd,
Lozengy gules and ermine (Rokeley), impaling two coats per pale,
dexter, Gules a bend engrailed azure between three leopards' faces or
jessant-de-lys azure (Dennis), and sinister, Qly, 1st and 4th, Argent a
chevron between three bats displayed sable (Collier), 2nd and 3rd,

Argent a greyhound courant in fess sable collared or between three
choughs proper (Williams)
Crest: A goat passant argent armed or   Mantling: Gules and
argent   Frame decorated with hourglasses, skulls and crossbones
For Charles Brune, who m. 1st, Margaret, dau. of John Dennis, of
Pucklechurch, Gloucs., and 2nd, Jane, dau. of Henry Collier, of
Hermitage, and d. 21 Oct. 1703.   (Burke's Commoners, Vol. 1.;
Visit. Dorset 1677)

3. All black background
On a lozenge   Azure three pillars or each with a florally decorated
capital and surmounted by a four-petalled flower (?Jeffery)
No motto
Unidentified

LYTCHETT MATRAVERS
1. All black background
Qly, 1st and 4th, Per pale, paly of six argent and sable and azure
(Trenchard), 2nd and 3rd, Or a cross gules in dexter chief a lion
rampant azure (Burke)
Mantling: Gules and vert   Motto: Resurgam   Cherub's head
above shield
Unidentified

2. All black background
Arms: As 1.
Crest: A dexter arm, vambraced and embowed proper, elbowed or,
holding a trenching knife proper   Mantling: Gules and
argent   Motto: Nosce teipsum
Unidentified

3. All black background
Qly, 1st and 4th, Trenchard, 2nd and 3rd, Argent a lion rampant
between three crescents surmounted by three estoiles gules, over all a
fess azure charged with a crescent argent (Dillon)
Crest: Dexter, A dexter arm, vambraced and embowed proper, cuffed or,
charged with a cross crosslet fitchy or and holding a trenching knife
proper   Sinister, From a chapeau gules and ermine a falcon rising
or   Mantling: Vert and argent   Motto: Nosce teipsum
Unidentified

4. All black background
Arms: As 3., but in 1st quarter of Trenchard coat a cross crosslet fitchy
or
Crest, mantling and motto: As 3.
Unidentified

MARNHULL

1. All black background

Qly, 1st, Vair a canton gules (Filiol), 2nd, Azure a lion rampant between seven crosses formy or (Walsh), 3rd, Barruly azure and or on a canton or a bend lozengy sable (Frome), 4th, Vair on a canton or a cross gules (Filiol)

Crest: (On a barred helm) A lion passant guardant or   Mantling: Gules and argent   On motto scroll: LEIVETENANT FILLOLL   Inscribed on frame: DIED THE 5 JUNE AND WAS BURIED THE 8 OF JUNE IN WORTHEN ANNO DOMINI 1631

2. All black background

Sable two lions passant paly of eight argent and gules (Strangways), impaling, Gules crusilly fitchy argent three demi-woodmen argent with clubs elevated proper, on a canton sinister azure tree fleurs-de-lys or (Wood)

Crest: A lion passant paly of eight argent and gules   Mantling: Gules and argent   In top angle of hatchment is the date 1663, and in the bottom angle the initials M.A.S.

For Mary Ann, dau. of John Strangways, who d. 7 Mar. 1663/4, aged 7.   (P.R.)

3. All black background

Or two chevrons gules on a canton gules an escallop or (Pope), impaling, Sable on a fess argent between three dragons' heads erased argent three estoiles of seven points sable (Buckler)

A decorative scalloped framework surrounds the shield

For John Pope, who m. Catherine Buckler of Woolcombe Matravers, and d. 25 Sept. 1653.   (Visit. Devon 1677; M.I.; P.R.)

(There is an identical hatchment at Stalbridge)

4. All black background

Three coats per pale, 1st, Sable on a bend argent three pierced molets gules, a crescent for difference (Glisson), 2nd, Argent a doubleheaded eagle displayed gules (for Bennett), 3rd, Gules on a bend or a lion passant sable (Gollop)

A decorative scalloped framework surrounds the shield

For Elizabeth (née Gollop), 2nd wife of Gilbert Glisson, Rector of Marnhull, d. 11 Feb. 1690/1. The Rev. Gilbert Glisson, m. 1st, Melior, née Bennet, who d. 17 Mar. 1685/6, and, 3rd Mary King. He d. 12 Dec. 1736.   (P.R.)

5. All black background

On a lozenge surmounted by an esquire's helm

Gules a fess indented or between three escallops ermine (Dive)

Crest: A wyvern gules   Mantling: Gules and argent   Motto: J'espere mieux

Probably for Beatrix, sister of Grace, wife of George Hussey, of
Marnhull, and daughter of Sir Lewis Dive; she d. before
1669.   (Hutchins; Gen. Mag. 1829)
(These hatchments are remarkable in that they all appear to be 17th
century; all are below average in size, ranging from 28 in. to 37 in.
square, and all are on wood panels)

MELBURY House
1. Dexter background black
Sable two lions passant paly of six argent and gules (Strangways),
impaling, Per pale argent and gules a griffin segreant counterchanged
within a bordure engrailed or (Ridout)
Crest: out of a ducal coronet or a ?boar's head proper between two wings
azure all semy of roundels argent   Mantling: Gules and
argent   Frame decorated with hour glasses, skull and crossbones
For Thomas Strangways who m. Susannah, dau. of John Ridout of
Bristol, and d. 21 Dec. 1713.   She d. 19 Aug. 1718.   (M.I. in
church)

MORDEN
1. All black background
Chequy or and azure on a chief gules a plume of three ostrich feathers
issuant or (Drax)
Crest: A demi-dragon or   Mantling: Gules and argent   Motto:
Mors janua vitae
Possibly for Richard Edward Erle Drax, who d. unm. 13 Aug. 1828.
(This hatchment was formerly at Charborough)

2. No background as arms on lozenge fill whole area of hatchment
Azure a garb or, a crescent for difference (Grosvenor)   In pretence:
Qly of 12, 1st, Drax, 2nd, Argent on a bend sable three eagles displayed
or (Ernle), 3rd, Sable two bars and in chief three roundels argent
(Hungerford), 4th, Per pale indented gules and vert a chevron or
(Heytesbury), 5th, Barry of six ermine and gules (Hussey), 6th, Azure
three garbs and a chief or (Peverell), 7th, Argent a dragon rampant
gules (   ), 8th, Sable on a chief argent three lozenges gules
(Molyns), 9th, Gules a chevron between three escallops and a bordure
engrailed argent (Erle), 10th, Ermine three battleaxes sable (Wykes),
11th, Argent six annulets, three, two and one gules (Plecy), 12th, Sable
two lions passant argent (Dymoke)
For Sarah Frances, dau. and heiress of Edward Drax, of Charborough,
who m. 1788, Richard Erle-Drax-Grosvenor (who assumed the
additional names and arms of Erle and Drax on his marriage), and d. 15
June 1822.   (B.P. 1949 ed.)
(This hatchment was recorded in 1952, but has since disappeared)

MOTCOMBE

1. Dexter background black

Sable a fess between three mascles argent (Whitaker), impaling, Per pale or and sable, on a fess engrailed argent between three greyhounds passant counterchanged a fleur-de-lys between two lozenges gules (White)

Crest: A horse passant or   Mantling: Gules and argent   Motto: Spero meliora   On centre of motto scroll in small letters: W.W   Oct 31st 1816

For the Rev. William Whitaker, of Motcombe House, who m. Hester White Parsons, and d. 31 Oct. 1816.   (Hutchins: G.M.)

OVER COMPTON

1. Dexter background black

Azure on a bend between two demi-lions rampant erased or three lozenges vairy argent and gules (Goodden), impaling, Azure a saltire voided between four spearheads erect or (Harbin)

Crest: A griffin's head erased or with wings endorsed vairy gules and argent, in its beak an olive branch proper   Mantling: Gules and argent   Motto: In caelo quies

For Robert Goodden, who m. Abigail, dau. of Wyndham Harbin, and d. 29 Jan. 1764.   (B.L.G. 1937 ed.; M.I.)

2. All black background

On a lozenge   Arms: As 1.

Motto: Jovis omnia plena

For Abigail, widow of Robert Goodden. She d. 24 Oct. 1772.   (Sources, as 1.)

3. All black background

Qly, 1st and 4th, Goodden, 2nd and 3rd, Argent on a bend gules between two demi-lions sable three lozenges vairy azure and or (Bishop), over all a crescent argent

Crest and mantling: As 1.   Motto: Resurgam

Probably for Robert, 2nd son of Robert and Abigail Goodden, who d. 3 Oct. 1828.   (M.I.)

4. Dexter background black

Qly, 1st and 4th, Goodden, 2nd and 3rd, Argent a fess between three nags passant sable (Culliford)   In pretence: Qly, 1st, Argent a lion rampant between three escallops sable (Jeane), 2nd, Argent a saltire engrailed sable, on a chief sable a lion passant argent (for Baker), 3rd, Sable a bend raguly between six estoiles or (Payne), 4th, Sable three swords in pile argent hilted or (Powlett)

Crest, mantling and motto: As 1.

For Wyndham Goodden, who m. 1794, Mary (d. 15 Apr. 1844), 2nd
dau. and co-heiress of John Jeane, of Binfords, Somerset, and d. 17 July
1839.   (B.L.G. 1937 ed.)

5. All black background
On a lozenge surmounted by a cherub's head   Qly, 1st and 4th,
Bishop (demi-lions erased), 2nd and 3rd, Goodden
Possibly for Elizabeth, dau. of Robert and Abigail Goodden, who d.
unm. 12 Feb. 1768; or her sister Mary, who d. unm. 22 Sept.
1812.   (M.I.)

PIDDLETRENTHIDE
1. All black background
Or a bend engrailed sable charged in dexter chief with a chaplet of oak
or, on a chief azure a three-arched two-turreted bridge argent, in centre
point a label gules for cadency (Bridge)
Crest: A chaplet of oak or between two wings sable each charged with a
single arched bridge argent   Mantling: Gules and
argent   Motto: Resurgam
Unidentified

2. Dexter background black
Bridge, as 1. but not cadency mark, impaling, Argent a chevron between
three moorhens sable (Moore)
Crest: As 1., but bridge with two turrets   Mantling: Gules and
argent   Mottoes:(above) Libertas (below) Deus et patria
For Robert Bridge, who m. Juliana, dau. of A. Moore; she d. 20 Aug.
1823.   (M.I.)

3. Dexter background black
Qly sable and argent in the 1st and 4th quarters three molets argent
(Newman), over all on an escutcheon gules a portcullis crowned or
(Newman Augmentation)
Crest: A dove volant or   Mantling: Gules and argent   Motto:
Lux mea Christus
Unidentified

PORTESHAM
1. Dexter background black
Argent a chevron sable in dexter chief a fleur-de-lys gules (Riccard),
impaling, Per bend indented azure and gules two fleurs-de-lys or
(   )
Crest: Two arms in armour embowed holding up a leopard's face
argent   Mantling: Gules and argent   Motto (above crest):
Possum
Unidentified

POWERSTOCK
1. All black background
Sable three lions passant between two cotises argent (Brown), impaling,
Ermine three piles sable each charged with three bezants (Larder)
Crest: A griffin's (or dragon's) head erased proper   Mantling: Gules
and argent
For Nicholas Browne of Powerstock, who m. Anne, dau. of Robert
Larder, of Loders, and was bur. 22 Sept. 1722.   (Hutchins)

PURSE CAUNDLE
1. All black background
Per pale sable and gules a chevron or between three lions rampant or, a
martlet on the chevron for difference (Hoskyns), impaling, Or two wings
conjoined gules, on a chief gules three martlets argent (Seymer)
Crest: A lion's head ducally crowned or, breathing fire
proper   Mantle: Gules and argent   Motto: In utrumque
paratus   Date on hatchment 1694   In dexter base a mailed arm
issuing from clouds holding a sword proper   In sinister base an arm
holding a branch proper
For John Hoskyns, of Purse Caundle, who m. Mary, dau. of Robert
Seymer, of Handford, and d. 18 June 1714.   (M.I.)

STALBRIDGE
1. All black background
Or two chevrons gules, on a canton gules an escallop or (Pope),
impaling, Sable on a fess between three dragons' heads erased argent
three estoiles sable (Buckler)
On a shield decorated with fleurs-de-lys at the corners
For John Pope, of Marnhull, who m. Catherine Buckler, and d. 25 Sept.
1653.   (See Marnhull 3.)
(There is an identical hatchment at Marnhull)

STAUNTON CAUNDLE
1. All white background
Sable a chevron between three hammers argent crowned or (Blacksmiths
Company)
Crest: A winged hourglass or above a duck or sitting on a nest
proper   Mantling: Gules and argent   Motto: With hamer and
hand all artes doe stand
Possibly for John Biddlecombe, blacksmith and clockmaker of Staunton
Caundle, who d. 28 May 1741.   (Note in church)

STUDLAND
1. Dexter background black
Sable a cross engrailed ermine between four fleurs-de-lys or (Bankes),
impaling, Ermine two bars gules (Nugent)

Crest: A moor's head affronté couped at the shoulders proper, on the head a cap gules and ermine adorned with a crescent, issuant therefrom a fleur-de-lys or   Mantling: Gules and argent   Motto: Resurgam
For the Rt. Hon. George Bankes, of Studland Manor, who m. Georgina, only dau. and heir of Sir Charles Edmund Nugent, G.C.H., K.C.B., Admiral of the Fleet, and d. 5 July 1856.   (B.L.G. 1937 ed.)

2. Dexter background black
Bankes, impaling, Or a chevron azure (Bastard)
Crest, mantling and motto: As 1.
For Edmund George Bankes, who m. 1847, Rosa Louisa, dau. of H. Bastard, of Stourpaine, and d. 28 Jan. 1860.   (B.L.G. 1937 ed.)

SYDLING ST NICHOLAS
1. Dexter background black
Two shields   Dexter, Sable a fess cotised between three martlets or ermined sable, the Badge of Ulster (Smith)   In pretence: Paly of six or and azure a fess countercompony argent and sable
(Curtis)   Sinister, A wyvern sejant or (Morland)
Crest: missing   Mantling: Gules and argent
For Sir John Smith, 1st Bt., who m. 1st, Elizabeth, dau. and heiress of Robert Curtis, of Wilsthorpe, Lincs., and 2nd, Anna Eleanora, dau. of Thomas Morland, of Court Lodge, Kent, and d. 13 Nov.
1807.   (B.P. 1875 ed.)
(This hatchment was in poor condition when recorded in 1953, and has since disappeared)

2. Sinister background black
Qly, 1st and 4th, Smith, 2nd and 3rd, Curtis, in the 1st quarter the Badge of Ulster   In pretence: Qly, 1st and 4th, Azure two bars or on a chief or two escallops gules (Marriott), 2nd, Per fess embattled azure and gules three suns in splendour or (Pearson), 3rd, Or a lion rampant gules (Bosworth)   Motto: Semper fidelis
For Elizabeth Anne, 2nd dau. and co-heiress of the Rev. James Marriott, of Horsmonden, Kent, who m. 1797, Sir John Wyldbore Smith, 2nd Bt., and d. 27 Feb. 1844.   (B.P. 1875 ed.)

3. Dexter background black
Qly of six, 1st and 6th, Smith, 2nd, Curtis, 3rd, Marriott, 4th, Pearson, 5th, Bosworth; in fess point the Badge of Ulster, impaling, Qly, 1st and 4th, Gules three cross crosslets fitchy argent issuant from three crescents or (Pinney), 2nd and 3rd, Or a doubleheaded eagle sable armed or (Pretor)
Crest: A greyhound sejant gules collared and lined or, charged on the shoulder with a mascle argent   Mantling: Gules and argent   Motto: As 2.

For Sir John James Smith, 3rd Bt., who m. 1828, Frances, eldest dau. of
John Frederick Pinney, of Somerton Erleigh, and d. 3 Sept.
1862.   (B.P. 1875 ed.)

THORNCOMBE
1. Dexter background black
Or a chevron between three bulls sable (Bragge), impaling, Sable three
falcons argent belled or (   )
Crest: Out of a coronet or a bull's head sable attired or   Mantling:
Gules and or
Inscribed on frame: Captn John Arthur Bragge J.P. born 28th June 1835,
died 29th July 1922, Crimea, Sebastopol, 4th Royal Irish Dragoon
Guards
For Captain John Arthur Bragge, who d. 29 July 1922.   (Inscr. on
hatchment frame)

UP CERNE
1. All black background
On a lozenge surmounted by a skull
Argent on a bend sable three roses argent (Cary)   In pretence:
Sable a cross between four lions' heads erased argent (March)
For Catherine, dau. of Thomas March, widow of Nicholas Cary, d. 17
July 1776.   (Hutchins, iv. 157)

2. All black background
Azure on a cross quarterly ermine and or between four falcons argent
beaked and belled or a fret between four lozenges gules (White)   In
pretence: Sable a cross moline argent (Upton)
Crest: From a ducal coronet or a camel's head proper wreathed with
roses argent and gules   Mantling: Gules and argent   Motto:
(above crest) Albi Candide Judex (below) Resurgam
For Harriet, dau. and co-heiress of George Proctor Upton, of Yeovil, who
m. John White, and d. 15 Sept. 1862. He d. 11 Dec.
1830.   Hutchins, iv. 157-8)
(In view of being on shield not lozenge possibly first used for husband)

3. Sinister background black
Azure a chevron ermine between three anchors or (Batten), impaling,
Azure on a cross quarterly or and ermine between four falcons argent
beaked or a fret between four lozenges gules (White)
Crest: A sealion erect per fess gules and argent in its paws an anchor
or   Mantling: Azure and argent   Motto: Resurgam
For Grace Eleanor, dau. of John White, who m. John Batten, and d. 4
July 1883.   (B.L.G. 1937 ed.)

WHITCHURCH CANONICORUM
1. Dexter background black
Sable a chevron between three arrows points downwards argent (Floyer),
impaling, Per saltire azure and or a lion rampant counterchanged
(Gould)
Crest: A stag's head couped proper attired or in the mouth an arrow
argent   Mantling: Gules and argent
For Anthony Floyer, who m. 2nd, Sarah, dau. of John Gould, of Upwey,
and d. 17 Nov. 1701.   (Burke's Commoners, I, 606; M.I.)

WINTERBORNE CAME
1. All black background
On a lozenge surrounded by three cherubs' heads, one each side, and
one below, and bow above   Barry nebuly of six argent and gules a
bend engrailed azure (Damer)
Motto: In coelo quies
Probably for Caroline, dau. of Joseph Damer, who d. unm.
1829.   (B.P. 1949 ed.)

2. Sinister background black
Qly, 1st and 4th, Azure a chevron ermine between three arrows points
downwards barbed and flighted proper, on a chief argent two martlets
sable, on a canton gules a molet or (Dawson), 2nd and 3rd, Damer,
impaling, Qly, 1st and 4th, Sable on a bend cotised argent a rose
between two annulets gules (Conway), 2nd and 3rd, qly. i. & iv. Or on
a pile gules between six fleurs-de-lys azure three lions passant guardant
or, ii, & iii, Gules a pair of wings conjoined in lure or (Seymour)
Crests: Dexter, A cat's head affronté erased of a tabby
colour   Sinister, From a mural coronet a talbot's head azure
langued gules eared or and gules   Mottoes: (above) Tu ne cede
malis (below) Vitae via virtus   Crossed feathers in base
For Mary Georgiana Emma, dau. of Lord Hugh Seymour-Conway, who
m. 1825, the Rt. Hon. George Lionel Dawson, who took the additional
surname of Damer in 1829, and d. 30 Oct. 1848.   (B.P. 1949 ed.)

3. All black background
Arms: As 2.
Crest and mottoes: As 2.   Mantling: Gules and
argent.   Pendent below the shield are two medallions, one being
that of a military Commander of the Bath, the other being that of the
Military Order of Max Joseph of Bavaria
For the Rt. Hon. George Lionel Dawson-Damer, who d. 14 Apr.
1856.   (B.P. 1949 ed.)

GLOUCESTERSHIRE

by

Catherine Constant

Hempsted: For Rev. Samuel Lysons, 1804
(*Photograph by Mr. J. N. Tyre*)

INTRODUCTION

Most of the original work of recording the Gloucestershire hatchments was carried out by members of the Bath Heraldic Society, and all subsequent recording, checking and research have also been undertaken by Society members.

Only one hatchment has been recorded for the 17th century, that of Bernard Powlett of Alderley; and one of the present century, that of Viscount Bledisloe of Lydney. The latter is most unusual in that it was placed in the family chapel in the parish church some years before the death of Lord Bledisloe.

Several hatchments recorded at the beginning of the survey are now missing; others are sadly in need of restoration.

Mickleton has seven hatchments for the Graves family. Dyrham has nine; William Blathwayt, who was Secretary for War to William III, married Mary Wynter, and she brought him the Dyrham property. Stanway has seven, of which five are for women; the family would have wished the hatchments to hang in the church, but the minister would not allow this, so they hang in the Great Hall. Lady Guise told a similar story, how a minister did not want the family hatchments to hang in the church, but her father-in-law being the Lord of the Manor insisted, so they are still in the little church at Elmore. There was an advantage in having a father-in-law as Lord of the Manor, she said!

A canvas was found beneath several layers of wallpaper when this was stripped from a room in Home Farm House, Hempsted. It was the hatchment of a one-time rector of Rodmarton and Cherington, Samuel Lysons. He was father of Samuel Lysons, the antiquary. The hatchment was originally placed in Hempsted church and probably removed at the time of the church's restoration, and so it was lost to the church until found by Mr. Woodman in 1953.

At Newnham may be seen the hatchment of Lady Davy, widow of Sir Humphry Davy, the inventor of the safety lamp. The hatchment of Sir Humphry is in the Geological Museum in Penzance.

Although their deaths were 16 years apart, Isabel Somerset's hatchment, now in Blaise Castle Museum, and William Tonge's, at Alveston, were both painted by William Edkins, City Painter of Bristol.

George Pinney died at the Georgian House in Bristol. His hatchment hung originally in St George's Chapel, opposite his house, but when the church was closed the hatchment was transferred to his house, now a museum.

The Lord Mayor's Chapel in Bristol is the only chapel in England belonging to a corporation, and it is here that are hung hatchments of four of the mayors of Bristol.

It was with great interest and enthusiasm that the people of Gloucestershire shared my notes and told me the histories of the local families whose hatchments hang in the manor house or church. To these people I would like to express my grateful thanks.

Catherine Constant
9 Newlands Road,
Keynsham, Avon

ADLESTROP

1. Dexter background black
Qly, 1st and 4th, Gules a cross engrailed in dexter chief a lozenge argent (Leigh), 2nd and 3rd, Argent on a fess gules between three cinquefoils azure two pheons or (Lord), impaling, Argent on a cross sable a leopard's face or (Brydges)
Crest: A unicorn's head erased argent armed and maned
or   Mantling: Gules and argent   Motto: Tout vient de Dieu
For James Leigh, of Adlestrop, who m. 1755, Caroline, eldest dau. of Henry, 2nd Duke of Chandos, and d. 31 Mar. 1774.   (B.P. 1949 ed.; M.I.)

2. Dexter background black
Leigh, impaling, Argent a chevron between three moles sable armed gules (Twisleton)
Crest, mantling and motto: As 1.
For James Henry Leigh, of Adlestrop, who m. 1786, Julia Judith, eldest dau. of Thomas Twisleton, 13th Baron Saye and Sele, and d. 27 Oct. 1823.   (Sources, as 1.)

3. All black background
On a lozenge surmounted by the coronet of a baroness
Leigh, impaling, Qly, 1st and 4th, Argent a chevron sable between three molets gules (Willes), 2nd and 3rd, Or on a fess between three ravens and in centre chief a spearhead sable three crescents or (Williams)
On a mantle gules and ermine   Supporters: Two unicorns or, ducally gorged gules, pendent therefrom an escutcheon with the arms of Brydges
For Margarette, dau. of the Rev. William Shippen Willes, of Astrop House, Northants, who m. 1819, Chandos, 1st Baron Leigh, of Stoneleigh, and d. 5 Feb. 1860.   (B.P. 1949 ed.)

ALDERLEY

1. All black background   .
Qly of ten, 1st, Sable three swords in pile points downwards argent hilted or, a crescent for difference (Powlett), 2nd, Gules three water bougets ermine (   ), 3rd, Azure three bars or a bend gules, a crescent gules for difference (Poynings), 4th, Argent on a chief gules two molets or (St John), 5th, Gules two lions passant guardant argent (Delamere), 6th, Barry of six ermine and gules (Hussey), 7th, Azure a

fess between three fleurs-de-lys or (   ), 8th, Argent fretty and a
canton sable (Ireby), 9th, Argent six martlets three, two and one sable
(Delamore), 10th, Ermine a leopard's face sable between two flaunches
azure each charged with three crosses formy or (   )
Crest: A hawk rising belled or ducally gorged gules   Mantling:
Gules and argent (very full)   *c.* 3 ft. by 3 ft.   A very fine
hatchment
For Bernard Powlett, of Cottles, the son of William Powlett, who was
the son of Richard, and grandson of Lord George Powlett, 4th son of
William, 1st Marquess of Winchester; buried in the chapel at Atworth,
with his ancestors, 2 Jan. 1700.   (Mon. in Atworth church, per Misc.
Gen. et Her. Vol. IV, 2nd ser.; attribution of quarterings from same)

2. All black background
On a lozenge   Sable three lions passant in bend between four
bendlets argent, a martlet for difference (Browne), impaling, Powlett
For Mrs. Jane Brown, of Cottles, sister to Bernard Powlett, d. 26 July
1706.   (M.I. in Atworth church)

3. All black background
Qly, 1st and 4th, Argent a fess and in chief three cinquefoils sable
(Hale), 2nd and 3rd, Sable a fess engrailed between six cross-crosslets
fitchy or (?Blagden), impaling, Per fess or and argent a cross gules, in
the dexter canton a lion rampant sable and in the sinister canton a
dexter hand couped gules (Bourke)
Crest: A heron's head erased proper   Mantling: Gules and
argent   Motto: Resurgam
For Robert Hale Blagden Hale, who m. Theodosia (d. 23 Aug. 1845),
dau. of Joseph, 3rd Earl of Mayo, Archbishop of Tuam, and d. 20 Dec.
1855.   (B.L.G. 1937 ed. M.I.)

4. Dexter background black
Qly, as 3., impaling, Azure a unicorn passant argent, on a chief gules
three fleurs-de-lys or (   )
Crest: As 3.   Mantling: Gules and argent   Motto: Non est
mortale quod opto
Unidentified

ALVESTON
1. All black background
Qly, 1st and 4th, Sable a bend cotised between six martlets or (Tonge),
2nd and 3rd, Qly argent and gules on the second and third quarters a
fret or, over all a fess sable (Norris)   In pretence: Or three piles
conjoined in point sable (Bryen)
Crest: A martlet or   Mantling: Gules and argent   Motto: In
coelo quies   Inscribed in bottom corner: W. Edkins and son, pinxt,
Bristol

For William Norris Tonge, of Alveston, who m. 1804, Mary Ann, dau. of the Rev. John Bryen, of West Charlton, Somerset, and d. Apr. 1844.   (B.L.G. 5th ed.)

AUST
1. Dexter background black
Azure fretty argent on a fess gules three leopards' faces or, in dexter chief the Badge of Ulster (Cann), impaling, Argent two bars and in chief two roundels sable (Churchman)
Crest: From a mural coronet gules a plume of six feathers alternately argent and azure   Mantling: Gules and argent   Motto: Nil tam difficile
For Sir Robert Cann, 6th Bt., who m. Anne, dau. of Henry Churchman, of Aust, and d. 20 July 1765.   (B.E.B.)

BADMINTON House
1. Dexter background black
Qly, 1st, Qly France and England, a bordure compony argent and azure (Somerset), 2nd, Per pale azure and gules three lions rampant argent (Herbert), 3rd, Argent a lion rampant gules, on a chief sable three escallops argent (Russell), 4th, Or fretty gules a canton ermine (Noel), impaling, Gules a chevron ermine between ten crosses formy, six and four argent (Berkeley)
Crest: A portcullis chained or   Mantling: Gules and argent   Motto: Mutare vel timere sperno   Supporters: Dexter, A panther argent flames issuant from the mouth and ears proper, plain collared and chained or, semy of roundels, gules azure and vert   Sinister, A wyvern vert, in the mouth a sinister hand couped at the wrist gules
For Charles Noel, 4th Duke of Beaufort, who m. 1740, Elizabeth, dau. of John Berkeley, of Stoke Gifford, and d. 28 Oct. 1756.   (B.P. 1949 ed.)

2. Dexter 2/3 background black
Two cartouches   Dexter, within the Garter, Somerset   Sinister, within an ornamental wreath, Somerset, impaling, two coats per pale (1) Qly, 1st and 4th, Per pale, France and England, 2nd, Scotland, 3rd, Ireland, over all a baton sinister compony argent and azure (Fitzroy), (2) Qly, 1st and 4th, Vert three acorns or (Smith), 2nd and 3rd, Argent on a chevron engrailed between three horns gules three molets argent (Horne)
Duke's coronet   Crest, motto and supporters: As 1.
For Henry, 7th Duke of Beaufort, K.G., who m. 1st, 1814, Georgiana Frederica (d. 11 May 1821), dau. of the Hon. Henry Fitzroy, and 2nd, 1822, Emily Frances (d. 2 Oct. 1889), dau. of Charles Culling Smith, and d. 17 Nov. 1853.   (B.P. 1949 ed.)

BITTON

1. All black background

Or a lion rampant guardant gules (Creswicke), impaling, Or a bend
engrailed between two lions rampant gules (Dickinson)
Crest: From a ducal coronet or an arm in armour embowed holding a
dagger proper   Mantling: Gules and argent   Motto: In coelo
quies   Skull and crossbones in base
For Henry Creswicke, who m. Mary, dau. of Vickris Dickinson, of Queen
Charlton, and d. 4 June 1806. She d. July 1799.   (C. P. Ketchley)

BOXWELL

1. Dexter background black

Qly, 1st and 4th, Argent on a chevron between three stags' heads erased
sable three buglehorns stringed argent (Huntley), 2nd, Qly per fess
indented or and azure (Langley), 3rd, Gules eight mascles conjoined,
two, two, three and one or, a canton ermine (Ferrers)   In pretence:
Qly, 1st, Argent on a pile sable three crosses botonny argent (Webster),
2nd, Azure a bend engrailed between four annulets or (Twells), 3rd,
Argent a chevron between three cormorants sable (Warburton), 4th, Qly
argent and gules in the 2nd and 3rd qrs. a fret or (Dutton)
Crest: A talbot statant proper collared and lined or   Mantling:
Gules and argent   Motto: As the hart the water brooks
For the Rev. Richard Huntley, Rector of Boxwell, who m. 1790, Anne,
dau. and sole heir of the Ven. James Webster, Archdeacon of Gloucester,
and d. 16 Oct. 1831.   (B.L.G. 1937 ed.; M.I.)
(A very small hatchment, *c.* 18 in. by 18 in., including frame)

2. Dexter background black

Qly, 1st, Huntley, 2nd, Langley, 3rd, Ferrers, 4th, Webster, impaling,
Ermine on a fess sable three molets argent (Lyster)
Crest: As 1.   Mantling: Sable and argent   Motto: Je voul droit
avoir
For the Rev. Richard Webster Huntley, Rector of Boxwell, who m. 1830,
Mary, eldest dau. of Richard Lyster, of Rowton Castle, Salop, and d. 4
May 1857.   (B.L.G. 1937 ed.)

BRISTOL, Christ Church

1. Dexter background black

Argent a fess gules between three garbs sable (Tyndall), impaling,
Azure two keys in saltire or (Schimmelpenning)
Crest: A demi-lion rampant gules holding a garb or   Mantling:
Gules and argent
For Thomas Tyndall, who m. Marianne, dau. of Lambert
Schimmelpenning, and d. 23 July 1804, aged 40.   (M.I.)

2. All black background

On a lozenge surmounted by a cherub's head

Arms: As 1.
For Marianne, widow of Thomas Tyndall. She d. 15 Nov. 1805, aged
42.   (M.I.)

3. All black background
Tyndall, impaling, Ermine on a cross sable a castle triple-towered
argent (Hill)
Crest and mantling: As 1.
Unidentified

4. All black background
Tyndall arms only
Crest and mantling: As 1.
Unidentified

BRISTOL St George
1. Dexter background black
Qly, 1st and 4th, Gules three crescents or issuing from each a cross
crosslet fitchy argent (Pinney), 2nd and 3rd, Or a double-headed eagle
displayed vert, beaked and legged gules (Pretor), impaling, Ermine
three battleaxes sable (Weekes)
Crest: A dexter arm in armour embowed, the upper arm in fess, the hand
proper holding a cross crosslet fitchy gules   Mantling: Gules and
argent   Motto: Amor patriae
For John Pretor, who took name and arms of Pinney, m. 1772, Jane, dau.
of Major William Burt Weekes, of Nevis, and d. 23 Jan. 1818. She d. 21
Mar. 1822.   (B.L.G. 1937 ed.; M.I.)
(There is another hatchment for John Pinney in the parish church at
Somerton, Somerset)

BRISTOL SS Philip and Jacob
1. All black background (should be dexter black)
Argent a lion rampant azure (Jones), impaling, Azure a chevron between
three foxes' heads erased or (Foxcroft)
Crest: A sun in splendour or   Mantling: Gules and or   Motto:
Propositi tenax
For Thomas Jones, of Stapleton House, who m. Frances, dau. of Edward
Foxcroft, of Halsteads, and d. 11 Oct. 1837, aged 89.   (B.LG. 1937
ed.; M.I.)

2. All black background
On a lozenge   Arms: As 1.
For Frances, widow of Thomas Jones. She d. 28 Sept.
1853.   (Sources, as 1.)

3. All black background
On a lozenge surmounted by a cherub's head
Jones arms only
Motto: As 1.
Probably for Eliza, dau. of Thomas Jones, who d. 24 Dec.
1854.   (M.I.)

4. All black background
Azure three boars' heads couped argent (Gordon), impaling, Argent on a
fess gules three molets or (   )
Crest: Two cubit arms in fess with hands clasped the dexter or the
sinister azure above a heart gules   Mantling: Gules and
argent   Motto: Vivit post funera virtus
Unidentified

5. Dexter background black
Paly of six or and gules on a bend sable three molets or (Elton),
impaling, Sable a sword erect proper hilted or between two lions
rampant respectant or (Tierney)
Crest: An arm in armour proper holding a scimitar argent hilted
or   Mantling: Gules and argent   Motto: Quies in caelo
For Isaac Elton, of Stapleton House, who m. 2nd, 1768, Ann (d. 15 Aug.
1816), dau. of James Tierney of Crutched Friars, London, and d. 31
Mar. 1790.   (B.P. 1949 ed.)
(There is another hatchment for Isaac Elton at Whitestaunton,
Somerset)

BRISTOL The Lord Mayor's Chapel
1. Dexter background black
Azure a squirrel sejant or (Walter), impaling, Barry wavy of ten argent
and sable on a chevron embattled counter-embattled or five gouttes
gules (   )
Crest: A lion's head erased argent   Mantling: Gules and
argent   Motto: Mors mihi lucrum
For Henry Walter, Mayor of Bristol, 1715, who m. Mary and d. 25 Oct.
1737, aged 76.   (M.I.)

2. Dexter background black
Vairy argent and gules on a canton or a stag's head cabossed sable
(Becher), impaling, Azure, a fess nebuly in chief three estoiles or
(   )
Crest: A demi-lion rampant erased encircled with a ducal coronet
argent   Mantling: Gules and argent   Motto: Bis vivit qui bene
For John Becher, Mayor of Bristol, 1721, who d.

3. Dexter background black
Sable three crosses formy or on a chief argent three lions' heads erased sable (Benough), impaling, Argent a cross engrailed azure in the dexter chief a stag's head cabossed sable ( )
Crest: A lion's head erased gules   Mantling: Gules and argent   Motto: Deo duce
For Henry Bengough, Mayor of Bristol, 1792, who d. 10 Apr. 1818, aged 80. (M.I.)

4. All black background
Ermine three battleaxes sable (Gibbs), impaling, Or a stag trippant gules attired sable, on a canton sable a lymphad or (Parker)
Crest: An arm in armour embowed holding a battleaxe sable   Mantling: Gules and argent   Motto: Post funera virtus
For James Gibbs, Mayor of Bristol, 1842, who and d. 24 Feb. 1855, aged 62.   (M.I.)

5. Sinister background black
Gules three arrows argent, on a chief vert a boar's head erased argent ( )   In pretence: Gibbs
Cherub's head above   Motto: Post funera virtus
Unidentified

6. Sinister background black
Azure a saltire paly of ten or and ermine between four cross crosslets fitchy argent ( ), impaling, Argent a lion rampant gules between four roundels azure ( )
Motto: In coelo quies   Cherub's head above
Unidentified

BRISTOL Blaise Castle Museum
1. Sinister background black
Argent ten escallops, four, three, two and one sable, on a canton gules a molet pierced or (Kingscote), impaling, Qly France and England within a bordure compony argent and azure (Somerset)
Hatchment signed: William Edkins, City Painter, Bristol
For Isabella Frances Anne, 6th dau. of Henry, 6th Duke of Beaufort, who m. as his 1st wife, 1828, Thomas Henry Kingscote, of Kingscote, and d. 4 Feb. 1831.   (B.L.G. 1937 ed.)

2. Dexter background black
Gules on a chevron between three cinquefoils argent three leopards' faces sable, the Badge of Ulster (Smyth)
Crest: A griffin's head erased gules beaked and eared or, gorged with two bars or   Mantling: Gules and argent   Motto: Mors mihi lucrum
Unidentified

3. All black background
Arms: As 2.
Crest and mantling: As 2.   Motto: Qui capit capitur
Unidentified

4. All black background
On a rococo lozenge, with two palm branches in base
Sable a cross moline argent (Upton), impaling, Azure three pike erect
palewise in fess argent (Way)
For Eliza, dau. of Benjamin Way, of Denham Place, Bucks, who m.
1829, Thomas Upton, of Ingmire Hall, and d. 1 June 1870.   (B.L.G.
5th ed.)
(The last three hatchments were first recorded for the Survey in 1955;
they were then in the Long Ashton Estate yard)

BROMSBERROW
1. All black background
Qly, 1st, Azure a fess and in chief two molets or, a crescent or for
difference (Yate), 2nd, Gules a chevron between nine crosses formy six
and three argent (Berkeley), 3rd, Gules a stag's head cabossed or (Box),
4th, Sable a lion rampant argent (Price)   In pretence: Sable a cross
between four roses argent (Barnesley)
Crest: An elephant's head erased proper   Mantling: Gules and
argent   Motto: Mors janua vitae
For John Yate, of the Inner Temple, 2nd son of Richard Yate, of
Arlingham, who m. Jane, dau. of William Barnesley, and relict of John
Vanham, of Bibury, and d. 29 May 1749, aged 49.   (Bigland's
Gloucestershire)

2. Dexter background black
Qly, 1st, qly i. & iv. Azure a fess and in chief two molets or (Yate),
ii. & iii. Azure a chevron between three annulets or (Dobyns), 2nd, Yate,
3rd, Gules a cross between three crosses formy argent (Berkeley), 4th,
Box, stag's head couped, impaling, Qly, 1st, Argent a chevron between
three eagles' heads erased azure (Honywood), 2nd, Argent on a chevron
gules three talbots statant argent (Martin), 3rd, Sable three covered
cups within a bordure or (Boteler), 4th, Sable two bars or a chief argent
(Frognall)
Crests: An elephant's head erased proper tusks and ears or   Above
this, A falcon wings elevated and inverted proper, belled
or   Mottoes: (above top crest) Quod pudet hoc pigeat   (between
crests) Quo virtus vocat   (below shield) Omne bonum
desuper   Mantling: Gules and argent
For Robert Gorges Dobyns Yate, who m. Annabella Christiana, only
dau. of William Honywood, of Malling Abbey, Kent, and d. 26 May
1785, aged 33.   (M.I.)

NORTH CERNEY

1. Dexter background black
Argent a fess gules between three garbs sable (Tyndale), impaling,
Sable a chevron between three stags' attires argent (Cox)
Crest: A demi-lion argent holding a garb azure   Mantling: Gules
and argent   Motto: Un diem, un roy, un coeur
For Thomas Tyndale, who m. Elizabeth (d. 23 Mar. 1821, aged 87),
dau. of Charles Cox, and d. 29 July 1783, aged 52.   (M.I.s in S.
transept)

DIDBROOK

1. Dexter background black
Qly, 1st and 4th, Argent a greyhound passant and in chief a molet sable
(Holford), 2nd and 3rd, Azure a lion passant argent, on a chief indented
or three molets sable (Stayner), impaling, Or on a fess gules beween in
chief a bull's head erased and in base a galley sable a saltire argent
(Richardson)
Crest: A greyhound's head erased sable   Mantling: Gules and
argent   Motto: Resurgam
Unidentified

2. Dexter background black
Qly, 1st and 4th, Sable on a fess between three elephants' heads erased
argent three molets sable (Pratt), 2nd and 3rd, Or in chief an escallop
sable between two bendlets sinister gules (Tracy), impaling, Or on a
fess azure between in chief a bull's head erased and in base a galley
sable a saltire argent (Richardson)
Crest: An elephant's head erased argent   Mantling: Gules and
argent   Motto: In coelo quies   Skull below
Unidentified

DODINGTON

1. Dexter background black
Qly, 1st and 4th, Argent a fess embattled counter-embattled sable fretty
gules between three lions passant gules (Codrington), 2nd and 3rd,
Sable on a bend argent three roses gules, in sinister chief a dexter hand
couped argent (   ), impaling, Qly France and England a bordure
compony argent and azure (Somerset), the Badge of Ulster over
impalement line
Crest: From a ducal coronet or a dragon's head couped gules between
two dragons' wings chequy or and azure   Mantling: Gules and
argent   Motto: Immersabilis est vera virtus   On a wood panel
For Christopher William Codrington, of Dodington, M.P. for East
Gloucester, who m. 1836, Georgiana Charlotte Anne, dau. of Henry, 7th
Duke of Beaufort, K.G., and d. 24 June 1864.   (B.P. 1949 ed.)

DOWDESWELL

1. All black background
On a lozenge surmounted by a cherub's head
Argent a molet sable, on a chief gules a fleur-de-lys or (Rogers)
Motto: Vigila et ora
Probably for Hester Rogers, who succeeded to Dowdeswell estates on the
death of her uncle, Edward Rogers, and d. unm. 1 Apr.
1846.   (B.L.G. 5th ed.; M.I.)

2. All black background
Argent a bend wavy sable between six cocks gules (Coxwell)   In
pretence: Rogers
Crest: A dragon's head couped proper between two wings
gules   Mantling: Gules and argent   Motto:
Resurgam   Two palm branches in base
For the Rev. Charles Coxwell of Ablington House, Rector of
Dowdeswell, who m. 1796, Anne, youngest dau. of the Rev. Richard
Rogers, of Dowdeswell, and d. 30 Aug. 1854, aged 83.   (B.L.G. 5th
ed.; M.I.)

3. All black background
Per pale sable and gules a cross botonny fitchy between four fleurs-de-
lys or (Rich), impaling, Sable a castle triple-towered or (   )
Crest: On the stump of a tree couped and erased or a hawk with wings
endorsed argent preying on a pheasant proper   Mantling: Gules and
argent   Motto: In coelo quies
Possibly for Lionel Rich, of Upper Dowdeswell, who was bur. 26 Apr.
1736, aged 71. His wife, Mary, was bur. 7 Feb. 1734, aged
69.   (M.I.)

DOYNTON

1. All black background
Argent a chevron sable between three molets pierced gules
(Davy)   Shield surrounded with the Order of Guelph, with the
Badge of the Order pendent below, together with the badge of the Order
of the Bath, and a medal inscribed Rolica, Vimiera, Talavera   On
either side of main shield a small shield   Dexter, Davy, impaling,
Or a fess between three roundels gules (   ) S.Bl.   Sinister,
Davy, impaling, Qly, 1st, Sable a wolf salient and in chief three molets
pierced argent, on a canton or a cross formy gules (Wilson), 2nd, Argnt
a fess gules between three elephants' heads erased sable (Fountaine),
3rd, Argent three lozenges conjoined in fess gules a bordure sable
(Montagu), 4th, Or an eagle displayed vert (Monthermer) D.Bl
For General Sir William Gabriel Davy, C.B., K.C.H., of Tracy Park,
who m. 1st   , and 2nd, Sophia, dau. of Richard Fountayne Wilson,
of Melton Park, York, and d. 25 Jan. 1856. She d. 5 Dec.
1866.   (B.L.G. 7th ed.; Tracy Park deeds)

DUMBLETON

1. Dexter background black

Qly of six, 1st, Azure a lion rampant guardant between nine fleurs-de-lys argent over all a bend gules (Holland), 2nd, Argent a chevron gules between three water bougets sable (   ), 3rd, Gules a lion rampant argent between three crescents or (Salmesbury), 4th, Gules six bezants, three, two, one (Zouche), 5th, Azure six lions rampant three, two, one or (Longespee), 6th, Argent two bars azure a bordure engrailed sable (Parr), impaling, Argent three bars and in chief three lions rampant sable langued gules (Willetts)

Crest: From a ducal coronet or a demi-lion rampant guardant argent collared gules holding a fleur-de-lys argent   Mantling: Gules and argent   Motto: Resurgam

For Swinton Colthurst Holland, who m. Anne, dau. of the Rev. William Willetts, of Newcastle-under-Lyme, Staffs, and d. 27 Dec. 1827, aged 50. She d. 20 Feb. 1845, aged 75.   (M.I.)

2. Sinister background black

Sable a chevron between three stags' attires argent, in fess point the Badge of Ulster (Cocks), impaling, Gules a garb or in chief two helms argent garnished or (Cholmeley)

Crest: On a mount vert a buck lodged reguardant, collared, chained and attired or   Mantling: Gules and argent   Motto: Virtus omnia vincit

For Elizabeth, 2nd dau. of James Cholmeley, of Easton who m. Sir Robert Cocks, 4th Bt., and d. 30 Jan. 1749. He d. 4 Apr. 1765.   (B.E.B.; B.P. 1949 ed.)

3. Dexter background black

Qly, 1st and 4th, Sable a chevron between three stags' attires argent (Cocks), 2nd and 3rd, Vert a fess dancetty ermine (Somers), over all the Badge of Ulster, impaling, to dexter, Argent a fess gules double cotised wavy azure (Eliot), and to sinister, Azure a lion rampant argent between seven fleurs-de-lys or (Pole)

Baron's coronet   Crest: As 2.   Motto: Prodesse quam conspici   Supporters: Two lions ermine langued gules collared dancetty vert   All on a mantle gules and ermine

For Charles, 1st Baron Somers, who m. 1st, 1759, Elizabeth (d. 1 Jan. 1771), dau. of Richard Eliot, of Port Eliot, Cornwall, and 2nd, 1772, Anne (d. 1833), dau. of Reginald Pole, of Stoke, and d. 4 Jan. 1806.   (B.P. 1949 ed.)

DYRHAM

1. All black background

Or two bends engrailed sable (Blathwayt)   In pretence: Sable a fess and in chief a crescent ermine (Wynter)

Crest: On a rock proper an eagle rising sable   Mantling: Gules and
argent   No motto
For William Blathwayt, of the City of London, Secretary of State to
King William III, who m. 1686, Mary, dau. and heir of John Wynter,
and d. Aug. 1717. She d. Nov. 1691.   (B.L.G. 1937 ed.)

2. Dexter background black
Qly, 1st, Blathwayt, 2nd, Wynter, 3rd, Azure a lion rampant argent
crowned or (Gerard of Trent), 4th, Argent a saltire gules
(Gerard)   In pretence: Or three dice sable each charged with an
annulet or (Ambrose)
Crest and mantling: As 1.   Motto: Mors janua vitae
For William Blathwayt, of Dyrham Park, who m. 1718, Thomasina,
dau. of Jonathan Ambrose, of London, and d. 1742.   (B.L.G. 1937
ed.)

3. All black background
On a lozenge surmounted by a cherub's head
Arms: As 2.
Motto: In coelo quies   Skull below
For Thomasina, widow of William Blathwayt. She d. 1774.   (B.L.G.
1937 ed.)

4. Sinister background black
Qly of six, 1st and 6th, Blathwayt, 2nd, Ambrose, 3rd, Wynter, 4th,
Gerard of Trent, 5th, Gerard, impaling, Azure a fess wavy argent
charged with a cross formy gules in chief two estoiles or (Jenkinson)
Crest, mantling and motto: As 2.
For Penelope, dau. of Sir Robert Jenkinson, Bt., who m. 1747, as his 1st
wife, William Blathwayt, of Dyrham Park, and d. July
1755.   (B.L.G. 1937 ed.)

5. Sinister background black
Qly, as 4., impaling, Argent on a bend engrailed gules a bezant between
two swans proper (Clark)
Crest, mantling and motto: As 2.
For Elizabeth le Pepre (née Clark) who m. 1758, as his 2nd wife,
William Blathwayt, of Dyrham Park, and d. Aug. 1764.   (B.L.G.
1937 ed.)

6. Dexter background black
Qly, as 4.   In pretence: Argent a lion rampant azure (Creighton)
Crest and mantling: As 1.   Motto: In coelo quies
For William Blathwayt, of Dyrham Park, who m. 3rd, Mary Creighton,
of London, and d. May 1787. She d.s.p. 30 Nov. 1823, aged
100.   (B.L.G. 1937 ed.)

7. Dexter background black

Qly, as 4., but Gerard of Trent within a bordure ermine, impaling, Argent on a fess gules cotised azure between three Catherine wheels sable three sheep argent (Scott)
Crest, mantling and motto: As 6.
For William Blathway, of Dyrham Park, who m. 1790, Frances, dau. of William Scott, of Great Barr, Staffs, and d.s.p. May 1806.   (B.L.G. 1937 ed.)

8. Dexter background black

Qly, as 4., impaling, Or on a cross sable a patriarchal cross or (Vesey)
Crest and mantling: As 1.   Motto: Virtute et veritate
For George William Blathwayt, of Dyrham Park, who m. 1822, Marianne, dau. of the Rev. Thomas Vesey, and d. 14 May 1871.   (B.L.G. 1937 ed.)

9. Dexter background black

Qly of six, 1st and 6th, Argent three ermine spots between two bends engrailed sable, each bend charged with three cross crosslets fitchy or, all between two buglehorns sable stringed gules (Blathwayt), 2nd, Ambrose, 3rd, Wynter, 4th, Gerard of Trent, as 2., 5th, Gerard, impaling, Azure on a fess cotised or three lions rampant sable (Taylor)
Crest, mantling and motto: As 8.
For William Blathwayt, son of Jeremiah Crane and Penelope Blathwayt, who took the name of Blathwayt: he m. Frances, dau. of James Taylor, and d.s.p. 25 Feb. 1839, aged 44.   (B.L.G. 1937 ed.)
(Since these hatchments were first recorded all have been replaced, repainted or restored)

ELMORE

1. All black background

On a lozenge surmounted by a cherub's head and with skull below
Qly, 1st, Gules seven lozenges vair, three, three and one, on a canton argent a pierced molet sable (Guise), 2nd, Sable a fess between six martlets argent (Wysham), 3rd, Qly gules and azure a cross flory or (Snell), 4th, Or a chevron chequy gules and azure between three cinquefoils gules (Cooke), in centre chief the Badge of Ulster   In pretence: Qly, 1st and 4th, Or two bars gemel gules, on a chief azure three leopards' faces or (Wright), 2nd and 3rd, Argent a chevron between three griffins passant sable (Finch)
For Elizabeth, dau. and heir of Thomas Wright, who m. 1770, Sir John Guise, 1st Bt., and d. 1808.   (B.P. 1949 ed; Guise family)

2. All black background

Two shields   Dexter, within the motto and the collar of the Order of the Bath, Guise, with canton or, and Badge of Ulster in centre

chief   Sinister, within an ornamental wreath, as dexter, impaling,
Argent a fret sable (Vernon)
Crest: From a ducal coronet or a swan rising proper ducally gorged and
chained or, charged with a lozenge vair   Mantling: Gules and
argent   Motto: Quo honestior eo tutior   Supporters: Dexter, A
swan proper crusilly gules, collared and chained or   Sinister, A
wolf sable billetty, collared and chained or   Frame inscribed
'General Sir John Wright Guise, Bt., G.C.B., born July 20th 1777. Died
April 1st 1865.' He m. 1815, Charlotte Diana, youngest dau. of John
Vernon, of Clontarf Castle, co. Dublin.   (B.P. 1949 ed.)

3. Dexter background black

Guise, as 2., with Badge of Ulster, impaling, Qly, 1st and 4th, Gules a
fess chequy or and gules between eight billets or (Lee), 2nd, qly i. & iv.
Per pale indented argent and sable, ii. & iii. Azure a fleur-de-lys or, over
all a crescent or for difference (Warner), 3rd, Vert a cross engrailed
argent (Warner)
Crest: As 2., but no lozenge   Mantling, motto and supporters: As
2.
Frame inscribed 'Sir William Guise, Bt., F.L.S., F.G.S. Born 19th
August 1816. Died 24 Sept. 1887.' He m. 1844, Margaret Anna Maria,
eldst dau. of the Rev. Daniel Henry Lee-Warner, of Tyberton Court,
Herefordshire.   (B.P. 1949 ed.; M.I.)

FRAMPTON-ON-SEVERN
1. Dexter background black

Qly of 16, 1st, Chequy or and azure on a bend gules three lions passant
guardant or (Clifford), 2nd, Azure on a chevron engrailed between three
birds or three cinquefoils azure, on a chief or a fleur-de-lys between two
spearheads azure (Winchcombe), 3rd, Argent on a chevron between three
hawks' bells gules three bars argent, on a chief gules a hawk's lure
between two martlets or (Bell), 4th, Azure a lion rampant and in chief
three escallops argent (Clutterbuck), 5th, as 1st, 6th, Ermine three bars
gules (Hussey), 7th, Argent three crescents sable (Hedley), 8th, Sable a
doubleheaded eagle displayed a bordure engrailed argent (Hoare), 9th,
Gules on a bend argent in dexter chief a martlet sable (Foliot), 10th,
Argent on a fess nebuly sable three hares' heads erased argent
(Harewell), 11th, Argent a chevron between in chief two crosses formy
and in base a saltire sable (Beaupyne), 12th, Argent three cocks sable
legged, crested and wattled gules (?Delamore), 13th, Argent a chevron
between three eagles displayed azure (?Clopton), 14th, Argent two bars
gules fretty or (Clopton), 15th, Qly per fess indented gules and or in the
first quarter a lion passant argent (Besyn), 16th, Ermine on a chief sable
three battleaxes argent (Sheppard)   In pretence: Gules a cross
lozengy or between four roses argent (Packer)
Crest: A dexter hand couped at the wrist in fess or holding a fleur-de-lys
argent   Mantling: Gules and argent   Motto:
Resurgam   Winged skull in base

For Nathaniel Winchcombe, who in 1801, assumed by Royal Licence,
the name and arms of Clifford. He m. 1782, Mary, dau. and heir of
Daniel Packer of Painswick, and d. 16 Sept. 1817.   (B.L.G. 1937
ed.)

FRETHERNE
1. All black background
On a lozenge surmounted by a countess's coronet
Qly, 1st and 4th, Qly gules and or, on a bend argent three lions passant
sable (Pery), 2nd and 3rd, Per chevron engrailed or and sable, in chief
three roundels and in base a stag trippant counterchanged (Hartstonge),
impaling, Gules three horses' heads erased argent (Horsley)
Supporters: Dexter, A lion rampant ermine   Sinister, A hind proper
ducally gorged and chained or   All on a mantle gules and ermine
For Margaret Jane, dau. of Capt. Nicholas Horsley, who m. 1842, as his
2nd wife, William, 2nd Earl of Limerick, and d. 25 Nov.
1875.   (B.P. 1949 ed.)
(The hatchment of the 1st Earl is at Limerick, Eire)

2. All black background
On a floriated lozenge   Azure a lion rampant or crowned argent
(Darell), impaling, Vairy argent and gules, on a canton or a stag's head
cabossed gules (Becher)
For Amelia Mary Anne, only dau. of William Becher, who m. 1809, Sir
Harry Verelst Darell, 2nd Bt., and d. 5 Jan. 1878.   (B.P. 1949 ed.)

3. Sinister background black
Darell, in dexter chief the Badge of Ulster   In pretence: Azure a
sword erect in pale argent hilted or between two lions rampant
respectant or, on a chief ermine two trefoils slipped vert (Tierney)
Shield suspended by a lover's knot
For Harriet Mary, only dau. of Sir Edward Tierney, Bt., who m. 1843,
as his 2nd wife, the Rev. Sir William Lionel Darell, 4th Bt., Rector of
Fretherne, and d. 27 June 1873.   (B.P. 1949 ed.)

4. Identical to 3.

HEMPSTED
1. All black background
Per fess azure and gules from a fess argent issuing to the base the rays of
the sun proper (Lysons), impaling, Gules three martlets between two
chevronels argent (Peach)
Crest: The sun rising out of clouds proper   Mantling: Gules and
argent   Motto: Resurgam
For the Rev. Samuel Lysons, Rector of Rodmarton and Cherington, who
m. Mary, dau. of Samuel Peach, of Chalford, and d. 15 Mar. 1804, aged
73.   (B.L.G. 5th ed.)

HORTON
1. All black background
On a lozenge surmounted by a cherub's head
Or a cross engrailed per pale gules and sable (Brooke), impaling,
Argent a lion passant gules, on a chief gules a ducal coronet or (Jones)
For Frances, 2nd dau. of John Jones, of Luckington, Wilts., who m.
1774, Thomas Brooke, of the Manor of Horton, and d. 20 Feb. 1832. He
d. 2 Sept. 1813.   (B.L.G. 1937 ed.)

LYDNEY
1. All black background
Sable two bars ermine in chief three crosses formy or (Bathurst)
Viscount's coronet   No helm   Crest: An arm embowed in
armour the hand holding a club proper   Motto: Tien ta
foy   Supporters: Two bulls gules ringed and lined or
For Charles, 1st Viscount Bledisloe, who d. 3 July 1958.   (M.I.)

MICKLETON
1. Dexter background black
Gules crusilly an eagle displayed or armed and ducally crowned argent
(Graves), impaling, Gules a bend ermine (Walwyn)
Crest: A demi-eagle displayed encircled with a ducal coronet or and
holding in the beak a cross crosslet gules   Mantling: Gules and
argent   Motto: Superna quaerite   Skull below
For Morgan Graves, who m. Anne, dau. of James Walwyn, of
Longworth, co. Hereford, and d. 26 Dec. 1770, aged 63.   (B.L.G. 5th
ed.; M.I.)

2. All black background
On a lozenge   Arms: As 1.
For Anne, widow of Morgan Graves. She d.   (Source, as 1.)

3. All black background
Graves, as 1., but crusilly argent, impaling, Argent a cross engrailed
between four roundels azure, each roundel charged with a pheon argent
(Fletcher)
Crest, mantling and motto: As 1.   Skull below
For Walwyn Graves, who m. Sarah Fletcher, and d. 2 Nov. 1813, aged
69. She d. 12 June 1813.   (M.I.)

4. Dexter background black
Qly of six, 1st, Graves, as 1., but crowned or, 2nd, Vert two lions
passant guardant argent on a chief or three fleurs-de-lys gules (Menseir),
3rd, Sable a fess engrailed argent between three hands bendwise couped
or (Bates), 4th, Azure a chevron ermine between three swans argent
(Swann), 5th, Sable on a bend argent three crows sable (Shilling), 6th,
Sable a chevron between three spearhads argent (Morgan)   In

pretence: Or a lion rampant sable between three oakleaves vert
(Shermer)
Crest: A demi-eagle displayed encircled with a ducal coronet or in its
beak a cross crosslet or   Mantling: Argent   Motto: As 1.
For the Rev. Richard Morgan Graves, who m. Elizabeth, dau. and co-
heir of Thomas Shermer of Hannington, Wilts., and d. 1815, aged
63.   (Sources, as 1.)

5. All black background
Arms: Qly of six, as 4., but 6th quarter Shermer nor Morgan
Crest: As 4.   Mantling: Argent   Motto: Graves disce mores
Probably for the Rev. Morgan Graves, who d.s.p. 1819, aged
40   (B.L.G. 5th ed.)

6. Dexter background black
Argent a bend chequy or and sable between two lions' heads erased
gules langued sable, on a chief azure three billets or, on the bend in
dexter chief the Badge of Ulster (Steele)   In pretence: Gules
crusilly an eagle displayed or crowned argent (Graves)
Crest: A demi-eagle displayed or, wings voided argent, holding a serpent
proper   Mantling: Vert and argent   Motto: Aquila non captat
muscas
For Sir John Maxwell Steele, 4th Bt., who m. 1838, Elizabeth Anne,
dau. of John Graves. He assumed the additional name of Graves in 1862,
and d. 25 Sept. 1872.   (B.P. 1875 ed.: B.L.G. 1937 ed. p. 1028)

7. All black background
On a decorative lozenge   Steele, with Badge of Ulster in centre
chief   In pretence: Gules crusilly an eagle displayed or armed
argent (Graves)
For Elizabeth, widow of Sir John Maxwell Steele, 4th Bt. She d. 29
Sept. 1877.   (Source, as 6.)

MISERDEN
1. Dexter background black
Qly, 1st and 4th, Or a fess dancetty between three cross crosslets fitchy
gules (Sandys), 2nd and 3rd, Sable ermined or a bend fusilly argent
(Bayntun), impaling, Per pale ermine and or ermined sable three
martlets sable a chief azure (Merryweather)
Crests: Dexter. A griffin segreant or   Sinister, A griffin's head erased
sable charged with a cross crosslet fitchy argent   Mantling: Gules
and argent   Motto: Resurgam
For the Rev. Sir Edwin Windsor Bayntun Sandys, who m. 1835, Mary
Anne, eldest dau. of William Stevens Merryweather, of Grovefield, co.
Gloucester, and d. 21 Dec. 1838.   (B.P. 1841 ed.; M.I.)

NEWLAND

1. All black background
Qly, 1st and 4th, Argent a cross sable between four choughs proper
(Edwin), 2nd and 3rd, Azure a chevron between three lions' heads
erased or (Wyndham)   To dexter of main shield, Edwin, impaling,
Argent on a chevron engrailed azure between three rooks sable three
suns or (Rooke) A.Bl.   To sinister of main shield, Edwin, impaling,
Sable a chevron between three spearheads argent (Jones) D.Bl.
Crests: Dexter, A chough proper   Sinister, A lion' head erased
between a fetterlock or   Mantling: Gules and argent   Motto:
Au bon droit   Long inscription on hatchment frame relating to the
Wyndham family
For Charles Wyndham, of Clearwell, who took the name of Edwin on
succeeding to the Edwin estate; he m. 1st, Eleanor, dau. of General
Rooke, of Bigsweir, and 2nd, Charlotte Jones, and d. 15 June 1801, aged
70.   (B.L.G. 7th ed.; M.I.)

2. All black background
On a lozenge   Qly, as 1., impaling, Jones
Crest: As sinister of 1.   Long inscription on hatchment frame mainly
relating to Charles Edwin, and his first marriage
For Charlotte, 2nd wife of Charles Edwin; she d.   (B.L.G. 7th ed.)

NEWNHAM

1. All black background
On a lozenge surmounted by a lover's knot
Sable a chevron engrailed or ermined sable between two annulets in
chief or and in base a flame proper encompassed by a chain sable issuing
from a civic wreath or, in centre chief the Badge of Ulster
(Davy)   In pretence: Gules on a chevron argent three molets gules
between in chief a fleur-de-lys and in base a martlet or (Kerr)
For Jane, dau. and co-heiress of Charles Kerr, who m. Sir Humphry
Davy, Bt., and d. Sept. 1855.   (B.E.B.)
(The hatchment of Sir Humphry Davy is at Penzance in the Geological
Museum)

ODDINGTON

1. Dexter background black
Gules a saltire between four garbs or, the Badge of Ulster (Reade),
impaling, Per pale azure and gules three lions rampant or (Hoskyns)
Crest: A falcon wings elevated and inverted proper   Motto: Mors
janua vitae   All on a mantle gules and argent   Cherubs' heads
at sides and skull below
For Sir John Reade, 6th Bt., who m. 1784, Jane (d. 17 Dec. 1847), only
dau. of Sir Chandos Hoskyns, 5th Bt., and d. 18 Nov. 1789.   (B.P.
1949 ed.)

2. An almost exact replica of 1.
Also for Sir John Reade, 6th Bt., who d. 18 Nov. 1789.

OXENTON
1. All black background
Ermine on a bend engrailed gules between two cocks or three pierced
molets or (Law), impaling, Qly, 1st and 4th, Or a bend countercompony argent and azure between two lions rampant gules (Stewart),
2nd and 3rd, Gules a saltire argent (Nevill)
Earl's coronet   Crest: A cock gules purfled and chained or, pendent
therefrom an escutcheon azure charged with a mitre and a bordure
or   Mantling: Gules and argent   Motto: Compositum jus fasque
animi   Supporters: Two eagles, wings elevated, sable the dexter
chained round the neck and pendent therefrom on the breast a mitre or;
the sinister with a like chain and pendent therefrom a covered cup
or   Badge of Order of Bath pendent below shield
For Edward, 1st Earl of Ellenborough, G.C.B., who m. 1st, 1813,
Octavia (d. 5 Mar. 1819), youngest dau. of Robert, 1st Marquess of
Londonderry, and 2nd, 1824, Jane Elizabeth, only dau. of Adm. Sir
Henry Digby, G.C.B., and d. 22 Dec. 1871.   (B.P. 1949 ed.; M.I.)

STANWAY House
1. All black background
On a lozenge   Argent a cross cotised with demi-fleurs-de-lys
between four molets pierced sable (Atkyns), impaling, Argent a chevron
sable between three roundels gules each roundel charged with an
escallop argent (Dacres)   Four skulls, one above, one below, and
one to dexter and sinister
For Anne, dau. of Sir Thomas Dacres, who m. as his second wife, Sir
Robert Atkyns, K.B., and d. Oct. 1712. He d. 12 Feb. 1710, aged
88.   (M.S. Ped. at Stanway House)

2. Dexter background black
Or in dexter chief an escallop sable between two bendlets gules in chief
a crescent gules for difference (Tracy), impaling, Qly per chevron
embattled or and azure three martlets counterchanged (Hudson)
Crest: On a chapeau gules and ermine an escallop sable between two
wings erect or   Mantling: Gules and argent   Motto: Mors
omnia vincit
For Robert Tracy, who m. Anna-Maria dau. of Sir Roger Hudson, and
d. 1767.   (Source, as 1.)

3. All black background
On a lozenge   Arms: As 2.
Motto: In coelo quies
For Anna Maria, widow of Robert Tracy. She d. 1785.   (Source, as 1.)

4. All black background
On a lozenge surmounted by a viscountess's coronet
Qly, 1st, Argent a fess and in chief three roundels gules (Devereux), 2nd
and 3rd, Qly France and England a bordure argent (Plantagenet), 4th,
Argent a cross engrailed gules between four water bougets sable
(Bourchier), impaling, Qly, 1st and 4th, Tracy, no crescent, 2nd and
3rd, Azure a cross crosslet fitchy or (Ethelred)
Motto: Virtutis comes invidia   Supporters: Dexter, A talbot argent,
ducally gorged, langued and eared gules   Sinister, A reindeer
proper, attired argent, ducally gorged and chained or
For Henrietta Charlotte, dau. of Anthony Tracy-Keck, who m. 1774,
Edward, 12th Viscount Hereford, and d. 23 June 1817.   (B.P. 1949
ed.)

5. All black background
On a lozenge surmounted by a baroness's coronet
Qly, 1st and 4th, Argent a fess azure within a double tressure flory
counter-flory gules (Charteris), 2nd and 3rd, Or a lion rampant gules
(Wemyss)   In pretence: Qly, 1st and 4th, Tracy as 4., but bendlets
sable 2nd and 3rd, Ethelred
Supporters: Two lions guardant gules
For Susan, dau, of Anthony Tracy-Keck, who m. 1771, Francis, Lord
Elcho, and d. 25 Feb. 1835. He d. 20 Jan. 1808.   (B.P. 1949 ed.)

6. Sinister background black
Two oval shields   Dexter, Qly, 1st and 4th, Wemyss, 2nd and 3rd,
Charteris, impaling, Gyronny of eight or and sable on a bordure
engrailed or eight crescents sable (Campbell)   Sinister, Qly, 1st and
4th, qly i. & iv. Argent a human heart gules imperially crowned proper,
on a chief azure three molets or (Douglas), ii. & iii. Azure a bend
between six cross crosslets fitchy or (Mar), all within a bordure or
charged with the royal tressure gules, 2nd and 3rd, Gules a lion
rampant argent, on a bordure argent nine roses gules barbed and seeded
proper (Dunbar)
Countess's coronet   Supporters: Dexter, A swan
proper   Sinister, A pegasus argent, winged or
For Margaret, dau. of Walter Campbell, of Shawfield, who m. 1794,
Francis, 8th Earl of Wemyss, and. 25 Jan. 1850.   (B.P. 1949 ed.)

7. All black background
Arms (on two oval shields): As 6., but only six crescents on Campbell
bordure
Earl's coronet   Crests: 1. A human heart gules imperially crowned
proper between two wings displayed or (Douglas)   2. A swan proper
(Wemyss)   Mottoes: 1. Je pense   2. Forward   Supporters:
As 6.

For Francis, 8th Earl of Wemyss, and 4th Earl of March, who d. 28
June 1853.   (B.P. 1949 ed.)

STOKE GIFFORD
1. All black background
Gules two chevrons ermine between three eagles displayed or (Parsons),
impaling, Or a lion rampant sable (Phillips)
Crest: A demi-griffin gules   Mantling: Gules and argent
For the Rev. John Parsons, Vicar of Marden, Wilts., who m. 1810,
Margaret (d. 16 July 1828), eldest dau. of George Phillips, and
d.   (B.L.G. 2nd ed.)

2. Dexter background black
Qly, 1st and 4th, France, 2nd and 3rd, England, all within a bordure
compony argent and azure (Somerset), impaling, Ermine a rose gules
barbed and seeded proper (Boscawen)   Shield surrounded with the
Garter
Duke's coronet   Crest: A portcullis chained or   Motto: Mutare
vel timere   Supporters: Dexter, A panther argent semy of roundels
gules, azure and vert, collared and chained or   Sinister, A wyvern
vert, collared and chained or   All on a mantle gules and ermine
For Henry, 5th Duke of Beaufort, K.G., who m. 1766, Elizabeth, dau. of
Admiral the Hon. Edward Boscawen, and d. 11 Oct. 1803.   (B.P.
1949 ed.)

3. All black background
On a curvilinear lozenge   Arms: As 2.
Duchess's coronet   Motto and supporters: As 2.
For Elizabeth, widow of Henry, 5th Duke of Beaufort, K.G., d. 15 June,
1828.   (B.P. 1949 ed.)
(These last two hatchments, recorded in 1953, are now missing)

STONEHOUSE
1. Dexter background black
Argent on a chevron gules between three lions' heads erased sable,
langued gules, crowned or, three bezants (Pettat), impaling, Gules a fess
wavy between three fleurs-de-lys or (Hicks)
Crest: A lion's gamb erect sable holding a bezant   Mantling: Gules
and argent   Motto: Resurgam   Skull in base
Unidentified
(In the ringing chamber of the tower)

TEMPLE GUITING
1. Sinister background black
Gules a lion rampant within a bordure engrailed or (Talbot)   In
pretence: Qly, 1st and 4th, Argent a wyvern gules (Drake), 2nd and 3rd,
Gules a fess chequy or and azure (Whittington)

Cherub's head above shield, which is flanked with sprays of berried foliage
For Charlotte Elizabeth, dau. and co-heir of the Rev. Thomas Drake, who m. 1789, George Talbot, and d. 1817.   (B.P. 1949 ed.)
(This hatchment, recorded in 1958, is now missing)

2. All black background
Talbot, as 1.   In pretence: Qly, 1st and 4th, Argent a wyvern (Drake), 2nd and 3rd, Gules three tyrwhitts or (Tyrwhitt)
Crest: On a chapeau gules and ermine a lion statant tail extended or   Mantling: Gules and argent   Motto: Humani nihil alienum
For George Talbot, who d. 7 Apr. 1836.   (B.P. 1949 ed.)

THORNBURY
1. Dexter background black
Qly of six, 1st, Gules on a bend between six cross crosslets fitchy argent the Augmentation of Flodden (Howard), 2nd, Gules three lions passant guardant in pale or a label of three points argent (Brotherton), 3rd, Chequy or and azure (Warren), 4th, Gules a lion rampant argent (Mowbray), 5th, Gules three escallops argent (Dacre), 6th, Barry of six argent and azure three chaplets or (Greystoke), impaling, Qly, 1st, Sable a lion passant argent on a chief argent three cross crosslets fitchy sable (Long), 2nd, Per fess or and gules a pale counterchanged, on the or three choughs proper (Tate), 3rd, Gules ten bezants, four, three, two and one, a canton ermine (Zouch), 4th, Argent two chevrons gules a label of five points azure (St Maur)
Crest: On a chapeau gules and ermine a lion statant guardant tail extended or charged with a label of three points argent   Mantling: Gules and argent   Motto: Sola virtus invicta
For Henry Howard, of Greystoke Castle, who m. 1849, Charlotte Caroline Georgiana, eldest dau. of Henry Lawes Long, of Hampton Lodge, Surrey, and d. 7 Jan. 1875.   (B.P. 1949 ed.)
(There is another hatchment for Henry Howard at Greystoke, Cumberland)

2. Dexter background black
Argent a chevron azure between three molets gules (Willis), impaling, Sable a griffin segreant or a bordure engrailed ermine
(Walker)   Crest: A dove argent beaked and legged
gules   Mantling: Gules and argent
For the Rev. Thomas Willis, Rector of Thornbury, who m. Ann Walker, and d. 26 1748, aged 58.   (per Sir Algar Howard)

TODENHAM
1. Sinister background black
Qly, 1st, Argent a chevron between three crescents gules in chief a label of three points sable (Pole), 2nd, Argent four pallets azure,(   ) 3rd,

Or a snake in pale wavy vert, (   ) 4th, Or three crescents gules
(Van Notten), over all the Badge of Ulster, impaling, Qly, 1st, Qly
gules and or on a bend argent three lions passant sable (Pery), 2nd, Per
chevron invecked or and sable, in chief three annulets and in base a stag
trippant counterchanged (Sexton), impaling, Sable three annulets or
(   ), 3rd, qly i. Sexton, ii. Sable three annulets or (   ), iii. Sable
on a bend between two cinquefoils argent three boars' heads sable
(Brettridge), iv. Azure a lion passant or (   ), 4th, qly i. Gules a
bend between six cross crosslets argent (Ormsby), ii. & iii. Sable
crusilly a lion rampant argent (Kinardsley), iv. Sable three chessrooks
and a chief or (Werdan)
Supporters: Two lions rampant reguardant proper   Shield
suspended from bow of green ribbon
For Louisa, dau. of Edmund Henry, 1st Earl of Limerick, who m. as his
1st wife, Sir Peter Van Notten-Pole, 3rd Bt., and d. 6 Aug. 1852, aged
54. (B.P. 1949 ed.; M.I.)

TREDINGTON
1. All black background
On a lozenge surmounted by an escallop
Per fess azure and or a lion rampant counterchanged, in chief a crescent
or for difference (Goodlake), impaling, Or a lion rampant sable,
langued gules, between three hollyleaves slipped proper, in chief a label
on a crescent or for difference (Surman)
Motto: Yet in my flesh shall I see God
For Elizabeth, only dau. of William Surnam, of Swindon and
Tredington, who m. 1807, John Hughes Goodlake, of Letcomb Regis,
and d. 26 Nov. 1843.   (B.L.G. 5th ed.)

WICKWAR
1. All black background
Argent on a fess between three mascles sable three cinquefoils argent
(Purnell), impaling, Gules a fess wavy between three fleurs-de-lys or
(Hickes)
Crest: A hound sejant proper the dexter paw resting on a mascle
sable   Mantling: Gules and argent   No motto, but on two
scrolls below: Mr. Purnell ob. Aug. 16, 1726 aet 46   Mrs. Purnell
ob. Apr. 5, 1743, aet 60
For Mr. John Purnell, of the Pool House, and his wife, Jane, youngest
dau. of John Hickes, of West End. He d. 16 Aug. 1726, and she d. 5 Apr.
1743.   (M.I. and inscription on hatchment)

WORMINGTON
1. All black background
Qly, 1st and 4th, Per pale gules and sable on a chevron engrailed or
ermined sable between three swans' heads erased ermine three fleurs-de-
lys azure (Gist), 2nd, Or three ?oakleaves proper in bend between two

chains sable and two chaplets vert (   ), 3rd, Per saltire or and
argent a cross crosslet azure between in pale two leopards' faces proper
and in fess two roses gules (   ), over all a label of three points
argent, impaling, Qly, 1st and 4th, Per bend or and vert in chief a tree
eradicated proper in base a seahorse naiant in water argent (Westenra),
2nd and 3rd, Argent three martlets gules a bordure or (Cairns)
Crests: Dexter, A swan's head erased ermine gorged gules charged with a
label sable, between two palm branches vert   Sinister, A demi-man
charged with a label sable, a cross crosslet gules in left hand, and a
chaplet vert in right hand, chained from wrists to waist, chains and belt
sable   Mantling: Gules and argent   Motto: Resurgam
For Samuel Gist Gist, who m. Mary Ann, dau. of Warner, 2nd Baron
Rossmore, and d. 15 Jan. 1815, aged 92.   (B.P.; M.I.)

HAMPSHIRE

by

John E. Titterton

Old Basing 3: For William, 2nd Baron Bolton, 1850
(*Photograph by Mr. J. E. Titterton*)

INTRODUCTION

There are 147 recorded hatchments in Hampshire at 50 different locations including four separate locations within the City of Winchester. Those detailed include ones which have disappeared since the survey began in 1952. At Avington only one out of three has survived and there are two out of six left at Barton Stacey. A curious coincidence is that for each of the three survivors there are further examples for the people concerned in other counties.

There are three 17th-century hatchments. The earliest identified one is at Martin for Sir Gabriel Lapp who died in 1688. This was found in a barn at the rear of the former village inn and given to the church. However at Heckfield there is a hatchment for a member of the Corham family which may be of an earlier date. The third hatchment is at Odiham in the Mayhill Junior School. The most recent is that of Colonel Bates at Wootton St Lawrence who died in 1958, with earlier 20th-century ones at Braemore.

At Freefolk there is the hatchment of King William III, which is dated 1701 (old style) who died in January 1702. The aristocracy is well represented. The hatchment of the 'Iron Duke', together with those of his wife and the 2nd Duke of Wellington are at Stratfield Saye. There are hatchments for nine further families of the Peerage and ten from the Baronetage. Appropriately at Winchester Cathedral there is that of a Bishop (Bishop North d. 1820).

The largest collection for one family is also the largest in the county. At Breamore in the Saxon and Norman church hang 12 hatchments of the Hulse family from the second to eighth baronets, spanning over a hundred years from 1800 to 1931. The next largest family collection is that of the seven Calthorpe hatchments in the now redundant church next to the Victorian Elvetham Hall, including one from early in the 18th century. Other notable family groups of hatchments are the five Tichbornes of Tichborne, and the four Brocases of

Bramley, both in beautiful family chapels. Large mixed collections are to be found at Froyle (9) and Lymington (11).

Hampshire can also boast the hatchments of an Admiral who saw action with Nelson, a General who fought with Wellington in the Peninsular War at Heckfield, the second longest serving Speaker of the House of Commons also at Heckfield, and a Warden of Winchester (in the College).

The work of Mr. E. Hepper who recorded the vast majority of these hatchments is greatly appreciated. He started work in 1952 while still a prep school boy and continued with the task until 1975 when business commitments took him abroad. Thanks are also due to Mr. A. Taylor, Mr. F. Carpenter, and Mr. W. Fletcher who made further contributions and checks and especially the late Mr. R. Boumphrey who checked all the hatchments over the last two years.

J. E. Titterton
7 Cecil Aldin Drive, Tilehurst
Reading, Berks.

ABBOTTS ANN

1. All black background

Gules the trunk of a tree eradicated and couped in pale sprouting two slips leaved all proper, in chief a label of three points or (Burrough) Crest: A griffin's head erased gules beaked or   Mantling: Gules and argent   *c.* 3 ft. by 3 ft.

Probably for the Rev. John Burrough, Rector of Abbotts Ann, 1730-74, who d.

AVINGTON

1. Sinister background black

Two oval shields, the dexter slightly overlapping the sinister

Dexter, within the Garter, Qly of seven, 1st, Vert on a cross argent five roundels gules (Grenville), 2nd, Or an eagle displayed sable (Leofric), 3rd, Argent two bars sable each charged with three martlets or (Temple), 4th, hidden, 5th, Ermine two bars gules (Nugent), 6th, Or a pile gules (Chandos), 7th, Argent on a cross sable a leopard's face or (Brydges)

Sinister, within ornamental wreath, as dexter, but 4th quarter, Gules on a chevron or three lions rampant sable (Cobham)   In pretence: Qly of eight, 1st and 8th, Argent on a cross sable a leopard's face or (Brydges), 2nd, Or a saltire and a chief gules, on a canton argent a lion rampant azure (Bruce), 3rd, Qly i. & iv. Or on a pile gules between six fleurs-de-lys azure three lions of England (Seymour Augmentation), ii. & iii. Gules two wings conjoined in lure tips downwards or (Seymour), 4th, Barry of six argent and azure in chief three roundels gules (Grey), 5th, Argent four bars gules over all a lion rampant or (Brandon), 6th and 7th, Qly France and England

Duchess's coronet   Supporters: Dexter, A lion rampant per fess embattled or and gules   Sinister, A horse argent semy of eagles displayed sable   All on a mantle gules and ermine   Cherub's head in top angle

For Anna Eliza, dau. and sole heir of James Brydges, 3rd and last Duke of Chandos, who m. 1796, Richard, 1st Duke of Buckingham and Chandos, K.G., and d. 15 May 1836.   (B.P. 1875 ed.)

(The hatchment of the 1st Duke of Buckingham is at Stowe)

2. Dexter background black

Qly, 1st, Or on a cross sable a leopard's face or (Brydges), 2nd, Qly France and England, 3rd, Or a pile gules (Chandos), 4th, Or a saltire and a chief gules (Bruce)   In pretence: Qly, 1st and 4th, Argent two

93

chevronels between three legs bent at the knee sable (Gamon), 2nd and
3rd, Gules three rabbits sejant proper (Coningsby)
Duke's coronet   Crest: The bust of a man in profile couped below
the shoulders proper, habited paly of six argent and gules semy of
roundels counterchanged   Motto: Maintien le droit   Supporters:
Two greyhounds proper   All on a mantle gules and
ermine   Winged skull in base
For James Brydges, 3rd and last Duke of Chandos, who m. 2nd, 1777,
Anne Eliza, dau. of Richard Gamon, and d. 29 Sept. 1789.   (B..P.)
(This hatchment was recorded in 1953, but has since disappeared; there
are also two hatchments for the 3rd Duke in the parish church of
Whitchurch, Middlesex)

3. Dexter background black

Sable a fess engrailed between three whelkshells or, a molet gules on
the fess for difference (Shelley), impaling, Argent a deer sejant in the
mouth a trefoil slipped proper (Bowen)
Crest: A griffin's head erased ducally gorged or   Mantling: Sable
and or   Motto: In coelo quies
For Edward Shelley, of Avington House, Hants, who m. 1827, Elizabeth,
dau. of Charles Bowen, of Kilnacourt, and d. 11 Nov.
1866.   (Foster's Peerage, 1880 ed.)
(This hatchment was recorded in 1953, but has since disappeared)

BARTON STACEY
1. Dexter background black

Qly, 1st and 4th, Sable a wolf rampant or charged on the shoulder with
a mascle gules, in chief an estoile or between two estoiles argent
(Wilson), 2nd and 3rd, Argent three bars gemel gules on a chief azure
three leopards' faces or, a canton ermine (Wright), impaling, Qly, 1st
and 4th, qly. i. & iv. Or a saltire and a chief gules, on a canton argent a
lion rampant azure (Bruce), ii. & iii. Argent a chevron gules between
three morions azure (Brudenell), 2nd and 3rd, Wright, but canton or
ermined sable
Crests: Dexter, A demi-wolf or charged with a chapeau
azure   Sinister, From a mural coronet chequy or and gules a
dragon's head vert charged with three leopards' faces between two bars
gemel and in chief a cross crosslet fitchy or   Mantling: Gules and
argent   Motto: Res non verba
For Sir Henry Wright Wilson, who m. 2nd, 1799, Frances Elizabeth, 2nd
dau. of Thomas, 1st Earl of Ailesbury, and d.s.p. 3 Dec.
1832.   (B.L.G. 1937 ed.)
(There is another hatchment for Sir Henry Wright Wilson at Crofton,
Yorkshire)

2. All black background

On a lozenge surmounted by a cherub's head   Arms: As 1.
Motto: In coelo quies
For Frances, widow of Sir Henry Wright Wilson, who d. 7 Feb.
1836.   (B.L.G. 1937 ed.)
(There is another hatchment for Frances Wilson at Crofton, Yorkshire)

3. Sinister background black

Qly, 1st and 4th, Argent six barrulets gules on a chief azure three
leopards' faces or (Wright), 2nd and 3rd, Argent a chevron between
three griffins passant sable (Finch)   In pretence: Or fretty azure
(Willoughby)
Motto: In coelo quies   Cherub's head above
Unidentified

4. All black background

On a lozenge surmounted by a cherub's head
Wright, as 3.
Motto: In coelo quies   Skull in base
Unidentified

5. Identical to 4., but Wright arms, Barry of 12 argent and gules, etc.

Unidentified

6. All black background

Or fretty azure (Willoughby)   In pretence, and impaling, Pily
counterpily of three points argent and sable the points ending in crosses
formy (Poynder)
Crest: A man's head couped at the shoulders affronté proper ducally
crowned or   Mantling: Gules and argent   Motto: Post funera
virtus
Unidentified
(Hatchments 3-6, recorded in 1953, are all now missing)

OLD BASING
1. All black background

Sable three swords in pile points in base argent pommels and hilts or
(Paulet)
Duke's coronet   Crest: A falcon rising or ducally gorged
azure   Mantling: Gules and ermine   Motto: Aymes
loyaulte   Supporters: Two hinds argent semy of estoiles argent
ducally gorged or
Probably for Charles, 5th Duke of Bolton, K.B., Lord Lieutenant of
Hampshire, who d. unm. 5 July 1765.   (B.P. 1939 ed.)

2. All black background

Sable three swords in pile points in base argent pommels and hilts or,
on a canton argent an escutcheon azure charged with a salmon hauriant
argent (Paulet), impaling, Paulet, no canton, but within a bordure or
Baron's coronet   Crest: A falcon rising belled or ducally gorged
azure in its beak a fish argent   Motto: In coelo quies
Supporters: Dexter, A hind proper ducally gorged and semy of estoiles
or   Sinister, A chough proper   All on a mantle gules and
ermine
For Thomas, 1st Baron Bolton, son of John Orde, of Morpeth. He m.
1778, Jean Mary Powlett (14 Dec. 1814), natural dau. of Charles, 5th
Duke of Bolton, assumed the additional name and arms of Powlett, and
d. 30 July 1807. Perhaps, in view of the background also used for his
widow.   (B.P. 1949 ed.)

3. Dexter background black

Powlett, as dexter of 2., impaling, Qly, 1st, Ermine on a bend sable
three pheons argent (Carleton), 2nd, Sable three bars argent in chief
three roundels argent (   ), 3rd, Argent a cross between four lions
rampant gules (Carlisle), 4th, Or a cross formy gules (Carlisle)
Baron's coronet   Crest: A falcon rising belled, ducally gorged azure
and charged on the breast and each wing with an estoile azure, in its
beak a salmon proper   Motto: Aimes loyaulte   Supporters:
Dexter, A hind proper ducally gorged or charged on the shoulder with a
rose argent barbed and seeded proper   Sinister, A chough proper
charged with a like rose argent
For William, 2nd Baron Bolton, who m. 1810, Maria, dau. of Guy, 1st
Baron Dorchester, and d. 13 July 1850.   (B.P. 1949 ed.)

4. Sinister background black

Barry of six sable and or on a chief or four pallets sable, over all on an
escutcheon ermine two bars gules (Burley), impaling, Argent on a fess
gules three lozenges or (Apletree)
Cherub's head above shield
Unidentified

5. Sinister background black

Qly, 1st and 4th, Argent on a fess gules three lozenges vair (Apletree),
2nd and 3rd, Argent a lion rampant gules, on a chief sable three
escallops argent (Russell), impaling, Qly, 1st and 4th, Sable on a bend
argent three rustres gules (   ), 2nd, Argent a lion rampant azure
(   ), 3rd, Azure six annulets, three, two and one or (Musgrave)
Motto: Resurgam   Cherubs' heads at top angles of shield
Unidentified

BISHOP'S WALTHAM
1. Sinister background black
Qly of 12, 1st Argent a maunch sable (Hastings), 2nd Sable two bars and in chief three roundels argent (Hungerford), 3rd, Per pale or and sable a saltire engrailed counterchanged (Pole), 4th, Qly France modern and England a label of three points throughout argent, on each point a canton gules (Clarence), 5th, Gules a saltire argent a label of three points throughout argent (Neville), 6th, Argent three lozenges conjoined in fess gules (Montacute), 7th, Azure a lion rampant guardant between eight fleurs-de-lys argent (Holland), 8th, Gules three lions passant guardant in pale or within a bordure argent (Holland), 9th, Gules a fess between six cross crosslets or (Beauchamp), 10th, Argent a fess and in chief three roundels gules (Devereux), 11th, Argent a cross engrailed between four water bougets gules (Bourchier), 12th, Qly France modern and England within a bordure or (for Plantagenet), impaling, Gules a fess and in chief two swans argent (Cobb)
Countess's coronet   Mantle: Gules and ermine   Motto: In veritate victoria   Supporters: Two lions guardant or each with a man's face bearded proper
For Frances, dau. of the Rev. Richard Chaloner Cobb, who m. Hans, 12th Earl of Huntingdon, and d. 31 Mar. 1820.   (B.P. 1963 ed.)

2. All brown background
Ermine on a saltire sable a rose or (Barton), impaling, Argent a fess engrailed between three wolves' heads couped sable (   )
Esquire's helmet with wreath, but no crest   Mantling: Gules and argent   Inscribed: In Memory of Robt. Barton Gent. & Sarah his wife
In a wood frame decorate with two skulls, two roses and four pairs of crossbones all gold
For Robert Barton, who d.   (Inscription)

BISTERNE
1. Dexter background black
Sable a lion passant guardant or between three helms proper (Compton), impaling, Ermine on a fess sable cotised gules five lozenges conjoined or (Richards)
Crest: A demi-dragon rampant erased gules the body encircled with a ducal coronet or   Mantling: Gules and argent   Motto: Non omnis morior
John Compton, of Minstead and Bisterne, who m. 1788, Catherine, dau. of the Rev. John Richards, and d. 1803. She d. 1805.   (B.L.G. 1937 ed.)

BRAMLEY
1. Sinister background black
Sable a lion rampant or (Brocas), impaling, Per fess or ermined sable and sable three pickaxes counterchanged (Pigott)

Motto: Resurgam   Shield suspended from a bow of ribbon and
flanked by cherubs' heads
For Anne Dolby, dau. of Paynton Pigott, of Archer Lodge, Hants, who
m. as his 1st wife, Bernard Brocas of Beaurepaire, and d.   (Burke's
Family Records; The Brocas Family of Beaurepaire)

2. Dexter background black
Sable a lion rampant guardant or (Brocas), impaling, Qly, 1st and 4th,
Or five escallops in cross azure (Barker), 2nd and 3rd, Azure an eagle
displayed wings inverted or on a chief embattled argent three roundels
gules (Raymond)
Crest: A moor's bust in profile proper crowned with an antique crown
and with an earring or gem gules   Mantling: Gules and
argent   Motto: Mors janua vitae
For Bernard Brocas, of Beaurepaire, who m. 2nd, Sophia Anne, dau. of
Daniel Raymond Barker, of Fairford Park, and d. 5 July 1839. She d.
1872.   (Sources, as 1.)

3. Dexter background black
Qly, 1st ad 4th, Sable a lion rampant guardant or (Brocas), 2nd and
3rd, Sable two lions passant guardant in pale argent (de Roches),
impaling, Or three water bougets azure (Rose)
Crest, mantling and motto: As 2.
For Bernard Brocas, who m. Jane, dau. of Sir John Rose, and d.
1861.   (The Brocas Family of Beaurepaire)

4. Dexter background black
Qly of 12, 1st, Sable a lion rampant guardant or (Brocas), 2nd, de
Roches, 3rd, Argent six staves raguly, three, two and one gules (   ),
4th, Argent a cross between four molets of six points gules (Banbury),
5th, Azure a fess between two chevrons or (Morell), 6th, Argent on a
cross flory engrailed between four martlets azure a bezant (Pexsall), 7th,
as 1st, 8th, Argent on a bend gules cotised sable three pairs of wings
conjoined in lure argent (Wingfield), 9th, Argent six roundels, three, two
and one gules (Harnage), 10th, Qly or and sable (   ), 11th, Gules
three bars argent a canton ermine (Walshe), 12th, Per chevron azure and
or three lions passant guardant counterchanged (Catelyn), impaling,
Qly, 1st and 4th, Or a lion rampant gules between eight wimbles sable
(   ), 2nd, and 3rd, Argent a bear sejant sable muzzled or (   )
Crest, mantling and motto: As 2.   Skull in base
Unidentified

BRAMSHAW
1. Sinister background black
Argent on a chevron sable three quatrefoils or (Eyre), impaling, Qly, 1st
and 4th, Per fess argent and ermine three piles one issuing from the chief
between the others reversed sable (Hulse), 2nd and 3rd, Argent a

chevron gules between three parrots' heads erased vert beaked gules
(Lethieullier)
No crest   Stylised gold decoration, and cherub's head above
For Frances, 3rd dau. of Sir Edward Hulse, 3rd Bt., of Breamore, who
m. 1803, as his 1st wife, George Eyre, of Warrens, and d. 29 Apr.
1820.   (B.L.G. 1937 ed.)

2. All black background

Eyre, impaling two coats per fess, in chief, Hulse, and in base, Gules on
a bend argent between two demi-lions couped or three fleurs-de-lys sable
(Hayes)   To dexter of main shield, Eyre impaling Hulse, A.Bl. To
sinister of main shield, Eyre impaling Hayes, A.Bl.
Crest: A leg in armour couped at the thigh proper garnished and spurred
or   Mantling: Gules and argent   Motto: Sola virtus invicta
For George Eyre, of Warrens, who m. 1st, 1803, Frances, dau. of Sir
Edward Hulse, 3rd Bt., and 2nd, Anna Maria, dau. of Horace Hayes, of
Brook Street, London, and d. 18 Jan. 1837.   (B.L.G.1937 ed.)

BREAMORE

1. Dexter background black

Argent three piles one issuing from the chief between two others reversed
sable, in centre chief the Badge of Ulster (Hulse), impaling, Per fess
embattled argent and gules on a canton azure the golden fleece proper
(Vanderplank)
Crest: A buck's head couped proper attired or between the attires a sun
or   Mantling: Gules and argent   Motto: Resurgam
For Sir Edward Hulse, 2nd Bt., who m. 1741, Hannah, dau. of Samuel
Vanderplank, of London, and d. 1 Dec. 1800.   (B.P. 1949 ed.; Hulse
family records)

.

2. All black background

On a lozenge   Arms: As 1.
Motto: Resurgam
For Hannah, widow of Sir Edward Hulse, 2nd Bt. She d. 16 Dec.
1803.   (Sources, as 1.)

3. Sinister background black

Hulse, as 1.   In pretence: Qly, 1st and 4th, Argent a chevron gules
between three parrots' heads erased vert beaked gules (Lethieullieur),
2nd and 3rd, Or a chevron between three pheons sable (Smart)
Motto: Resurgam   Cherub's head above
For Mary, dau. of Charles Lethieullieur, who m. 1769, Sir Edward
Hulse, 3rd Bt., and d. 24 Mar. 1813.   (Sources, as 1.)

4. All black background
Per fess argent and ermine three piles one issuing from the chief between
two reversed sable, in centre chief the Badge of Ulster (Hulse)   In
pretence: Qly, 1st and 4th, Lethieullieur, 2nd and 3rd, Smart
Crest: A buck's head couped proper attired or between the attires a sun
or and charged on the neck with three bezants   Mantling: Gules
and argent   Motto: Resurgam
For Sir Edward Hulse, 3rd Bt., who d. 30 Sept. 1816.   (Sources, as 1.)

5. Dexter background black
Two shields   Dexter, within the ribbon of the Order of Hanover,
Argent three piles one issuing from the chief between two others reversed
sable, on a canton azure a plume of three feathers argent issuing from a
mural coronet or (Hulse)   Sinister, within an ornamental wreath,
Hulse, impaling, Azure three round buckles or (   )
Crest: A buck's head couped proper attired or between the attires a sun
or   Mantling: Gules and argent   Motto: Esse quam
videri   Star of Order pendant between shields   Supporters: Two
horses reguardant argent, maned and tailed or, the dexter gorged with a
wreath vert, pendant therefrom a shield gules charged as the canton; the
sinister gorged with a wreath vert, pendant therefrom a shield or charged
with a bomb sable inflamed proper
For Field Marshal the Rt. Hon. Sir Samuel Hulse, P.C., G.C.H., who
m. Charlotte (d. 6 Feb. 1842), and d. 1 Jan. 1837.   Sources, as 1.)
(There is another hatchment for Sir Samuel at Wilmington, Kent)

6. Dexter background black
Qly, 1st and 4th, Hulse, as 1., 2nd and 3rd, Lethieullieur, over all the
Badge of Ulster, impaling, Sable on a cross quarterpierced argent four
eagles displayed sable (Buller)
Crest and mantling: As 5.   Motto: Resurgam
For Sir Charles Hulse, 4th Bt., who m. 1808, Maria, dau. of John
Buller, of Morval, Cornwall, and d. 19 Oct. 1854.   (Sources, as 1.)

7. All black background
On a lozenge suspended from a lover's knot
Arms: As 6.
Motto: Resurgemus
For Maria, widow of Sir Charles Hulse, 4th Bt. She d. 20 Jan.
1855.   (Sources, as 1.)

8. Dexter background black
Hulse, as 4., but with Badge of Ulster in dexter chief   In pretence:
Gules a molet or between three cinquefoils argent and a bordure

engrailed argent charged alternately with four crescents and four fleurs-de-lys azure (Hamilton)
Crest: As 4.   Mantling: Sable and argent   No motto
For Sir Edward Hulse, 5th Bt., who m. 1854, Katherine Jane (d. 23 Aug. 1928), only child of the Very Rev. Henry Parr Hamilton, F.R.S., and d. 11 June 1899.   (Sources, as 1.)

9. All red background
Arms: As 8. On a cartouche
For Katherine Jane, widow of Sir Edward Hulse, 5th Bt. She d. 23 Aug. 1928.   (Sources, as 1.)

10. Dexter background black
Hulse, as 8., impaling, Qly, 1st and 4th, Azure three bars gemel argent over all a winged cap or (Lawson), 2nd and 3rd, Gules a saltire double parted and fretted or between two rams' heads couped in fess argent
(   )
Crest: As 1., but charged with two bezants and a roundel argent   Mantling: Sable and argent
For Sir Edward Henry Hulse, 6th Bt., who m. 1888, Edith Maud (d. 1 Nov. 1937), dau. of Edward, 1st Baron Burnham, and d. 29 May 1903.   (Sources, as 1.)

11. All black background
Qly, 1st and 4th, Hulse, as 8., 2nd and 3rd, Lethieullieur
Crest and mantling: As 10.   Motto: Esse quam videri
For Sir Edward Hamilton Westrow Hulse, 7th Bt., who d. unm. 12 Mar. 1915.   (Sources, as 1.)

12. Dexter background black
Qly, 1st and 4th, Hulse, as 4., 2nd and 3rd, Hamilton, in centre chief the Badge of Ulster   In pretence: Gyronny of eight sable and or on a chief argent two pallets azure between two cantons gules each charged with a molet argent (Campbell)
Crest and mantling: As 10.   Motto: Esse quam videri
For Sir Hamilton John Hulse, 8th Bt., who m. 1908, Estelle Leonore (d. 13 Apr. 1933), dau. of William Lorillard Campbell, of New York, and d. 5 Dec. 1931.   (Sources, as 1.)

BURGHCLERE Old Church
1. Dexter background black
Per pale azure and gules three lions rampant argent, in centre chief a crescent argent for difference (Herbert), impaling, Qly, 1st and 4th, Argent three fusils conjoined in fess within a bordure gules (Montagu),

2nd and 3rd, Or an eagle displayed vert beaked and membered gules
(Monthermer)
Crest: A wyvern vert with flames issuing from the mouth
proper   Mantling: Gules and argent   Motto: Ung je serviray
For Charles Herbert, brother of Henry, 1st Earl of Carnarvon, who m.
1775, Caroline, dau. of Robert, 3rd Duke of Manchester, and
d.   She d. 1818.   (B.P. 1949 ed.)

2. All black background
Herbert, as 1.   In pretence: Qly, 1st and 4th, Chequy or and azure
a fess gules (Acland), 2nd and 3rd, Argent three cinquefoils gules
(Dyke)
Earl's coronet   Crest: A wyvern vert   Motto: Ung je
servirai   Supporters: Dexter, A panther guardant argent semy of
roundels or azure and gules, ducally gorged and chained or, charged on
the shoulder with an ermine spot and a crescent gules charged with a
label argent   Sinister, A lion rampant argent ducally gorged azure
chained or, charged as the dexter   All on a mantle gules and
ermine
For Henry George, 2nd Earl of Carnarvon, who m. 1796, Elizabeth (d. 5
Mar. 1813), dau. of Col. John Dyke Acland, and d. 16 Apr.
1833.   (B.P. 1949 ed.)

3. Dexter background black
Herbert, without crescent, impaling, Qly, 1st and 4th, Azure a cross
moline or (Molyneux), 2nd and 3rd, Gules on a bend between six cross-
crosslets fitchy argent the Augmentation of Flodden (Howard)
Earl's coronet   Crest: A wyvern vert   Motto: Ung je
serviray   Supporters: Dexter, A panther argent semy of roundels
sable, ducally gorged and chained or   Sinister, A lion argent
ducally gorged and chained or, on the shoulder an ermine spot
For Henry, 3rd Earl of Carnarvon, who m. 1830, Henrietta Anna, dau.
of Lord Henry Thomas Molyneux Howard, and d. 10 Dec.
1849.   (B.P. 1949 ed.)

BURITON
1. Sinister background black
Gules a fess chequy or and azure between ten billets four and six or
(Lee), impaling, Argent an annulet sable (Pym)
Crest: A squirrel sejant holding a tree proper   Mantling: Gules and
argent
Unidentified

2. All black background
On a lozenge surmounted by a cherub's head
Lee, impaling, Gules two bars ermine in chief a lion passant or
(Costomer)   Skull below
Unidentified

CHERITON
1. Dexter background black

Or on a chevron between three molets sable three lions passant
guardant or (Barrett), impaling, Sable on a chevron between three ears
of wheat or an annulet enclosed by a pair of arrows pointing to it sable
(Villebois)
Crest: A griffin's head erased argent langued gules pierced by an arrow
bendwise sinister point downwards or   Mantling: Gules and
argent   Motto: Resurgam
For Charles Reid Barrett, of Cheriton Lodge, who m. Charlotte, dau. of
William Villebois of Feltham Place, Middlesex, and d. 18 Mar. 1847,
aged 72.   (M.I. in churchyard)

CHRISTCHURCH
1. Dexter background black

Qly, 1st and 4th, Argent a fire of brands proper, 2nd and 3rd, Sable a
saltire couped argent (Brander), impaling, Gules two bars nebuly argent
over all on a bend sable three roundels argent (Gulston)
Crest: Out of flames a phoenix rising proper   Mantling: Gules and
argent   Motto: In silentio et spe
For Gustavus Brander, who m. Elizabeth, dau. of Francis Gulston, of
Widdial Hall, and d. 21 Jan. 1787, aged 67.   (M.I.)

2. Sinister background black

Per bend indented azure and or two fleurs-de-lys counterchanged, in
centre chief the Badge of Ulster (Shee), impaling, Azure a martlet
between three pierced molets or, within a bordure compony argent and
gules (Young)
Motto: Resurgam   Shield suspended from a lover's knot with a
cherub's head at each top corner of shield
For Jane, eldest dau. of William Young, of Hexton House, Herts, who
m. 1808, as his 1st wife, Sir George Shee, 2nd Bt. and d.
1832.   (B.P. 1868 ed.)

3. Sinister background black

Argent a chevron between three bugle horns stringed sable, on a chief
sable three lions rampant or (Hinxman), impaling, Ermine on a chevron
engrailed gules three escallops argent (Grove)
On a shield suspended by gold ribbons from a gold skull
For Elizabeth, dau. of Thomas Grove, of Ferne, Wilts., who m. 1740,
Joseph Hinxman, of North Hinton, Hants, and d.   (B.L.G. 2nd ed.)

4. Dexter background black

Hinxman, impaling, Azure three stirrups between two bendlets or
(   )

Crest: A demi-lion rampant or holding in its dexter paw a bugle horn
stringed sable   Mantling: Gules and argent
Unidentified

5. Dexter background black
Two shields   Dexter, within the Order of the Bath, Or a fess chequy
argent and azure within a double tressure flory counter-flory gules, in
centre chief a molet sable for difference (Stuart)   Sinister, Stuart,
with in pretence, Argent a saltire azure (Yorke)
Baron's coronet   Crest: A demi-lion rampant gules charged on the
shoulder with a molet argent   Mottoes: (above crest) Nobilis ira
(below shield) Avito iret honore   Supporters: Dexter, A horse argent
bridled gules   Sinister, A stag proper   Each gorged with a
wreath vert within a double tressure flory counter-flory gules
For Charles, Lord Stuart de Rothesay, G.C.B., who m. 1816, Elizabeth
Margaret, dau. of Philip, 3rd Earl of Hardwicke, and d. 6 Nov.
1845.   (B.E.P.)

DUMMER
1. Dexter background black
Qly, 1st and 4th, Gules a fess between six martlets argent (Croke), 2nd,
Qly gules and or in the first and fourth quarters a cross botonny argent
(Crosse), 3rd, Per chevron sable and argent in chief three leopards' faces
or (   )   Two escutcheons of pretence, the one surmounting the
other: Qly, 1st, Azure a lion rampant argent (   ), 2nd, Argent a
buglehorn sable stringed or (   ), 3rd, Gules a fleur-de-lys or
(   ), 4th, Sable a chevron ermine between three bells argent
(Bell)   Second escutcheon, surmounting the first, Qly, 1st and 4th,
Or a fess countercompony argent and azure surmounted by a bend
engrailed, all within a double tressure flory counter-flory gules
(Stewart), 2nd Argent on a chief gules two molets or (St John), 3rd, Qly
ermine and paly of six or and gules (   )
Crest: Two swans' necks addorsed erased argent, surrounded with an
annulet sable and each with an annulet or in its beak   Mantling:
Gules and argent   Motto: In coelo quies
Unidentified

ELING
1. Dexter background black
Per pale or and sable (Serle), impaling, Per bend sinister ermine and
sable ermined argent a lion rampant or (Edwards)
Crest: A tower in flames proper   Mantling: Gules and
argent   Motto: Resurgam
A small hatchment, *c.* 2½ ft. by 2½ ft.
For Lt.-Col. Wentworth Serle, son of Peter Serle of Testwood House,
who d. 13 Jan. 1837. Mary Ann, his widow, dau. of John Edwards of
Longparish, d. 20 June 1862.   (M.I.s)

2. All black background
Sable semy-de-lys a lion rampant argent (Phillips), impaling, Azure a
fess between three garbs or (   )
Crests: Dexter, A demi-lion rampant crowned holding a fleur-de-lys
or   Sinister, A fox sejant reguardant proper   Mantling: Gules
and argent   Motto: Resurgam
For the Rev. William Joseph George Phillips, Vicar of Eling, who m.
Susannah, and d. 1855. She d. 1848.   (M.I.)

3. Dexter background black
Per fess argent and sable a pale counterchanged and three bears sejant
sable, muzzled and chained or, the Badge of Ulster (Mill), impaling,
Azure a cross crosslet argent between four martlets or, on a chief argent
three escallops gules (Morshead)
Crest: A demi-bear sable muzzled collared and chained
or   Mantling: Gules and argent   Motto: Resurgam
For Sir Charles Mill, 10th Bt., who m. 1800, Selina, eldest dau. of Sir
John Morshead, Bt., of Trenant Park, Cornwall, and d.s.p. 26 Feb.
1835.   (B.E.B.)

ELLINGHAM
1. All black background
Or on a chief azure three lions rampant or (Lisle)
Crest: A stag statant argent attired or   Mantling: Gules and
argent   Motto: Resurgam
Unidentified

ELVETHAM
1. Dexter background black
Chequy or and azure a fess ermine (Calthorpe), impaling, Argent three
lions rampant and a chief gules (Yelverton)
Crest: A boar's head couped azure muzzled or   Mantling: Azure
and or   Motto: Gradu diverso via una
For Reynolds Calthorpe, who m. 2nd, Barbara, only dau. of Henry, 1st
Viscount Longueville, and d. 1719.   (B.P. 1949 ed.; M.I.)

2. All black background
Calthorpe, within the Order of the Bath
Crest and motto: As 1.   Supporters: Two wild men, wreathed at the
temples and loins, each holding in the exterior hand a club resting on
the ground proper   All on a mantle gules and argent
For Sir Henry Calthorpe, K.B., who d. unm. 1788.   (Source, as 1.)

3. Dexter background black

Qly, 1st and 4th, Calthorpe, 2nd and 3rd, Gules on a fess between three boars' heads couped or a lion passant azure (Gough)
Baron's coronet   Crests: Dexter, as 1.   Sinister, A boar's head couped argent pierced by an arrow gules   Motto: As
1.   Supporters: Two wild men, wreathed at the temples and loins, each holding in the exterior hand a club resting on the shoulder proper
Unidentified

4. All black background

Tierced in pairle   1st, Calthorpe, as 1., 2nd, Ermine a maunch gules (Calthorpe), 3rd, Gough, in centre chief the Badge of Ulster
Baron's coronet   Crest: A boar's head couped azure between two wild men wreathed at the temples and loins, each holding in the exterior hand a club resting on the shoulder proper   Motto: As
1.   Supporters: Two wild men as in the crest
Probably for Charles, 2nd Baron Calthorpe, who d. unm. 5 June 1807. (See Ampton, Suffolk for similar marshalling by his father, 1st Baron Calthorpe)   (Complete Peerage)

5. All black background

Qly, 1st and 2nd, as 4., 3rd, Gough, 4th, Argent three pallets gules over all a chevron azure charged with three trefoils slipped or (Carpenter), over all the Badge of Ulster, impaling, Qly, France and England, a bordure compony wavy argent and azure (Somerset)
Baron's coronet   Crest, motto and supporters: As 4.   All on a mantle gules and ermine
For Frederick, 4th Baron Calthorpe, who m. 1823, Charlotte Sophia, dau. of Henry Charles, 6th Duke of Beaufort, and d. 2 May
1868.   (Source, as 1.)

6. All black background

Calthorpe, as 1.   In pretence, and impaling, Azure a chevron between three cross crosslets fitchy or (Reynolds)
Crest, mantling and motto: As 1.
Probably for Priscilla, dau. and heiress of Sir Robert Reynolds of Elvetham, 1st wife of Reynolds Calthorpe (No. 1.) and d. 29 Aug.
1709.   (M.I.; V.C.H.)

7. All black background

Calthorpe, as 1.
Crest, mantling and motto: As 1.
Probably for Reynolds Calthorpe, son of No. 6., who d. 10 Apr.
1714.   (Sources as 6.)

FARLEY CHAMBERLAYNE

1. All black background

On a lozenge surmounted by two cherubs' heads
Argent on a chief gules two molets or, in fess point the Badge of Ulster
(St John), impaling, Azure a chevron ermine between three urchins or
(Harris)
Moto: Mors janua vitae   Festoons of naturalistic flowers to dexter
and sinister, and winged skull in base
For Jane, dau. and heir of Roger Harris, of Silksted, Hants, who m.
1761, as his 3rd wife, Sir Paulet St John, 1st Bt., and d.s.p. 26 Jan. 1791,
aged 85.   (B.P. 1949 ed.)

2. All black background

Qly, 1st, Argent on a chief gules two molets or (St John), 2nd, Gules a
fess between two chevrons vairy or and azure (Goodyear), 3rd, Sable a
chevron between three spearheads argent (   ), 4th, Sable a
spearhead between three scaling ladders argent, on a chief azure a tower
triple-towers argent (   ), over all the Badge of Ulster, impaling,
Barry wavy of eight argent and azure on a chevron embattled counter-
embattled or between three seahorses naiant argent manes and tails or
five gouttes sable (Tucker)
Crest: A falcon rising or collared gules   Mantling: Gules and
argent   Motto: Data fata secutus
For Sir Henry Paulet St John, 2nd Bt., who m. 1763, Dorothy Maria,
dau. and co-heiress of Abraham Tucker, of Betchworth Castle, Surrey,
and d. 7 Aug. 1784.   (B.P. 1949 ed.)

FREEFOLK

1. All black background

Argent a lion rampant sable, on a chief azure six molets, three and three
or (Portal), impaling, Argent three horses' heads erased sable a chief
gules (Slade)
Crest: A castellated portal flanked by two towers argent   Mantling:
Gules and argent   Motto: Constanter
For William Portal, of Ashe Park, later of Laverstoke, who m. 1789,
Sophia, dau. of John Slade, of Maunsell Park, Somerset, and d. 12 Feb.
1846.   (B.P. 1963 ed.)

2. Sinister background black

Azure on a fess argent between three pelicans or vulning themselves
proper three roundels sable (for Cullum), impaling, Gules a lion
couchant guardant or, on a chief argent three crescents gules (Deane)
No crest or mantling   Motto: Vigilate
For Jane, dau. and heir of Thomas Deane, of Freefolk, who m. 1728, as
his 1st wife, John Cullum (later 5th Bt.), and d. 1729.   (B.P. 1855
ed.)

3. All black background

Qly, 1st and 4th, qly i. & iv. France, ii. & iii. England, 2nd, Scotland, 3rd, Ireland   In pretence: Or billetty a lion rampant azure (Nassau)

Royal crown, crest and supporters   Motto: Dieu et mon droit

Initials and date below W R 1701

For H.M. King William III, who d. 8 March 1702.

FROYLE

1. Sinister background black

Qly, 1st and 4th, Argent a fess wavy azure between three wolves' heads erased proper, in centre chief the Badge of Ulster (Miller), 2nd and 3rd, Or a fess dancetty gules between three estoiles sable (Comber)   In pretence: Per bend sinister ermine and sable ermined argent a lion rampant or (Edwards)

Motto: Resurgam   Cherub's head above shield

For Elizabeth Edwards, who m. as his 2nd wife, Sir Thomas Miller, 5th Bt., and was buried at Froyle, 4 Apr. 1800.   (B.P. 1949 ed.; Complete Baronetage)

2. All black background

Qly, 1st and 4th, Miller with Badge of Ulster in centre chief of 1st quarter, 2nd and 3rd, Comber   In pretence: Edwards

Crest: A wolf's head erased argent collared wavy azure   Mantling: Gules and argent   Motto: Resurgam   Skull below

For Sir Thomas Miller, 5th Bt., who d. 4 Sept. 1816.   (B.P. 1949 ed.)

3. Dexter background black

Miller, with Badge of Ulster over line of impalement, impaling two coats per fess, in chief, Gules two bars ermine in chief three fleurs-de-lys or (Gilbert), and in base, Barry or and azure a bordure nebuly ermine, on a canton argent a chaplet vert flowered gules (Holmes)

Crest and mantling: As 2.   Motto: In coelo quies

For Sir Thomas Combe Miller, 6th Bt., who m. 1824, Martha, dau. of the Rev. Thomas Holmes, of Bungay, Suffolk, and d. 29 June 1864.   (B.P. 1949 ed.)

4. Dexter background black

Qly, 1st and 4th, Miller, 2nd, Comber, 3rd, Per bend ermine and sable ermined argent a lion rampant or a bordure argent (Edwards), over all the Badge of Ulster, impaling, Per pale indented sable and argent a saltire counterchanged (Scott)

Crest, mantling and motto: As 3.

For Sir Charles Hayes Miller, 7th Bt., who m. 1856, Katherine Maria, 2nd dau. of James Winter Scott, of Rotherfield Park, Hants, and d. 12 Jan. 1868.   (B.P. 1949 ed.)

5. All black background
Argent a chevron gules between three pinecones vert, on a canton gules
a fleur-de-lys argent, in centre chief the Badge of Ulster
(Pepperell)   In pretence: Azure three garbs or (for Royall)
Crest: From a mural coronet argent a dexter arm in armour embowed
the hand proper holding a flag argent, and on a scroll above the word,
Peperi   Mantling: Gules and argent   Motto: Virtute parta
tuemini
For Sir William Pepperell, Bt., who m. 1767, Elizabeth, dau. of Isaac
Royall, and d. 18 Dec. 1816.   (B.E.B.)

6. All black background
On a lozenge surmounted by a cherub's head
Qly, 1st and 4th, Argent on a fess engrailed between three choughs sable
three lions rampant argent, in chief a crown or (Nicholas), 2nd and 3rd,
Azure on a fess or three cross crosslets sable (   )   In pretence:
Qly, 1st and 4th, Argent on a fess between three annulets gules three
covered cups or (Draper), 2nd and 3rd, Argent a chevron between three
buglehorns sable stringed gules (   )
For Mary, dau. of William Draper, who m. William Nicholas, and d.
1791.   (M.I.)

7. All black background
On a lozenge   Vert on a fess engrailed between three owls argent
another fess engrailed gules (Moody)   In pretence: Qly, 1st, Argent
on a cross gules an imperial crown proper (Nicholas), 2nd, Argent on a
fess azure between three choughs proper three lions rampant argent
(Nicholas), 3rd, Argent on a fess engrailed between three annulets gules
three covered cups argent (Draper), 4th, Argent a chevron between three
buglehorns azure stringed gules (   )
For Mary Annabel, dau. of William Nicholas, who m. Richard Vernon
Moody, of Southampton, and d. Dec. 1829, aged 73.   (M.I.)

8. All black background
On a rococo lozenge suspended from a lover's knot
Qly of 16, 1st and 16th, Vert on a fess engrailed between three owls
argent another fess gules (Moody), 2nd, Or a lion rampant proper
ducally crowned argent (   ), 3rd, Per chevron or and gules in chief
two lions combatant sable (Lee), 4th, Gules three swords argent
pommels and hilts or fesswise in pale that in the centre pointing sinister
the others dexter, within an orle of eight molets and a bordure engrailed
argent (   ), 5th, Sable three pallets ermine, on a canton azure a lion
rampant argent (Newberry), 6th, Argent a fess wavy between three
choughs proper (Nicholas), 7th, Argent on a cross gules an imperial
crown proper (Nicholas), 8th, Argent on a fess between three crows
sable three lions rampant argent (Nicholas), 9th, Argent on a chevron
sable between three choughs proper two lions passant respectant argent

(Nicholas), 10th, Gules a chevron between three wells or (   ), 11th,
Azure three fishes fesswise in pale argent (   ), 12th, Or three bulls'
heads cabossed in fess sable (   ), 13th, Azure on a fess or three cross
crosslets sable (   ), 14th, Argent on a fess engrailed between three
annulets gules three covered cups or (Draper), 15th, Argent a chevron
between three buglehorns sable stringed gules (   )
For Mary Elizabeth Moody, who d. 29 July 1855 or her sister Rebecca
Anabella, who d. 2 April 1860. They were the daughters of Richard
Moody and his wife Mary. No. 7.   (M.I.)

9. All black background
On a lozenge   Arms, as 8., but with the following differences, 2nd,
lion rampant gules, 3rd, lions combatant proper, 12th, bulls' heads
proper, 13th, cross crosslets brown, 15th, buglehorns brown
Identification as 8.

HARTLEY WINTNEY, St Mary
1. Dexter background black
Within the Order of the Bath, Gules on two serpents intertwined a dove
rising, wings displayed and inverted, holding in its beak an olive branch
proper (Sloper), impaling, Argent a chevron between three molets sable
(Willes)
Crest: A dove rising in its beak an olive branch proper   Motto: In
pace ut sapiens   Supporters: Dexter, A female figure, in the left
hand a rod of Aesculapius, in the dexter a mirror   Sinister, A
soldier, with shako, blue coat, white breeches, and cross belts, with
drawn cutlass in sinister hand proper   All on a mantle gules and
argent
For General Sir Robert Sloper, K.B., who m. Jane, dau. of Lord Chief
Justice Sir John Willes, and d. 1802.   (B.L.G. 2nd ed.)
(There is a pencil note on edge of canvas: Put up Aug. 5, 1803)

2. Dexter background black
Vert a saltire engrailed argent (Hawley), impaling, Azure a cock's head
erased argent a chief per fess embattled argent and or (Jepson)
Crest: A winged thunderbolt proper   Mantling: Gules and
argent   Motto: Et suivez moy
For Henry William Toovey Hawley, of West Green House, who m.
1794, Catherine, dau. of Rev. George Jepson, and d.   (B.L.G.
5th ed.)

3. All black background
On a lozenge surmounted by a cherub's head
Arms: Hawley, impaling, Per fess argent and azure a fess embattled or,
in base a cock's head erased argent combed and langued gules
(Jepson)   Motto: Resurgam   All on a mantle gules and argent

For Catherine, widow of Henry William Toovey Hawley, who d.
(B.L.G. 5th ed.)

HECKFIELD
1. All black background
On a lozenge   Sable a chevron argent between two trefoils slipped
in chief and in base an orb or (Lefevre)   In pretence: Qly, 1st and
4th, Lefevre, 2nd and 3rd, Ermine on a bend engrailed or a bend gules
charged with three eagles displayed argent (Selman)
For Helena, only child of John Lefevre, of Heckfield Place, who m.
Charles Shaw, M.P. for Reading, who took the name of Lefevre, and d.
17 Aug. 1834, aged 68.   (B.P. 1875 ed.)

2. Sinister background black
Qly, 1st and 4th, Lefevre, 2nd and 3rd, Argent a chevron sable ermined
argent, on a canton gules a talbot's head erased or (Shaw), impaling,
Argent a chevron sable between three hinds' heads erased gules
(Whitbread)
Viscountess's coronet   Motto: Sans changer   Supporters: Dexter,
A talbot gules langued azure charged with a mace or   Sinister, A
talbot sable charged with a mace or
For Emma Laura, dau. of Samuel Whitbread, who m. 1817, Charles, 1st
Viscount Eversley, and d. 20 June 1857.   (B.P. 1875 ed.)

3. All black background
Two oval shields   Dexter, within the Order of the Bath,
Lefevre   Sinister, within an ornamental wreath, Lefevre, impaling,
Whitbread
Viscount's coronet   Crest: Six arrows interlaced saltirewise three
and three proper with an annulet or   Motto and supporters: As 2.
For Charles, 1st Viscount Eversley, who d. 1888.   (B.P. 1875 ed.)

4. All black background
Qly, 1st and 4th, Argent a cross sable between four eagles displayed
gules (Corham), 2nd and 3rd, Vert a fess between three antelopes
statant or langued gules (Bornicomb)
Crest: A cat-a-mountain statant or charged with a martlet
gules   Mantling: Gules and argent
A small hatchment, on wood panel, *c.* 2 ft. by 2 ft. only
Unidentified

5. Dexter background black
Within the Order of the Bath, and badge pendent below, Argent a bull
passant proper, armed and unguled or, in chief a crescent or, a bordure
vert bezanty, on a canton azure a harp or stringed argent (Cole),
impaling, Azure a chevron or ermined sable between three urchins or, on

a chief or an eagle displayed sable holding in the dexter claw a sceptre and in the sinister an orb or (Harris)
Crest: A demi-dragon vert in the dexter claw an arrow argent in the sinister an escutcheon, azure a harp or   Motto: Deum cole regem serve   Supporters: Two dragons reguardant vert each holding an arrow argent
For General Sir Galbraith Lowry Cole, G.C.B., who m. 1815, Frances, dau. of James, 1st Earl of Malmesbury, and d. 4 Oct. 1842.   (B.P. 1875 ed.)

6. All black background
An oval shield and a lozenge   Shield, within the Order of the Bath, Sable a fess chequy argent and azure between three bezants, in chief a crescent sable (Pitt)   Lozenge, Pitt, impaling, Or a fess between three wolves' heads couped sable langued gules (Howe)
Supporters: Dexter, A hawk wings inverted or charged with a crescent sable   Sinister, A unicorn argent similarly charged   Cherub's head above   All on a mantle gules and ermine
For Mary, dau. of Emanuel Scrope, 2nd Viscount Howe, who m. 1763, Lt.-Gen. Sir William Augustus Pitt, K.B., and d. 26 May 1819.   (B.P. 1875 ed.)

KINGSWORTHY
1. All black background
Per fess or and azure a fess embattled counter-embattled between three fleurs-de-lys all counterchanged (Wall)
To dexter of main shield, Wall, with in pretence, Azure a falcon volant or (Binns) S.B1   To sinister of main shield, Wall, impaling, Qly, 1st, Gules a fess and in chief two pelicans vulning or (Lechmere), 2nd, Vert fretty or (Whitmore), 3rd, Argent a chevron engrailed between three chess rooks sable (Rook), 4th, Argent three wolves' heads erased proper (   ) D.B1.
Crest: From a mural coronet or a demi-wolf argent collared with a fess embattled counter-embattled gules   Mantling: Gules and argent   Motto: Resurgam
For Samuel Wall, of Worthy Park, who m. 1st, 1812, Eliza, dau. and co-heiress of John Binns, of Leeds, and 2nd, 1837, Eliza Ann, dau. of Sir Anthony Lechmere, Bt., of the Rhyd, and d. 1843.   (B.L.G. 2nd ed.)

KNIGHTS ENHAM
now ENHAM ALAMEIN
1. All black background
Azure on the waves of the sea a ship with sails set oars in action proper, on a chief sable three boars' heads couped or (Dewar), impaling, Argent three battering rams in pale proper headed sable (Bertie)
Crest: An anchor erect sable, and above it on scroll, Dum spiro spero   Mantling: Gules and argent   Motto: In coelo quies

For George Dewar, who m. Caroline, dau. of Peregrine, 2nd Duke of
Ancaster, and d. 12 July 1785.   (Burke's Family Records)

2. Dexter background black
Azure a galley with sail set oars in action proper on a chief argent three
boars' heads couped proper (Dewar)
Crest: An anchor and chain erect or   Mantling: Azure and
or   Motto: Dum spiro spero
For Albermarle Dewar, of Doles Hall, who m. Jane, dau. of Felix
O'Beirne, and d. 5 June 1862.   She d. 10 Mar. 1905.   (As 1.;
M.I.)

LYMINGTON
1. Dexter background black
Argent a fess flory gules between three rooks sable (Rooke), impaling,
Vert a lion passant or between three estoiles argent, on a chief or two
lions rampant respectant supporting a sinister hand couped gules
(Burrard)
Crest: On a trumpet or a rook close sable   Mantling: Gules and
argent   Motto: Resurgam
For W. Rooke, of the H.E.I.C., who m. Marianne, dau. of William
Burrard, and sister of Sir George Burrard, 3rd Bt., and d. 6 Aug.
1831.   (B.P. 1939 ed.)

2. All black background
On a lozenge suspended from a lover's knot
Argent a fess flory counter-flory gules between three rooks sable (Rooke),
impaling, Azure a lion passant between three estoiles argent, on a chief
or two lions rampant respectant supporting a sinister hand couped gules
(Burrard)
Cherub's head in base
For Mariane, widow of W. Rooke, d.   (Sources, as 1.)

3. Dexter background black
Rooke, as 1., impaling, Vert a lion rampant argent and in chief two piles
engrailed gules, all within a bordure engrailed argent charged with
popinjays azure beaked and armed gules (Home)
Crest, mantling and motto: As 1.
Unidentified

4. Dexter background black
Per pale sable and gules gutty argent a lion rampant tail forked ermine
(Kingston), impaling, Rooke, as 1.
Crest: A dexter arm in armour grasping a scimitar proper embrued
gules   Mantling: Sable and argent   Motto: Fortes fortuna juvat
For Lucy Henry Kingston, who m. Frances Sophia, dau. of Sir Giles
Rooke, and d.   (Sources, as 1.)

5. Dexter background black
Two shields   Dexter, within collar of Order of the Bath and with
military star of Order pendent below, Argent a lion rampant gules
debruised by a fess or charged with two lions rampant respectant
supporting a sinister hand couped gules, in chief two dexter hands
couped gules and in centre chief the Badge of Ulster
(Burrard)   Sinister, within an ornamental wreath, as dexter, with
Burrard in pretence
Crests: Dexter, A naval crown or issuing therefrom a cubit arm erect
proper, the hand grasping a trident in bend sinister points downwards or,
and a sprig of oak proper   Sinister, An arm in armour embowed the
hand grasping the broken butt of a spear proper   Motto:
Persevere   Supporters: Two lions rampant reguardant argent
standing on anchors sable, each gorged with a naval crown vert, chained
proper, and holding a trident or
For Sir Harry Burrard Neale, 2nd Bt., Admiral of the White, G.C.B.,
G.C.M.G., who m. 1795, Grace Elizabeth, dau. and co-heir of Robert
Neale, of Shaw House, Wilts., when he assumed the surname and arms
of Neale, and d.s.p. 7 Feb. 1840.   (B.P. 1949 ed.)

6. Dexter background black
Qly, 1st and 4th, Argent an eagle displayed sable charged on the breast
with an escutcheon gules (Reid), 2nd, Gyronny of eight sable and or
(Campbell), 3rd, Or a lion rampant sable ducally crowned or (   ),
impaling, Argent a chevron between three harts lodged gules (   )
Crest: An eagle rising wings addorsed and inverted
proper   Mantling: Gules and argent   Mottoes: (above crest)
Sublime (below shield) Resurgam
Unidentified

7. All black background
Or an eagle's head erased gules in its beak an olive branch vert
(Munro), impaling, Azure a chevron between three molets pierced
argent (   )
Crest: An eagle close or beaked gules   Mantling: Gules and
argent   Motto: Non inferiora
For James Munro, who m. 2nd, Elizabeth Vassall (née Athill), and d.
26 Oct. 1894.   (M.I.)

8. All black background
Or a chevron wavy between three bucks trippant and a chief sable
(Rogers)
Crest: A buck's head couped proper collared or   Mantling: Gules
and argent   Motto: Resurgam   Beside the shield are two
cannons, a sword hilt, a ramrod, and the red and blue ensigns
Unidentified

9. Dexter background black
Argent a bend gules cotised sable (Frampton), impaling, Argent three
boars' heads couped proper (   )
Crest: A greyhound sejant argent collared gules   Mantling and
motto: As 8.
Unidentified

10. Dexter background black
Argent two bars and in chief three cocks gules, in fess point the Badge of
Ulster (Blakiston), impaling, Azure a lion rampant argent (Rochfort)
Crest: A cock gules   Mantling: Gules and argent   Motto: Do
well and doubt not
For Sir Matthew Blakiston, 2nd Bt., who m. 1782, Anne, dau. of John
Rochfort, of Clogrenane, co. Carlow, and d. 20 Sept. 1806.   (B.P.
1949 ed.)

11. All black background
Azure in chief a sun in splendour and in base a chalice or (Vassall)
Crest: A ship with mast and shrouds proper the masts flagged gules, at
the stern a red ensign   Mantling: Gules and argent   Motto:
Resurgam
For John Vassall, who d. 23 Mar. 1827.   (B.L.G. 2nd ed.; M.I.)

MARTIN
1. Dexter two-thirds black
Or a mermaid, comb, glass and hair proper (Lapp), impaling two coats
per pale, 1st, Argent two bars azure and in chief three escallops sable
(Errington), 2nd, Argent a fess azure between three crescents gules, in
fess point a crescent gules for difference (Patteshall)
No crest or motto   Shield surrounded by oval framing of interlocked
circles, with a knot above and a bow below   A small hatchment, *c.*
2 ft. by 2 ft.
For Sir Gabriel Lapp, of Durnford, son of Robert Lapp, of Rodbourne,
who m. 1st, Mary Erington, of Durnford, and 2nd, . . . Patteshall, and d.
1 Feb. 1668. (M.I.)

MICHELDEVER
1. All black background
Azure a fess and in chief a bear's head couped argent muzzled gules, in
fess point the Badge of Ulster (Baring), impaling, Gules crusilly or three
fishes hauriant argent (Herring)
Crest: A molet of six points or between two wings argent   Mantling:
Gules and argent   Motto: Spes mea in Deo
For Sir Francis Baring, 1st Bt., who m. 1766, Harriet, dau. of William
Herring, and d. 12 Sept. 1810.   (B.P. 1949 ed.)

2. Sinister background black
Qly, 1st and 4th, Baring with Badge of Ulster in 1st quarter, 2nd and
3rd, Herring, impaling, Gules a chevron between three molets or (Sealy)
Crest: A molet or ermined sable between two wings
argent   Mantling: Gules and argent   Motto: Resurgam
For Mary Ursula, dau. of Charles Sealy, of Calcutta, who m. 1794, Sir
Thomas Baring, 2nd Bt., and d. 26 July 1846.   (B.P. 1949 ed.)

3. All black background
Arms: Qly, 1st and 4th, Baring, 2nd and 3rd, Herring, over all the
Badge of Ulster, impaling, Azure a chevron or between three molets
argent (Sealy)
Crest: As 2.   Mantling: Gules and argent   Motto: Probitate et
labore
For Sir Thomas Baring, 2nd Bt., who d. 3 Apr. 1848.   (B.P. 1949
ed.)

NURSLING
1. All black background
Azure a chevron engrailed ermine, on a chief argent two stags' heads
cabossed gules attired or (Nibbs), impaling, Argent on a bend azure
three buckles or (Leslie)
Crest: A stag's head cabossed gules attired or   Mantling: Gules and
argent   Motto: In caelo quies
Probably for Thomas Nibb, of Nursling, who m. Sarah (Lesslie) and d.
1882, aged 70.   (M.I.)

ODIHAM
1. All black background
Argent on a chevron azure between three lynxes' heads erased sable
three crescents ermine (Nicolls)
Crest: A rabbit sejant sable collared or in the paws a water bouget
argent   Mantling: Gules and argent   Motto: Resurgam
For Samuel Nicholls, of The Priory, Odiham, Sergeant-at-Law and
Executor of Dean Swift, who d.   (Church guide)

2. Dexter background black
Argent a bat displaying sable (   ), impaling, Sable a saltire or in
chief a rose argent (   )
Crest: A bat displayed sable   Mantling: Gules and
argent   Motto: Resurgam
Unidentified

Mayhill Junior School
1. All black background
Gules a chevron argent between three men's heads proper each in an
esquire's helmet sable garnished or (May)

Crest: A man's head proper in a helmet as in the arms   Mantling:
Gules and argent, tasselled or   Motto (over crest): Fiat voluntas
Dei   Dated 1673
Unidentified

OVINGTON

1. Dexter background black
Qly, 1st and 4th, Or a chief indented gules (Dyer), 2nd and 3rd, Argent
a cross fleuretty sable (Swinnerton), over all the Badge of
Ulster   In pretence: Qly, 1st and 4th, Or a chief indented azure
(   ), 2nd and 3rd, Argent a fess dancetty between three crows sable
beaked and membered gules (   )
Crest: From a ducal coronet a goat's head argent attired
or   Mantling: Gules and argent   Motto: O hen fon
ned   Crosses of the Orders of San Hermenegelda and Isabel da
Catolica hang below shield which is flanked by the Blue and Red
Ensigns
For General Sir Thomas Richard Swinnerton Dyer, 7th Bt., who m.
1814, Elizabeth, only dau. and heir of James Standerwicke, of Ovington
House, and d.s.p. 12 Apr. 1838.   (B.P. 1949 ed.)

RINGWOOD

1. All black background
Or a lion rampant gules (Mowbray)
Crest: A tree or   Mantling: Gules and argent   Motto: Resurgam
For James Mowbray, of Burley Manor, who d. unm. 20 July 1801, aged
67.   (M.I. in church)

2 . All black background
Qly, 1st and 4th, Sable a lion passant guardant or between three
esquires' helms argent (Compton), 2nd and 3rd, Argent three fusils
gules (Hoby)
Crest: A demi-dragon gules gorged with a ducal coronet
or   Mantling: Gules and argent
For Hoby Compton, son of Henry Compton and Elizabeth Hoby, d.
unm. 1714.   (B.L.G. 1937 ed.)

3. Dexter background black
Qly of 19, 1st, Compton, with a molet for difference, 2nd, Argent a
chevron azure, on a bordure azure eight roundels argent (   ), 3rd,
Argent on a chevron azure three fleurs-de-lys or (   ), 4th, Argent a
fess engrailed between six billets, three and three gules (Aylworth), 5th,
Gules a lion rampant argent between four crosses botonny fitchy sable
(Warre), 6th, Azure three leopards' heads affronté or (   ), 7th, Barry
of six or and sable a bend ermine (Meritt), 8th, Gules a pair of wings
conjoined in lure argent, over all a bend azure (Kentisbere), 9th, Argent
two bars sable in chief a molet gules (   ), 10th, Gules a chevron

between 12 crosses formy a bordure argent (Berkeley), 11th Argent on a
saltire gules five molets or (Peverell), 12th, Per pale azure and gules
three lions rampant argent (Herbert), 13th, Or three keys erect two and
one gules (   ), 14th, Argent a cross botonny gules (   ), 15th,
Argent on a bend gules cotised azure between six martlets sable three
wings argent (   ), 16th, Or on a chief sable three martlets
or(   ), 17th, Gules a chevron between six feathers three and three
argent (   ), 18th Azure a chevron between three stags' heads
cabossed or (   ), 19th, Argent on a bend azure three boars' heads
erased argent (Hartley), impaling, Per pale gules and argent three lions
rampant counterchanged a bordure ermine (Willis)
Crest: A demi-dragon gules ducally gorged or   Mantling: Gules and
argent
For Henry Compton, who m. Eleanor, dau. of John Willis, of Ringwood,
and d.s.p. 1724.   (B.L.G. 1937 ed.)

4. All black background
Compton arms only   To dexter of main shield, Compton, impaling,
Ermine a millrind sable (Mills) S.B1.   To sinister of main shield,
Compton, impaling, Azure (   ) D.B1.
Crest and mantling: As 2.   Motto: Mors janua vitae
For Henry Compton, who m. 1747, Lucretia Mills (d. 10 July ·1771),
and d. 4 Sept. 1786.   (B.L.G. 1937 ed.)

5. All black background
Qly, 1st and 4th, Compton, 2nd and 3rd, Mills
Crest and mantling: As 2.   Motto: In coelo quies
Probably for Henry Compton, who d. unm. 9 Jan. 1787.   (B.L.G.
1937 ed.)

ROMSEY
1. Dexter background black
Argent three battering rams in pale sable garnished or (Bertie),
impaling, Azure a pelican in her piety or (Piers)
Crest: (over a peer's helm) A Saracen's head couped at the shoulders
proper ducally crowned or   Mantling: Gules and
argent   Motto: Loyalte me oblige   Supporters: Dexter, A monk
habited proper girdled or holding in his right hand a staff
or   Sinister, A savage wreathed about the temples and loins with ivy
proper
For Captain Lord Montagu Bertie, 3rd son of Robert, 1st Duke of
Ancaster, who m. Anne, dau. of William Piers, and d. 1753.   She d.
1782.   (B.E.P.)

ROPLEY

1. Dexter background black
Ermine on a saltire sable a rose or (Barton), impaling, Or a fess cotised gules (?Delamare)
Crest: An owl proper   Mantling: Gules and argent   Motto: In coelo quies
Probably for Charles Barton, J.P., Major North Hants Militia, who m. Martha, and d. 1821, aged 69.   (M.I. in church)

SHERBORNE ST JOHN

1. Sinister background black
Gules three swords fesswise in pale points to the dexter argent hilts and pommels or (Chute), impaling, Sable a bend ermine cotised flory or (Keck)   To dexter of main shield, Or two bendlets gules, in fess point an escallop sable, and in chief a crescent sable for difference (Tracy), impaling, Keck, D.B1.   To sinister of main shield, Chute, impaling, Keck S.B1.
Motto: Fide viventi justi
For Katharine Keck, widow of Ferdinand Tracey, who m. Edward Chute, of the Vyne, and d.   (B.L.G. 1937 ed.)

2. All black background
Chute, impaling, Keck
Crest: A dexter cubit arm vested gules cuffed argent grasping a broken sword proper   Mantling: Gules and argent   Motto: Fide viventi justi
For Edward Chute, of the Vyne, who d. 1722.   (B.L.G. 1937 ed.)

3. All black background
Qly of nine, 1st, Chute, 2nd, Qly or and gules ( ), 3rd, Azure a chevron argent between three mascles or (Chaloner), 4th, Or on a saltire sable five cinquefoils or (Skory), 5th, Argent a chevron between three billets gules ( ), 6th, Gules on a mount vert encircled by the walls of a castle argent an eagle rising or ( ), 7th, Gules three eagles displayed argent ( ), 8th, Sable a bend ermine cotised flory or (Keck), 9th, Argent a fess nebuly sable between three lozenges gules, in centre chief a lion passant azure, armed and langued gules ( )
Crests: Dexter, A dexter cubit arm in armour grasping a broken sword proper   Sinister, From a mural coronet gules a demi-maiden crined or habited ermine   Mantling: Gules and argent   Motto: In coelo quies
For either Anthony, d. 1754, eldest son of Edward Chute, or his younger brother, John, d. 1776.   (B.L.G. 1937 ed.)

4. All black background
Qly of six, 1st, Chute, 2nd, Qly or and gules ( ), 3rd, Skory, 4th, Argent a chevron between three billets gules ( ), 5th, Gules a fess

argent flory counter-flory or (   ), 6th, Gules three eagles displayed
argent(   )
Crest and mantling: As 2.
For Chaloner Chute, eldest brother of Edward Chute,
d.   (B.L.G. 1937 ed.)
Copies of Nos. 1, 3 and 4 hang in the tea-rooms at the Vyne.

SHIRLEY
1. All black background
Within the Order of the Bath, Ermine on a chevron azure between three
bulls' heads erased sable two swords argent pommels and hilts or the
points upwards transfixing at the fess point a laurel wreath or, in centre
chief point the representation of the Trafalgar medal
(Bullen)   Pendent below shield are badges of the Order of the Bath
and of Hanover, also the Trafalgar medal
Crest: From a naval coronet or the sails argent, the rim inscribed
Trafalgar, a bull's head or charged with an anchor sable between two
wings vert   Motto: A rege et victoria   Supporters: Dexter, A
soldier of the Royal Marines, habited proper, his exterior hand
supporting a staff proper, thereon a flag azure inscribed with the words,
Monmouth, Brittania, Ramillies   Sinister, A sailor of the Royal
Navy, habited proper, his exterior hand supporting a staff, thereon a flag
azure inscribed with the words, Camperdown, Trafalgar, 1st June, or
For Admiral Sir Charles Bullen, G.C.B., G.C.H., who d. 2 July 1853,
aged 86.   (M.I.)

SILCHESTER
1. All black background
On a lozenge   Qly, 1st and 4th, Or a fess chequy argent and azure
between three lions rampant gules (Stewart), 2nd and 3rd, Per bend
embattled argent and gules (Boyle)   In pretence: Argent a saltire
gules charged with a crescent or (Fitzgerald)
Countess's coronet   Motto: Nil desperandum   Supporters:
Dexter, A knight in armour proper, kneecaps and elbow caps or, with a
crest of ostrich feathers, argent, gules, argent   Sinister, A woman,
garbed gules, wearing a cloak azure and ermine crowned proper
For Eleanor, dau. and heiress of Robert Fitzgerald, of Castle Dod, co.
Cork, who m. 1733, William, 3rd Viscount Mountjoy (later 1st Earl of
Blesinton), and d. 1 Oct. 1774.   (B.P. 1949 ed.)

SOBERTON
1. Dexter background black
Qly, 1st and 4th, Ermine a chevron cotised gules between three fleurs-
de-lys gules (Minchin), 2nd and 3rd, Azure three swords in pile argent
hilted or (Poulet)   In pretence: Argent a fess chequy or and azure in
chief a lion passant gules (Stewart)   Also impaling two coats per
fess, in chief, Gules three swans proper in base azure a salmon fesswise

(Guitton), and in base, Or a lion rampant within a double tressure flory counter-flory gules (Maitland)
Crest: From a ducal coronet or an arm proper holding a baton argent   Mantling: Gules and argent   Motto: Regarde la mort
For Henry Minchin, of Holywell, Soberton, who m. 1st, 1796, Elizabeth (d. 1813), dau. of John Guitton, of Little Park, and 2nd, Edith Maitland, who d.s.p., and 3rd, Caroline Mackett, and d.   (B.L.G. of Ireland 1912 ed.)

SOUTHWICK
1. Sinister background black
Qly, 1st and 4th, qly 1. and 4., qly i. & iv. Or on a bend sable three pheons or (Thistlethwayte), ii. & iii. Gules a fess argent between three fleurs-de-lys or (Whithead), 2. and 3., Or on a chief azure three doves proper (Frederick), 2nd and 3rd, Vert a lion rampant or (Norton), impaling, Gules a chevron embattled counterembattled or between the top and stump of a tree proper and three birds argent, in base a salmon swimming in water proper (Guitton)
Mantling: Gules and argent   Motto: In coelo quies
For Mary Anne, dau. of John Guitton, of Little Park, Wickham, who m. 1803, Thomas Thistlethwayte, of Southwick Park, and d. 1821.   (B.L.G. 1937 ed.)

STRATFIELD SAYE
1. Sinister background black
Two shields   Dexter, within the Garter, Qly, 1st and 4th, Gules a cross in each quarter five roundels in saltire argent (Wellesley), 2nd and 3rd, Or a lion rampant gules (Colley), and for Augmentation in chief an escutcheon charged with the Union   Sinister, within an ornamental wreath, as dexter, impaling, Qly or and gules in the 1st quarter an eagle displayed vert (Pakenham)   The two shields are encircled with the collar of the Order
Duchess's coronet   Supporters: Two lions gules langued azure, each gorged with an antique crown and chained or   All on a mantle gules and ermine
For Catherine, dau. of Edward, 2nd Baron Longford, who m. Arthur, 1st Duke of Wellington, K.G., and d. 25 Apr. 1831.   (B.P. 1949 ed.)

2. All black background
Two oval shields   Dexter, within the Garter, Qly, 1st and 4th, Wellesley, 2nd and 3rd, Or a lion rampant gules ducally gorged vert (Colley), in chief an escutcheon charged with the Union   Sinister, within an ornamental wreath, as dexter, impaling, Qly, 1st and 4th, Pakenham, 2nd, Argent on a bend indented between two bendlets sable each charged with three bezants three fleurs-de-lys argent (Cuffe), 3rd, Ermine a griffin segreant azure armed or (Aungier)

Duke's coronet   Crest: From a ducal coronet or a demi-lion gules
holding a forked pennon per pale argent and gules charged with the
cross of St George   Motto: Virtutis fortuna comes   Supporters:
Two lions gules each gorged with an antique crown and chained or
For Arthur, 1st Duke of Wellington, K.G., who d. 14 Sept.
1852.   (B.P. 1949 ed.)
(There is also a hatchment for the Duke of Wellington in the parish
church at Walmer, Kent)

3. Dexter background black
Two shields   Dexter, within the Garter, as 1.   Sinister, within
an ornamental wreath, as dexter, impaling, Qly, 1st and 4th, Azure
three cinquefoils argent (Fraser), 2nd and 3rd, Gules three bars ermine
(Gifford), over all an escutcheon, Argent three escutcheons gules (Hay)
Duke's coronet   Crest, motto and supporters: As 2.
For Arthur Richard, 2nd Duke of Wellington, K.G., who m. 1839,
Elizabeth, dau. of George, 8th Marquess of Tweeddale, and d.s.p. 13
Aug. 1884.   (B.P. 1949 ed.)

EAST STRATTON
1. Dexter background black
Qly, 1st and 4th, Azure a fess or in chief a bear's head couped proper,
bridled and ringed or (Baring), 2nd and 3rd, Gules a cross formy fitchy
or between three fishes hauriant argent within an orle of cross crosslets
or (Herring), over all the Badge of Ulster, impaling, Qly, 1st, Gules on
a bend between six cross crosslets fitchy argent the Augmentation of
Flodden (Howard), 2nd, Gules three lions passant guardant in pale or
in chief a label of three points argent (Brotherton), 3rd, Chequy or and
azure (Warren), 4th, Gules a lion rampant argent (Mowbray), at fess
point a molet sable for difference
Crest: A molet or ermined sable between two wings argent   Motto:
Probitate et labore   Supporters: Two bears proper muzzled and
each charged on the shoulder with a portcullis chained or
For Francis, 1st Baron Northbrook, who m. 2nd, 1841, Arabella, 2nd
dau. of Kenneth Alexander, 1st Earl of Effingham, and d. 6 Sept.
1866.   (B.P. 1949 ed.)

TICHBORNE
1. Dexter background black
Vair a chief or, the Badge of Ulster (Tichborne), impaling, Azure a fess
dancetty the two upper points terminating in fleurs-de-lys or (Plowden)
Crest: A hind's head couped proper between two wings
gules   Mantling: Gules and argent   Motto: Pugna pro patria
For Sir Henry Tichborne, 7th Bt., who m. 1778, Elizabeth Lucy (d. 24
Jan. 1829), eldest dau. of Edmund Plowden, of Plowden, Salop, and d.
14 June 1821.   (B.P. 1949 ed.)

2. Dexter background black
Tichborne, with Badge of Ulster, impaling, Or a cross sable in the first
quarter a lion rampant gules (Burke)
Crest and motto: As 1.   Mantling: Azure and
argent   Supporters: Two lions rampant gules
For Sir Henry Tichborne, 8th Bt., who m. 1806, Anne (d. 12 Aug. 1853),
4th dau. of Sir Thomas Burke, 1st Bt., and d. 3 June 1845.   (B.P.
1949 ed.)

3. Dexter ⅔ background black
Qly, 1st and 4th, Argent two bars sable between three pierced molets
azure (Doughty), 2nd and 3rd, Tichborne, over all the Badge of Ulster
Crests: Dexter, A cubit arm erect vested or charged with a cross crosslet
sable, holding in the hand proper a molet azure   Sinister, a hind's
head couped proper between two wings gules   Mantling: Gules and
argent   Mottoes: Pugna pro patria   Resurgam
To sinister of main shield: On a double-headed eagle displayed sable a
shield sable charged with six swallows, three, two and one argent
(Arundell)   The shield ensigned with a coronet of a Count of the
Holy Roman Empire   Motto: Deo data
For Sir Edward Doughty, 9th Bt., who m. 1827, Katherine (d. 12 Dec.
1872), dau. of James Everard, 9th Baron Arundell of Wardour, and d. 5
Mar. 1853.   (B.P. 1949 ed.)

4. Dexter background black
Qly, 1st and 4th, Tichborne, 2nd and 3rd, Doughty, with a canton
azure, over all the Badge of Ulster
Crests: 1. A hind's head proper between two wings gules   2. A cubit
arm erect vested per pale embattled or and argent charged with a cross
formy gules, holding in the hand proper a pierced molet of six points
sable   Mantling: Azure and argent   Motto: Pugna pro
patria   Supporters: Two lions rampant guardant gules
Probably for Sir James Francis Doughty-Tichborne, 10th Bt., who m.
1827, Harriet Felicite (d. 12 Mar. 1868), dau. of Henry Seymour of
Knoyle, Wilts., and d. 11 June 1862.   (B.P. 1949 ed.)

5. Dexter background black
Vair a chief or, a martlet on the chief for difference (Tichborne),
impaling, Argent a lion rampant guardant gules (Nunez)
Crest and mantling: As 1.   Motto: Resurgam
Probably for Roger Robert Tichborne, son of Sir Henry Tichborne, 7th
Bt., who m. 1822, Rebecca (d. 26 Jan. 1859), dau. of A. F. Nunez, of
Belmont Park, Hants, and Amsterdam, and d. at Malvern, 3 Nov.
1849.   (B.P. 1949 ed.)

UPTON GREY
1. All black background
Per pale argent and gules a chevron between three lions rampant
counter-changed (Limbrey)
Crest: A unicorn passant gules, armed, maned, unguled and tip of tail
or   All on a mantle gules and ermine
For John Limbrey, who d. 22 Dec. 1801, aged 98.   (Miss N. Sclater-
Booth)

WARNFORD
1. Dexter background black
Argent a lion rampant between three crosses gules surmounted by three
molets azure, over all a fess sable (Dillon), impaling, Or a cross gules
in dexter chief a lion rampant sable (De Burgh)
Crest: On a chapeau azure and ermine a falcon rising
proper   Mantling: Gules and argent   Motto: Auxilium ab alto
For Luke Dillon, who m. Margaret Augusta, dau. of John, 11th Earl of
Clanricarde, and d. 1825.   (B.P. 1868 ed.; church guide)

2. Sinister background black
On a lozenge surmounted by a cherub's head
Argent two bars gules, on a canton gules a lion of England (Lancaster),
impaling, Gules three fountains a chief nebuly or (Burne)
Mantling: Gules and argent   Motto: In coelo quies
For Elizabeth, dau. of Thomas Burne, who m. the Rev. Richard Hume
Lancaster, Rector of Warnford from 1802 to 1853, and d. 21 May 1822,
aged 30. He d. 25 June 1853, aged 80.

WEYHILL
1. All black background
Argent on a chevron azure a martlet argent within a bordure engrailed
azure charged with eight molets argent (Lockton)
No crest   Mantling: Gules and argent   Motto: Resurgam
Probably for the Rev. John Lockton, of Clanville, who d. 11 Sept. 1807,
aged 72.   (M.I.)

2. Dexter background black
Gules a lion rampant argent (Stacpoole), impaling, Or on a cross
between four ermine spots sable five bezants (Wasey)
Crest: On a ducal coronet a pelican in her piety all
proper   Mantling: Gules and argent   Motto: Resurgam
For Lt.-Col. Hugh Stacpoole, of Clanville Lodge, who m. Jane, dau. of
John Wasey, of Prior's Court, Berkshire, and d. 1840, aged
56.   (M.I.)

WINCHESTER College
1. All black background
Argent a chevron between three chapeaux gules and ermine (Barter)
Crest: An arm in armour embowed the hand holding a club
proper   Mantling: Gules and argent   Motto: Resurgam
For Warden Robert Specott Barter, who d. 1861.   (In the Exchequer
Room, Chamber Court)

WINCHESTER Hampshire Record Office
(formerly St Thomas's church)
1. Dexter background black
Sable a bow and arrow or (Cubitt), impaling, Qly, 1st and 4th, Azure a
chevron engrailed ermine (Gerard), 2nd and 3rd, Argent two bars gules
on a canton per pale sable and gules a boar's head couped or
(Pakeman)
Crest: An arm embowed holding in the hand proper an arrow
argent   Motto: Resurgam
For the Rev. George James Cubitt, Rector of St Thomas, who m. Emily,
dau. of Col. Edward Garrard and d. 20 Aug. 1855.   (Alumni
Cantab)

WINCHESTER Cathedral
1. Sinister background black
Gules two keys endorsed in bend, the upper argent, the lower or,
between them a sword in bend sinister argent the point in chief hilted or
(See of Winchester), impaling, Azure a lion passant or between three
fleurs-de-lys argent, in dexter chief a crescent argent (North)
On a shield within the Garter, surmounted by a mitre or, and with a key
and bishop's crook or in saltire behind the shield
For the Rt. Rev. the Hon. Brownlow North, Bishop of Winchester, who
d. 12 July 1820.   (B.P. 1963 ed.)
(In the Venerable Chapel)

WINCHESTER Chilcomb House
1. All background black
Two oval shields   Dexter, within the Order of the Bath, and badge
of Order pendent below, Argent a chevron between three coots sable, a
crescent for difference (Coote)   Sinister, within an ornamental
wreath, Coote.   In pretence, Azure a chevron ermine between three
bulls passant argent (Rodbard), also impaling, Paly of six argent and
sable on a chief gules a lion passant or (Bagwell)
Crest: A coot proper charged with a crescent or   Mantle: Gules and
argent   Motto: Vincit veritas   Supporters: Dexter, A wolf sable
collared gules from the collar pendent an escutcheon gules charged with
an estoile and an increscent in fess argent   Sinister. the same, but
the escutcheon charged with a decrescent and an estoile in fess of eight
points argent

For General Sir Eyre Coote, G.C.B., who m. 1st, 1786, Sarah, dau. and
co-heir of John Rodbard, and 2nd, 1805, Katherine, dau. of John
Bagwell, of Marlfield, Tipperary, and d. 1823, aged 63.   (B.L.G.
1937 ed.; M.I. in Rockbourne church)
(This hatchment was formerly in Rockbourne church)

2. Dexter background black
Coote, with a crescent sable for difference, impaling, Qly, 1st and 4th,
Argent two pallets sable a chevron gules, on a canton gules a battleaxe
erect or (Dawson), 2nd and 3rd, Argent on a chevron between three
lozenges sable a lion passant or (Massey)
Crest, mantling and motto: As 1.
For Eyre Coote, of West Park, who m. 1828, Elizabeth Rosetta, dau. of
James Hewitt Massey-Dawson, and d. 30 May 1834.   (B.L.G. 1937
ed.)
(This hatchment was formerly in Rockbourne church)

3. Sinister background black
Qly of 12, 1st, Gules three lions' faces or jessant-de-lys azure, over all a
bend engrailed azure (Tennyson), 2nd, Argent a cross between four
roundels sable (Clayton), 3rd, Azure three pierced molets or (Hilyard),
4th, Argent two bars azure (Hilton), 4th, Argent a fess gules between
three popinjays vert, beak legs and collars gules (Thweng), 6th, Argent
a lion rampant azure (Brus), 7th, Gules three arches argent (Arches),
8th, Argent two bars gules, on a canton gules a lion statant guardant or
(Lancaster), 9th, Argent on a saltire engrailed sable nine annulets or
(Leke), 10th, Vair a fess gules (Marmion), 11th, Argent two bars azure,
a label of three points gules on each point three bezants (Grey), 12th,
Azure three cinquefoils pierced or (Bardolf), impaling, Sable ermined
argent on a cross voided argent four millrinds sable (Turner)
For Mary, dau. and heiress of John Turner, of Caistor, Lincs., who m.
1775, George Tennyson, of Bayons Manor, and Usselby Hall, Lincs.,
and d. 20 Aug. 1825.   (B.L.G. 5th ed.)

4. All black background
Arms, as 3., except, 3rd quarter, molete not pierced, 5th quarter, beaks
vert
Crests: Centre, A dexter arm in armour embowed proper holding a
broken spear argent   Dexter, A bear's paw couped argent holding a
roundel sable   Sinister, A cockerel gules   Mantling: Azure and
or   Motto: Nil temere
For George Tennyson, who d. 4 July 1835, aged 85.   (B.L.G. 5th
ed.)

5. Identical to Old Basing 3., except that the escutcheon on the Paulet
coat is sable not azure, there is no crest, and the hatchment is
rectangular, *c.* 4 ft. wide and 2 ft. high
For William, 2nd Baron Bolton, d. 13 July 1850.

WOOTTON ST LAWRENCE
1. Dexter background black
Argent a chevron gules between three crescents sable (Wither)   In
pretence, and impaling, Sable a pheon argent (Nicoll)
Crest: A demi-hare, in its mouth two ears of wheat
proper   Mantling: Gules and argent   Motto: Mors mihi lucrum
For William Wither, of Manydown, who m. Elizabeth, dau. of Richard
Nicoll, and d.s.p. 25 Sept. 1733, aged 55.   (Burke's Commoners;
M.I. in church)

2. All black background
Qly, 1st and 4th, Wither, with a molet or for difference, 2nd and 3rd, Or
a lion rampant with two heads azure vulned in the shoulder gules
(Mason)
Crest: As 1., but charged with a molet for difference   Mantling: As
1.   Motto: In coelo quies
Unidentified

3. All black background
Qly, 1st and 4th, Wither, as 2., 2nd and 3rd, Per pale ermine and azure
a lion passant gules crowned or on a bordure engrailed gules eight
fleurs-de-lys or (Bigg), impaling, Barry wavy of six azure and or, on a
chief or three pheons sable (Blachford)
Crests: Dexter, as 2.   Sinister, A rhinoceros proper   Mantling:
As 1.   Motto: Resurgam
For Lovelace Bigg, of Chilton Foliat, Wilts., who assumed name and
arms of Wither on succeeding to estates, and m. 2nd, 1766, Margaret,
dau. of Bridges Blachford, of Osborne, I.o.W., and d. 24 Feb. 1813, aged
7.   (Sources, as 1.)

4. Dexter background black
Qly, as 3., impaling, Or on a chevron gules between three lions passant
sable a crescent argent (   )
Crests and mantling: As 3.   Motto: The gift of God is eternal life
Unidentified

5. Dexter background black
Argent on a fess between in chief two quatrefoils and in base a fleur-de-
lys azure a quatrefoil between two fleurs-de-lys argent (Bates), impaling,
Qly gules and argent on the first and fourth quarters a cross moline
argent (Crosse)
Crest: A stag's head erased azure attired or charged on the neck with two
quatrefoils in pale and pierced by two arrows in saltire
or   Mantling: Azure and argent   Motto: Labore et virtute
For Colonel Arthur Sydney Bates, of Manydown Park, who m. Mary da
Costa, dau. of Lt.-Col. Charles Crosse, and d. 7 May 1958. She d. 18
Jan. 1962.   (M.I.)

ISLE OF WIGHT

by

Robert Adams

St Helens 5: For George Charles, 4th Baron Vernon, 1835
(*Photograph by Mr. R. Brinton, published with the consent of the Vicar and Churchwardens of St Helens*)

INTRODUCTION

Ecclesiastically, the 26 ancient parishes of the Isle of Wight were for centuries cared for by the Bishop and Diocese of Winchester. In 1927 they were transferred to the new Bishopric of Portsmouth.

Forty-six hatchments are recorded, but recently this number has been seriously depleted by the destruction by fire of the fine series of 13 which had been removed into store from the now disused St Thomas' church, Ryde. They included those for George Player, who rebuilt the church in 1827, and for the 2nd Earl Spencer, K.G., and his wife.

The two oldest, and the only 17th-century hatchments are at Carisbrooke; Margaret Leigh, widow of Barnabas Leigh of the old landowning family of Shorwell and Alvington, died in 1655, and Grace Harvey, born Leigh, died in 1661. Two 20th-century hatchments have been recorded, 1915 and 1929, both formerly at St Thomas', Ryde.

All the hatchments are in churches except the one at Chale to the Rev. Sir Henry Worsley-Homes, 8th Bt. of Appuldurcombe and Westover, who died in 1811.

There are, not surprisingly, Royal memorials, but no such hatchments at Whippingham, the church that served Osborne House, and the Royal Naval College.

A hatchment for John Nash, the architect, is at East Cowes. One for a member of the Urry family, formerly in Freshwater Church (depicted in Alexander Monro's drawing of 1839 in the Carisbrooke Castle Museum), was probably a casualty of the restoration of the church in 1873. This was the church for Farringford, but there are no hatchments, only memorials to the family of Alfred, Lord Tennyson.

I acknowledge with thanks the help in recording of the late Mr. Robert Whittingham of Carisbrooke.

Robert Adams,
Wellow, Isle of Wight

BONCHURCH, Old Church
1. All black background
Qly, 1st and 4th, Gules two bars ermine in chief a lion passant guardant
or (Hill), 2nd and 3rd, Argent on a chief gules two stags' heads
cabossed or (Popham), impaling, two coats per fess, in chief, Qly, 1st
and 4th, Or a cross gules between four falcons sable (for Worsley), 2nd
and 3rd, Paly of six or and azure, on a chief gules three crosses formy or
(Meux), and in base, Azure a lion rampant per fess or and argent
(Bettesworth)
Crests: Dexter, A boar's head couped sable in the mouth a sprig of oak
leaves proper   Sinister, A stag's head erased proper   Mantling:
Gules and argent   Mottoes: (above crests) Memento
pauper   (below shield) Virtus me defendit   Red, white and blue
flags in saltire behind shield
For Vice-Admiral Henry Hill, who m. 1st, Anne, dau. of the Rev. James
Worsley, Rector of Gatcombe, and 2nd, Caroline, dau. of Joseph
Bettesworth, of Ryde, and d. 7 June 1849, aged 77.   (M.I. in
Shanklin old church)

BRADING
1. Sinister background black
Qly, 1st and 4th, Azure a stork between three cross crosslets fitchy or
(Oglander), 2nd and 3rd, Ermine on a canton sable a crescent argent
(Strode), over all the Badge of Ulster, impaling, Per pale or and sable
(Serle)   Two cherubs' heads above
For Sukey, only dau. of Peter Serle, of Testwood, Hants, who m. 1765,
Sir William Oglander, 5th Bt., of Nunwell, and d. July 1804.   (B.P.
1875 ed.)

2. All black background
Arms: As 1.
Crest: A bear's head couped or   Mantling: Gules and
argent   Motto: In coelo quies
For Sir William Oglander, 5th Bt., of Nunwell, who d. 5 Jan.
1806.   (B.P. 1875 ed.)

3. Dexter background black
Oglander, in dexter chief the Badge of Ulster, impaling, Argent a fess
gules between three eagles displayed sable within a bordure wavy gules
(Leeds)

Crest: A boar's head couped behind the ears or langued
gules   Mantling: Gules and argent   Motto: (above the crest)
Servare munia vitae
For Sir Henry Oglander, 7th and last Bt. of Nunwell, who m. 1845,
Louisa, dau. of Sir George William Leeds, Bt., and d. 8 Apr.
1874.   (B.P. 1875 ed.)

4. All black background

Qly, 1st and 4th, Argent on a fess sable between three bucks' heads
erased sable attired or a fret between two doves argent (Knight), 2nd
and 3rd, Gules on a chevron argent between three doves or three pheons
sable (Page)   In pretence: Qly, 1st and 4th, Vert on a chevron
between three annulets or three eagles displayed sable (for Minefey),
2nd and 3rd, Argent on a chevron gules between three roundels vert
each charged with a fleur-de-lys argent three birds volant or (   )
Crest: A buck's head erased sable attired or   Mantling: Gules and
argent
For Richard Knight, of Landguard, who m. 1692, Ann Minefey, and d. 2
Jan. 1721, aged 58.   (M.I.; P.R.; Salisbury Marr. Lics.)

CALBOURNE

1. Dexter background black

Qly, 1st and 4th, qly i. & iv. Barry wavy of six or and azure, on a
canton gules a lion passant guardant or (Holmes), ii. & iii. two coats
per pale, Argent a chief gules (Worsley), Argent a chevron between
three falcons close sable (Worsley), 2nd and 3rd, two coats per pale,
Holmes, Argent three otters passant in pale sable (   ), the Badge of
Ulster on 2nd quarter   In pretence: Gules three fleurs-de-lys and in
chief three boars' heads couped or (?Delgarno)
Crests: Dexter, From a naval coronet or an arm in armour embowed the
hand holding a trident proper   Centre, A wyvern gules winged
azure   Sinister, a dragon's head erased or   Mantling: Gules and
argent   Mottoes: Vectis, and, In coelo quies
For Sir Leonard Thomas Worsley-Holmes, 9th and last Bt., who m.
1813, Anne Redstone, dau. of John Delgarno, of Newport, and niece of
Leonard, Lord Holmes, and d. 10 Jan. 1825.   (B.E.B.)

CARISBROOKE

1. All black background

Qly, 1st and 4th, Argent on a chief embattled sable three roundels
argent (Leigh), 2nd, Argent three roundels gules (Bessell), 3rd, Sable a
lion passant guardant argent crowned or (Leigh), impaling, Argent a fess
between three nags passant sable (Culliford)
Crest: A horse argent maned or   Mantling: Sable and
argent   On scroll above crest: Obit 27 Junii 1655   Cherubs'
heads at sides of shield

For Margaret, dau. of John Culliford, of Encombe, Purbeck, Dorset, and widow of William Bulkley, of Burgate, Hants, who m. Barnabas Leigh, of North Court, Shorwell, and d. 27 June 1655. (The Ancestor, vols. 10 & 11; P.R.)

2. All black background
Or a chevron between three lions' heads affronté erased gules (Harvey), impaling, Leigh
Crest: A leopard statant gules   Mantling: Gules and argent   On either side of shield the date 16 and 61
For Grace, eldest dau. of Barnabas Leigh, who m. John Harvey, of Alvington, d. and was buried 4 Sept. 1661   (P.R.)

3. Dexter background black
Argent three bendlets sable over all a lion rampant gules armed and langued azure (Young), impaling, Gules three molets within a tressure flory counterflory or (Sutherland)
Crest: From a ducal coronet a dragon's head or   Mantling: Gules and argent   Motto: Sans peur
For Major-General Robert Young, who m. Jannette Sarah Sutherland, and d. at Clatterford House, 17 Nov. 1815, aged 46. She d. 19 Oct. 1851, aged 77. (P.R.)

CHALE, Blackgang Chine Museum
1. Dexter background black
Qly of six, 1st and 6th, qly i. & iv. Barry wavy of six or and azure, on a canton gules a lion passant or (Holmes), ii. & iii. Argent a chevron between three falcons sable (Worsley), 2nd, Worsley, 3rd, Or on a cross engrailed gules a lion's head erased or (Worsley), 4th, Argent on a chief embattled sable three roundels argent (Leigh), 5th, Argent three fishes hauriant between six cross crosslets fitchy sable (Hackett), in chief the Badge of Ulster   In pretence: Holmes
Crest: Out of a naval coronet or an arm in armour embowed holding a trident proper   Mantling: Gules and argent   Motto: Vectis
For the Rev. Sir Henry Worsley-Holmes, 8th Bt., who m. Elizabeth Troughear, eldest dau. of Leonard, Lord Holmes, and d. 7 Apr. 1811.   (B.E.B., B.E.P.)
(This hatchment was formerly in St Thomas' Church, Newport)

EAST COWES
1. Dexter background black
Sable on a chevron between three greyhounds statant three sprigs of ashen leaves proper (Nash), impaling, Sable a fess engrailed between three crosses formy fitchy and a bordure engrailed argent (Bradley)
Crest: A greyhound sejant argent   Motto: Resurgam   Palm sprays in base

For John Nash, the eminent architect, who m. 1798, Mary Anne
Bradley, of Abingdon Street, Westminster, and d. at East Cowes Castle,
13 May 1835.   (D.N.B.; John Summerson)

2. Dexter background black
Qly, 1st and 4th, Or three lions rampant gules (Tudor), 2nd and 3rd,
Sable a chevron ermine between three martlets argent collared or
(Jervys)   In pretence: Or a lion rampant within a bordure sable
(Jones), impaling, Azure a fess between three fleurs-de-lys or (   )
Crests: Dexter, A demi-lion rampant gules collared flory or, crowned
with an antique crown or, charged on the shoulder with a crescent
argent, in the dexter paw a sword with blade wavy argent hilted or,
surmounted by the motto, Pendifices discum   Sinister, A lion
rampant azure between the paws a mirror proper, surmounted by the
motto, Oddiwerth nyni   Motto: (below shield) Constantia et
vigilantia
For George Tudor, of East Cowes Castle, who m. Elizabeth Mary, dau.
and heiress of John Jones, of London, and d. 24 Dec. 1857.   (Misc.
Gen. et Her. , 3rd Series, I, 21-22)

GODSHILL
Dexter background black
Qly, 1st and 4th, Argent a chief gules (Worsley), 2nd and 3rd, Argent a
chevron between three falcons sable (Worsley), over all the Badge of
Ulster, impaling, Qly, 1st and 4th, Barry of ten or and sable (Thynne),
2nd and 3rd, Argent a lion rampant tail nowed gules armed and
langued azure (Botevile)
Crest: A wolf's head proper langued gules   Mantling: Gules and
argent   Motto: In coelo quies
For Sir Robert Worsley, 4th Bt., of Appuldurcombe, who m. 1690,
Frances, only dau. of Thomas, 1st Viscount Weymouth, and d. Aug.
1747.   (B.E.B.)

2. Dexter background black
Qly, 1st, Argent a chevron between three falcons sable (Worsley), 2nd,
Or on a cross invecked gules a lion's head or (Worsley), 3rd, Argent on
a chief embattled sable three roundels argent (Leigh), 4th, Sable three
hakes hauriant between six cross crosslets fitchy argent (Hackett), over
all the Badge of Ulster, impaling, Per bend embattled argent and gules
(Boyle)
Crest and mantling: As 1.   Motto: Ut sursum desuper
For Sir Thomas Worsley, 6th Bt., who m. 1749, Elizabeth, dau. of John,
5th Earl of Cork and Orrery, and. d. 23 Sept. 1768.   (B.E.B.)
(Recorded in 1956 this hatchment is now missing)

3. All black background

Qly of six, 1st and 6th, Argent a chief gules (Worsley), 2nd, Argent a chevron between three falcons sable, in fess point the Badge of Ulster (Worsley), 3rd, Or on a cross invecked gules a lion's head erased or (Worsley), 4th, Leigh, 5th, Hackett

Crest: A wyvern proper langued and tailed gules   Mantle: Gules and ermine   Motto: Ut sursum desuper

For Sir Richard Worsley, 7th Bt., who m. Dorothy, dau. of Sir John Fleming, Bt., and d. 5 Aug. 1805.   (B.E.B.; H. A. M. Worsley)

4. All black background

Qly, 1st and 4th, Argent a fret sable (Tollemache), 2nd and 3rd, Azure an imperial crown proper between three molets argent, all within a double tressure flory counterflory or (Murray), over all the Badge of Ulster, impaling, Qly, 1st and 4th, Gules three serpents nowed in triangle argent with a bordure engrailed or (Lewis), 2nd and 3rd, Azure a wolf rampant argent (   )

Earl's coronet   Crest: A horse's head couped argent with wings expanded or semy of roundels sable   Motto: Confido, conquiesco   Supporters: Two antelopes proper horned sable   All on a mantle gules and ermine

For Wilbraham, 6th Earl of Dysart, who m. 1773, Anna Maria, dau. of David Lewis, of Malvern Hall, and d.s.p. 9 Mar. 1821.   (B.P. 1939 ed.)

5. Sinister background black

Qly, 1st and 4th qly i. & iv. Azure three pelicans argent (Pelham), ii. & iii. Gules two pieces of belt erect argent buckled or (Pelham), 2nd and 3rd, Argent a chevron between three crosses floretty sable (Anderson)   In pretence: Qly, 1st and 4th, Per bend sinister or and sable a lion rampant counterchanged (Simpson), 2nd and 3rd, Argent a chevron between three falcons sable (Worsley)

Motto: Vincit amor patriae   Supporters: Dexter, A bay horse reguardant charged on the body with three antique buckles in bend sinister or   Sinister, A water spaniel reguardant proper charged on the body with three crosses flory in bend sable   Cherub's head above

For Henrietta Anna Maria Charlotte, 2nd dau. of the Hon. John Bridgeman Simpson, who m. 1806, Charles 2nd Baron Yarborough (cr. Earl of Yarborough 1837) and d. 30 June 1813.   (B.P. 1949 ed.)

6. All black background

Arms: As 5., but 1st and 4th quarters of escutcheon of pretence, Per bend dexter, not sinister

Earl's coronet   Crests: Dexter, A peacock in pride proper   Centre, A water spaniel passant or   Sinister, An antique buckle or   Supporters and motto: As 5., but horse charged with buckles in bend sinister sable

For Charles, 1st Earl of Yarborough, who d. 5 Sept. 1846.   (B.P.
1949 ed.)

NEWCHURCH

1. Dexter background black
Qly, 1st and 4th, Gules two lions rampant in pale argent, on a canton
sable a fret or (Bocland), 2nd and 3rd, Gules a lion salient or
(Dillington), impaling, Sable a bend within a bordure embattled argent
(Bisset)
Crest: On a chapeau gules and ermine a talbot sejant or langued
gules   Mantling: Gules and argent
For Lt.-Gen. Maurice Bocland, M.P., of Knighton House, Newchurch,
and of Lymington, who m. 1st, Jane Fox, of Ireland, and 2nd, Sophia,
dau. of Major William Bisset, of Southampton, and d. 16 Aug.
1765.   (M.I.; Misc. Gen. et Her., 2nd ser., vol. I)

RYDE

1. Sinister background black
Two cartouches   Dexter, Qly argent and gules a fret or, over all on
a bend sable three escallops or (Spencer)   Sinister, Spencer,
impaling, Sable two bendlets between six crosses formy or (Bingham)
Countess's coronet   Supporters: Dexter, A griffin per fess ermine and
or ermined sable, gorged with a collar flory counter-flory sable thereon
three escallops argent chained argent   Sinister, A wyvern ermine
gorged and chained as the dexter
For Lavinia, dau. of Charles, 1st Earl of Lucan, who m. 1781, George
John, 2nd Earl Spencer, K.G., and d. 8 June 1831.   (B.P. 1963 ed.)

2. All black background
Two cartouches as 1., but surrounded with the Garter chain, with the
George pendent below   Earl's coronet
Crest: From a ducal coronet or a griffin's head argent gorged with a
collar gemel gules between two wings expanded and elevated
argent   Motto: Honi soit qui mal y pense   Supporters: As 1.
For George John, 2nd Earl Spencer, K.G., who d. 10 Nov.
1834.   (Source, as 1.)
(There is an identical hatchment at Brington, Northants)

3. All black background
On a lozenge surmounted by the coronet of a baroness
Qly, 1st and 4th, Or two bars sable (Venables), 2nd, Argent a fret sable
(Vernon), 3rd, Or on a fess sable three garbs or (Vernon)   In
pretence: Chequy or and sable, on a canton gules a lion rampant or
(Warren)
No crest, mantling or motto   Supporters: Dexter, A lion gules
collared and chain reflexed over the back or   Sinister, A boar sable
ducally gorged and chain reflexed over the back or

For Frances Maria, only dau. of Adm. Rt. Hon. Sir John Borlase
Warren, Bt., who m. George Charles, 4th Baron Vernon, and d. 17 Sept.
1837.   (B.P. 1963 ed.)
(For Lord Vernon's hatchment, see St Helen's, No. 5.)

4. Sinister background black

Two coats on the dexter, per pale, 1st, Chequy argent and azure, on a
chief argent a molet azure, in the dexter canton the Badge of Ulster
(Clifford), 2nd, Argent a lion passant guardant gules (   ), impaling,
Qly, 1st, Azure a chevron ermine between three escallops argent
(Townshend), 2nd, Qly gules and argent in the first quarter a molet
argent (Vere), 3rd, Or on a cross azure five pheons argent (Harrison),
4th, Sable a lion passant guardant between three tilting helms argent
(Compton)
For Elizabeth Frances, sister of John, 4th Marquess Townshend, who m.
1813. Adm. Sir Augustus William James Clifford, 1st Bt., and d. 10 Apr.
1862.   (B.P. 1939 ed.)

5. Dexter background black

Azure a cinquefoil ermine (Astley), impaling two coats per pale, 1st,
Qly, 1st and 4th, Argent a molet azure (Assheton), 2nd and 3rd, Azure
two bars between three pheons argent (Smith), and 2nd, Argent a lion
rampant gules (   )   In centre chief between the two sinister
coats is a crescent gules
Crest: From a ducal coronet or three ostrich feathers   Mantling:
Gules and argent   Motto: Fide sed cui vide
For William Buckler Astley, who m. 1818, Elizabeth, dau. of Thomas
Assheton Smith, of Tedworth House, Hants, d. 13 Sept. 1849.   (B.P.
1868 ed.)

6. All black background

On a lozenge   Arms: As 5.
For Elizbeth, widow of William Buckler Astley, d. 19 Oct.
1851.   (Source, as 5.)

7. Dexter background black

Gules two tilting spears in saltire between in chief a molet and in base a
crescent or, all within a bordure engrailed argent charged with four
fleurs-de-lys and four annulets alternately azure (Lind), impaling, Sable
a pale or gutty-de-sang (Player)
Crest: Two laurel branches in saltire proper   Mantling: Gules and
ermine   Motto: Resurgam
For Dr. John Lind, M.D., who m. 1789, Elizabeth Lydia, dau. of
William Player of Ryde, and d. 3 Sept. 1831.   (B.L.G. 2nd and
1937 ed.)

8. Sinister background black
Player, impaling, Argent a chevron gules between three boars' heads in
the mouth of each a cross crosslet fitchy sable (Thresher)
On a lozenge   Motto: Resurgam
For Mary Ann, dau. of William Thresher of Fareham, Hants, who m.
1784, George Player of Ryde, and d. 25 Apr. 1839.   (B.L.G. 1937
ed.)

9. All black background
Arms: As 8.
Crest: A dexter arm in armour proper grasping a broken spear
gules   Motto: Resurgam
For George Player, who d. 30 Apr. 1843.   (B.L.G. 1937 ed.)

10. All black background
On a lozenge   Qly, 1st and 4th, Qly argent and sable three
escallops gules and or counterchanged (Brigstocke), 2nd and 3rd, Player
No crest, mantling or motto
For Mary Harriette Player Brigstocke, of Stone Pitts, d. unm. 21 Nov.
1904. (B.L.G. 1937 ed.)

11. Sinister background black
On a lozenge   Qly, 1st and 4th, Brigstocke, 2nd, Azure a pale or
gutty-de-sang (Player), 3rd, Argent on a cross between four demi-lions
rampant gules a bezant (Benett), impaling, Argent in chief two fleurs-de-
lys gules and in base a martlet sable (Fairbridge)
No crest, mantling or motto
For Mary, youngest dau. of Charles Aiken Fairbridge, of Cape Town,
who m. 1895, William Player Brigstocke, of Ryde House, and d. 4 Sept.
1915.   (B.L.G. 1937 ed.)

12. All black background
Arms: As 11.
Crest: A raven proper in one claw an escallop or   Motto (in Greek):
Be wise as serpents and harmless as doves
For William Player Brigstocke, who d. 5 Mar. 1929.   (Source, as
11.)

13. All black background
On a lozenge   Qly, 1st and 4th, Argent on a cross between four
demi-lions rampant gules a bezant (Benett), 2nd and 3rd, Paly of six
argent and vert (Langley)
No crest, mantling or motto
For Wilhelmina Amelia Benett, of Fareham, who d. unm. 1865.
(All these hatchments were in store when destroyed by fire on 7 Feb.
1986)

ST HELENS
1. All black backbround
Qly argent and azure on a bend sable three martlets or (Grose),
impaling, Sable gutty argent a canton ermine (Dennett)
Crest: A demi-lion rampant or   Motto: Cedo non pereo
Palm and other branches crossed in saltire at base of shield
For Sir Nash Grose, of the Priory, St Helens, Judge of the Court of
King's Bench, who m. Mary, dau. of Henry Dennett, yeoman, and d. 13
Mar. 1814, aged 73.   (D.N.B.; M.I.)

2. All black background
Qly, 1st and 4th, Grose, 2nd and 3rd, Dennett
Crest: As 1.   Motto: Ob patriam vo. . .nando.
For Captain Edward Grose, 1st Regt. of Guards, only son of Sir Nash
and Lady (Mary) Grose, who d. on the field of Quatre Bras, 16 June
1815, aged 31.   (M.I.)

3. Sinister background black
Qly, 1st and 4th, Argent a bend between three rowels sable (Smith),
2nd and 3rd, two coats per pale, Grose, and, Vert a chevron argent
between three greyhounds or (Nash)   In pretence: Azure five garbs
in saltire or (Fielder)
Motto: Mors janua vitae
For Mary Fielder, who m. Edward Grose-Smith, of the Priory, St
Helens, and d. 26 Dec. 1833, aged 64.   (M.I.)

4. All black background
Arms: As 3.
Crest: A boar's head gules   Motto: Mors janua vitae
For Edward Grose-Smith, who d. 6 June 1843, aged 74.   (M.I.)

5. Dexter background black
Qly, 1st and 4th, Azure two bars argent (Venables), 2nd, Argent a fret
sable (Vernon), 3rd, Or on a fess azure three garbs or (Vernon)   In
pretence: Chequy or and azure on a canton gules a lion rampant argent
(Warren)
Baron's coronet   Crests: Dexter, A boar's head erased sable ducally
gorged or   Centre, On a chapeau gules and ermine a wyvern argent
with wings displayed chequy or and azure   Sinister, A wyvern wings
endorsed standing on a fish trap, devouring a child and pierced through
with an arrow in fess proper   Motto: Deo fides
For George Charles, 4th Baron Vernon, who m. 1802, Frances Maria,
only dau. of Admiral Sir John Borlase Warren, Bt., and d. 18 Nov.
1835.   (B.P. 1949 ed.)
(For hatchment of widow, see Ryde No 3.)

SHANKLIN Old Church
1. All black background
Qly, 1st, qly i. & iv. Argent on a chief gules three stags' heads cabossed or (Popham), ii. & iii. Argent a stag's head cabossed proper a chief indented sable (Alchorne), 2nd, Vert a chevron argent between three escallops or (Shapleigh), 3rd, Alchorne, 4th, Ermine on a chief sable three lozenges or (Cheke)
Crest: A stag's head erased proper argent   Motto: Memento pauper   Mantling: Gules and   Wide double frame, the outside covered with black crepe
Unidentified

2. All black background
Qly of 23, 1st and 23rd, Popham, but two stags' heads, 2nd, Sable three roundels argent (Clarke), 3rd, Gules two wings conjoined in lure points downwards over all a bend sable (Kentisbeare), 4th, Per pale azure and gules three lions rampant or (Rous), 5th, Argent a fess between three martlets sable (Edmondes), 6th, Gules on a bend argent three escallops sable (Knoyle), 7th, Sable three fusils two and one argent (Payne), 8th, Argent a saltire gules between four eagles displayed azure (Hampden), 9th, Per pale argent and gules a bend sable (?Bedford), 10th, Sable a chevron between three spearheads argent (Gam), 11th, Gules a chevron ermine (   ), 12th, Argent three cocks gules (   ), 13th, Sable a chevron between three fleurs-de-lys argent (   ), 14th, Gules three chevronels argent (   ), 15th, Sable three fleurs-de-lys or (   ), 16th, Or an eagle displayed sable (   ), 17th, Gules a chevron argent between three swords erect argent hilted or (   ), 18th, Argent a lion rampant sable crowned gules (   ), 19th, Or a lion rampant sable (Dudley), 20th, Or two lions passant in pale sable (Somery), 21st, Gules a cinquefoil pierced ermine (Paganel), 22nd, Argent a cross flory azure (Malpas)   In pretence: Argent in centre chief a molet sable (   )
Motto: resurgam   On a shield surmounted by two cherubs' heads   Olive and palm branches in base   Double frame, outer covered in black crepe
Probably for John Popham of Kitehill and Shanklin, who m. Mary, dau. of James Perry and d. June 1816   (B.L.G. 5th ed.)

VENTNOR
1. All black background
On an asymmetrical lozenge surmounted by a cherub's head
Gules gutty or a tower argent (Hambrough), impaling, Sable a fess between two chevrons ermine, in centre chief a covered cup argent (Holden)
Motto: Resurgam   Palm branches crossed in saltire below shield
For Catherine, only surviving child of Robert Holden, who m. John Hambrough, of Pipewell Hall, Northampton, and Hanwell, Middlesex, and d. 1844.   (B.L.G. 5th ed.)

2. Dexter background black
Qly, 1st and 4th, Gules a tower argent within an orle of cross crosslets
and gouttes or (Hambrough), 2nd and 3rd, Sable on a fess or between
two chevrons ermine two fleurs-de-lys vert (Holden), impaling, Azure on
a chevron engrailed argent between three escallops ermine a cross
crosslet fitchy between two annulets azure (Townsend)
Crest: On a mount vert a horse courant argent   Mantling: Gules
and argent   Motto: Honestum utili praefer
For John Hambrough, of Steephill Castle, who m. 1820, Sophia, dau. of
Gore Townsend, of Honington Hall, Warwickshire, and d. 4 Feb.
1863.   (B.L.G. 5th ed.: M.I.)
(There is another hatchment for John Hambrough in the parish church
at Stanwell, Middlesex)

3. All black background
On an asymmetrical lozenge suspended from a lover's knot
Arms: As 2.
Palm and olive branches crossed in saltire below
For Sophia, widow of John Hambrough, d. 16 Feb. 1863.   (Sources,
as 2.)

4. All black background
Qly, 1st and 4th, Azure on a pale rayonny or a lion rampant gules
(Coleman), 2nd and 3rd, Argent three bars and a canton gules
(Fuller)   In pretence: Qly, 1st and 4th, Or two lions passant
between two flaunches azure, on a fess gules three bezants (Noble), 2nd
and 3rd, Argent three bendlets azure a chief ermine (   )
Crest: A caltrap or between two wings erect argent   Motto:
Resurgam
For Benjamin Freeman Coleman, of Burton Overy, Leicestershire, who
d. 25 Jan. 1838, aged 79.   (M.I.; P.R.)

YARMOUTH
1. All black background
Qly, 1st and 4th, Barry wavy of six or and azure, on a canton gules a
lion passant guardant or (Holmes), 2nd and 3rd, Or three otters passant
in pale sable (   )
Crest: From a naval coronet or an arm embowed in armour proper
holding a trident sable prongs or   Mantling: Gules and argent
For Henry Holmes, M.P. for Yarmouth, who m. Mary, natural dau. of
Admiral Sir Robert Holmes, Bt., and d. 23 June 1738.   (B.E.P.)

2. Dexter background black
Qly, as 1., impaling, Argent on a chief embattled sable three roundels
argent (Leigh)
Baron's coronet   Crest: From a ducal (five leaves) coronet or an
arm embowed in armour proper holding a trident sable prongs or
        Mantling: Gules and argent   Motto: Vectis

Supporters: Two seahorses argent ridged gules
For Thomas Holmes, cr. 1760, Baron Holmes of Kilmallock, who m.
1st, Ann Apsley (d. 1743), and 2nd, Catherine Leigh, and d.s.p.
1764.   (B.E.P.; M.I.)

3. Dexter background black
Argent a bend sable between an eagle displayed vert langued gules and
a cross crosslet sable (Rushworth)   In pretence: Qly, as 1.
Crest: An eagle displayed vert langued gules   Mantling: Gules and
argent   Motto: In coelo quies
For Edward Rushworth, who m. Catherine, dau. of Leonard, Lord
Holmes, and d. 15 Oct. 1817. She d. 9 Dec. 1829.   (B.E.P.; M.I.)

SOMERSET

by

Catherine Constant

Crowcombe 3: For Mary Carew, 1757
(*Photograph by Mr. J. Constant*)

INTRODUCTION

Most of the original work of recording the Somerset hatchments was carried out by members of the Bath Heraldic Society, and all subsequent recording, checking and research have also been undertaken by Society members.

More than half the hatchments belong to the 19th century, none for the present. There is only one for the 17th century, that of Thomas Carew of Crowcombe, who died in 1661.

There is a very interesting and unusual hatchment-type memorial at Bridgwater, dating from the 17th century. It is quite small, and closely resembles a hatchment except that it has no frame, is of stone and mounted on the wall. It commemorates, though there is no inscription, George Bond, who married Gertrude Saunders.

All the hatchments at Nailsea Court were the property of a previous owner and are so far untraced. None relate to Somerset families.

Three hatchments of the Smyth family of Long Ashton are now in the Blaise Castle Museum in Bristol; they were originally recorded in the Long Ashton estate yard.

The remains of the original hatchment for John Hudleston were found at Kelston and were reproduced by the Rev. Everhard Rowe, founder of the Bath Heraldic Society. Norton Malreward's hatchment has also been restored.

There are two hatchments for Isaac Elton, one at Whitestaunton and another at SS Philip and Jacob, Bristol.

Hester, Countess of Chatham, was the wife of William Pitt the Elder and lived on the estate of Burton Pinsent. She died in 1805, and her hatchment hangs in Curry Rivel church.

Crowcombe has nine hatchments. The one for Mary Drewe, first wife of Thomas Carew, has 16 quarterings, and impales the arms of Drewe quartering Sparrow. Thomas died in 1766 after the death of his second wife. This is recorded by three different hatchments.

Goathurst also has nine hatchments, which show the intermarriages of the Halswells, Tyntes, Kemeys and Whartons.

147

The Wharton maunch, emblazoned as a bouget on Jane Hassell's escutcheon of pretence, has a bordure charged with lions' gambs in saltire. The bordure is an augmentation of honour granted by Edward VI for defeating the Scots at the Battle of Solway Moss. The lion supporter crowned and fretty is the Scots lion trapped in a net. The Wharton arms, with a maunch instead of a bouget, appear on an unidentified hatchment in the church.

Catherine Constant
9 Newlands Road,
Keynsham, Avon

ABBOTSLEIGH
1. Background, dexter green, sinister brown
Azure a chevron ermine between three lozenges argent each charged with
a fleur-de-lys sable (Miles), impaling two coats per fess, in chief, argent
a cross gules charged with a lion rampant sable (Whetham), and in
base, Gules three birds proper between two chevronels argent (Peach)
Crest: A dexter arm in armour embowed the hand proper grasping an
anchor sable   Mantling: Gules and or   Motto: In coelo quies
For Philip John Miles, of Leigh Court, who m. 1st, 1795, Maria (d. 20
July 1811), dau. of the Very Rev. Arthur Whetham, Dean of Lismore,
and 2nd, Clarissa (d. 22 June 1868), dau. of Samuel Peach Peach, and
d. 24 Mar. 1845, aged 71.   (B.P. 1939 ed.; M.I.)
(This hatchment has been incorrectly restored since it was first recorded
in 1954; the Whetham arms were then, Argent a cross sable (no lion),
the birds on the Peach coat were martlets and argent, the mantling was
gules and argent, and the background was dexter black)

BAGBOROUGH
1. Dexter background black
Argent on a chief gules two bucks' heads cabossed or (Popham),
impaling, Per fess gules and argent six martlets counterchanged
(Fenwick)
Crest: A buck's head erased or   Mantling: Gules and
argent   Motto: Mens pristina mansit   No frame
For Francis Popham, who m. 1809, Susan, dau. of Nicholas Fenwick, of
Lemmington, Northumberland, and d. 28 May 1858, aged
78.   (B.L.G. 1937 ed.; M.I.)

2. All black background
On a lozenge surrounded by escallops and gilt scrollwork
Arms: As 1.   No frame
For Susan, widow of Francis Popham, d. 23 Jan. 1865, aged
77.   (Sources, as 1.)

BARROW GURNEY
1. Sinister background black
Qly, 1st and 4th, Gules a fess between three cross crosslets fitchy or
(Gore), 2nd, Sable on a bend cotised argent three lions passant sable
(Browne), 3rd, Gules on a chevron between three cinquefoils argent

three leopards' faces gules (Smyth), impaling, Sable a pillar ducally
crowned between two wings expanded attached at the base or (Little)
Motto: Resurgam   Two cherubs' heads above
For Harriet, dau. of Richard Little, of Grosvenor Place, who m. 1798,
the Rev. Charles Gore, of Barrow Court, and d. 17 July 1840.   (B.P.
1949 ed. under Temple of Stowe; M.I.)

2. All black background
Arms: As 1.
Crest: A wolf rampant ducally gorged or   Mantling: Gules and
argent   Motto: Resurgam
For the Rev. Charles Gore, of Barrow Court, who d. 21 Apr.
1841.   (Sources, as 1.)

BATH, Masonic Temple
1. All black background
Or on a chief sable a doubleheaded eagle displayed or (   )
Crest: From a ducal coronet a talbot's head or
Mantling: Gules and ermine   Motto: Resurgam   Palm branches
flanking lower part of shield; skulls and crossbones in dexter and sinister
corners   *c.* 20 in. by 20 in. including frame
Label on back reads: This hatchment is the property of Bro. Percy Wells
P.M. No. 48.
Unidentified

BISHOP'S LYDEARD
Dexter background black
Qly, 1st, Argent over water proper a bridge of five arches gules, in chief
an eagle displayed sable (Lethbridge), 2nd, Gules a chevron between
three leopards' faces or (Periam), 3rd, Azure three stirrups leathered or
a bordure gules bezanty (Giffard), 4th, Sable on a fess between three
greyhounds' heads couped or three molets sable (Buckler), over all the
Badge of Ulster
Crests: Dexter, from a mural coronet or a demi-eagle displayed
sable   Sinister, from a ducal coronet or two arms in armour
embowed proper holding a leopard's face or   Mantling: Gules and
argent   Mottoes: (above crest) Truth   (below shield) Spes mea
in Deo   Supporters: Two eagles sable
Unidentified

BROCKLEY
1. All black background
Ermine three fusils conjoined in fess sable (Pigott)
Crest: A wolf's head erased proper collared or   Mantling: Gules
and argent   Inscribed below: Colonel John Pigott, d. 23 Dec. 1727
For John Pigott, of Brockley Court, M.P. for Somerset, 1705-7, who d. 23
Dec. 1727.   (B.L.G. 1937 ed.; inscr. on hatchment)

2. Dexter background black
Pigott, impaling, Argent on a chevron gules three martlets or, on a chief gules a chamber piece or (Coward)
Crest: A wolf's head erased proper collared argent   Motto: Quies in coelo   Inscribed below: John Pigott, Esq. d. 30th Dec. 1794.
For John Bigg-Pigott, of Brockley, who m. 1740, Ann, sister and co-heir of Thomas Coward, of Sparkgrove, Somerset, and d. 30 Dec. 1794.   (Sources, as 1.)

3. All black background
Arms: As 2.
Crest: As 2.   Motto: Mors janua vitae   Inscribed below: John Pigott, Esq. died 28 July 1816.
For John Pigott, of Brockley, son of John Bigg-Pigott, who d. unm. 28 July 1816.   (Sources, as 1.)
(Hatchment bears the arms of John Pigott's parents)

CHARLTON MUSGROVE
1. All black background
Qly, 1st and 4th, Ermine on a cross sable five millrinds argent (Turner), 2nd and 3rd, Ermine four bars gules in chief a demi-lion rampant proper (Frewen)
Crests: Dexter, A lion passant guardant argent in the dexter paw a millrind sable   Sinister, A demi-lion rampant proper collared or in its paws a caltrap gules   Mantling: Gules and argent   Motto: Resurgam   Skull and crossbones in base
Unidentified

2. All black background
On an asymmetric lozenge flanked by two olive branches
Arms: As 1.
Motto: Resurgam
Unidentified

CHEDZOY
1. Sinister background black
Paly of six argent and azure, on a bend gules three cinquefoils or (Stradling), impaling, Gules a chevron argent between three swans proper (Lyte)
Motto: Dyw a dygon heb dyw hebdym   Cherub's head above shield
Inscribed below motto: Mercy Parsons Stradling, died April 27 1854, aged 32.

CLAVERTON
1. Dexter background black
Azure three swans' heads erased argent (Hedges)   In pretence:
Sable a fess or between three wolves' heads erased argent (Wolferstan)

Crest: A swan's head erased argent   Mantling: Gules and
argent   Motto: In coelo quies
For Thomas Hedges, of Widcombe House, who m. Elizabeth, dau. of
Stanford Wolferstan, of Statfold Hall, Staffs, and d.s.p. 29 Dec. 1798.
She d. 12 Apr. 1811.   (Burke's Commoners, I, 189; M.I.)

EAST COKER, Coker Court

1. All black background (formerly dexter background black)
Qly, 1st, Azure a cross patonce argent between four pierced molets or
(Helyar), 2nd, Argent on a bend sable three roses argent (Cary), 3rd,
Argent a chevron engrailed and in chief four roses per pale azure and
gules (Weston), 4th, qly i. & iv. Or a cross vair (   ), ii. & iii. Per
pale argent and or a cross patonce gules between four escallops azure
(   ), impaling, Ermine on a chevron engrailed gules two escallops
argent (Grove)
Crest: A cock sable, wattled, combed, legged and beaked gules standing
in front of a cross flory fitchy or   Mantling: Gules and
argent   Motto: In labore quies
For William Helyar, who m. Harriet Grove, and d. 10 Dec. 1841; also
used for his wife, who d. 14 Dec. 1867.   (Pedigree at Coker Court)

WEST CRANMORE

1. Sinister background black
Ermine on a canton sable a crescent argent (Strode), impaling, Sable a
stag's head cabossed between two flaunches or (Parker)
Motto: Mors janua vitae   Cherub's head above
For Margaret Sophia, dau. of Sir Henry John Parker, Bt., of Talton, co.
Worcs., who m. John Strode, of Southill, and d. 25 Aug.
1805.   (B.L.G. 2nd ed.; M.I.)

2. All black background
Arms: As 1.
Crest: A demi-lion rampant or   Mantling: Gules and
argent   Motto: In coelo quies
For John Strode, who d. 1807, aged 69.   (Sources, as 1.)

3. Dexter background black
Qly, 1st and 4th, Strode, 2nd and 3rd, Argent a griffin segreant gules
charged with a cross potent or within a bordure engrailed gules
(Chetham)   In pretence: Qly, 1st and 4th, Argent a lion passant
sable between three fleurs-de-lys gules (Evans), 2nd and 3rd, Sable five
mascles in cross or (Brandreth)
Crests: Dexter, A demi-lion rampant or   Sinister, From a mural
coronet argent, a demi-griffin gules charged with a bezant holding a
cross potent azure between its paws   Mantling: Sable and
argent   Motto: Mors janua vitae

For Thomas Chetham-Strode, who m. 1816, Catherine Brandreth
Backhouse, dau and co-heiress of the Rev. D. Evans, D.D., and d. 11
Sept. 1827.   (B.L.G. 2nd ed.)

4. Dexter background black

Qly, as 3., impaling, Per pale vert and argent three greyhounds courant
counterchanged, on a chief or a garb in bend sable surmounted by a
sword in bend sinister between two cross formy gules (Thomlinson)
Crests: As 3.   Motto: Malo mori quam foedari
For Richard Chetham-Strode, who m. Frances, dau. of the Rev. Robert
Thomlinson, Rector of Cley, Norfolk, and d.s.p. 19 July
1828.   (B.L.G. 2nd ed.)

CROWCOMBE

1. All black background

Qly, 1st and 4th, Or three lions passant in pale sable (Carew), 2nd,
Argent a chevron between three billets gules (Kelly), 3rd, Argent a
cross gules between four crows proper (   ), impaling, Azure a
chevron between three lions' heads erased or (Wyndham)
Crest: Issuant from a mainmast roundtop surrounded with palisadoes or
a lion rampant sable   Mantling: Gules argent   Motto: J'espor
bien
For Thomas Carew, who m. Margery, dau. of Sir John Wyndham, and
d. 1661. She d. 1660.   (Burke's Commoners, Vol. I)

2. Sinister background black

Qly of 16, 1st, Carew, 2nd, Gules a maunch ermine the hand proper
holding a fleur-de-lys or (Mohun), 3rd, Azure a chevron between three
griffins' heads erased or (Jennings). 4th, Argent a chevron between three
billets gules (Kelly), 5th, Gules a saltire engrailed argent between four
bezants (Ansell), 6th, Argent two wings conjoined in base points
upwards gules (Barnhowse), 7th, Argent six roses three, two and one
gules (   ), 8th, Argent a chevron between three escallops sable
(   ), 9th, Gules three lozenges conjoined in fess ermine (   ),
10th, Azure three garbs or (Peverel), 11th, Or a bend gules (   ),
12th, Argent a cross gules between four crows proper (   ), 13th, Or
a pile gules (Chandos), 14th, Gules a lion rampant argent (   ),
15th, Gules a bend fusilly argent (Raleigh), 16th, Gules on a chevron
between three martlets argent a cross formy sable (   ), impaling,
Qly, 1st and 4th, Ermine a lion passant gules (Drewe), 2nd and 3rd,
Sable ermined argent three roses argent (for Sparrow)
No crest, but escallop sable charged with three roses argent above
shield   Mantling: Gules and argent   Motto: J'espere
bien   Supporters: Dexter, A lion rampant sable crowned
gules   Sinister, An antelope gules armed or   Frame decorated
with skulls and crossbones

For Mary, dau. of Francis Drewe, of Grance, Devon, who m. as his 1st
wife, Thomas Carew, and d. 1738, aged 36.   (B.L.G. 1937 ed.; M.I.)

3. Sinister background black

Carew, impaling two coats per pale, 1st, Ermine a lion passant gules
(Drewe), 2nd, Argent on a chevron engrailed gules between three bugle
horns stringed sable three molets pierced argent (Horne)
To dexter of main shield, Carew impaling Drewe S.B1   To sinister
of main shield, Carew impaling Horne S.B1
Motto: J'espere bien   Cherub's head above   Frame decorated
with skulls and crossbones
For Mary, dau. of John Horne, who m. as his 2nd wife, Thomas Carew,
and d. July 1757.   (B.L.G. 1937 ed.; M.I.)

4. All black background

Carew, impaling two coats per pale, 1st, Drewe, 2nd, Horne
Crest and mantling: As 1.   Motto: J'espere bien   Supporters: As
2.   Frame decorated with skulls and crossbones
For Thomas Carew, who d. Mar. 1766, aged 64.   (B.L.G. 1937 ed.:
M.I.)

5. Dexter backgound black

Carew   In pretence: Carew
Crest: As 1.   Motto: J'espere bien   Supporters: As 2.
For George Henry Warrington (who took the name and arms of Carew
on succeeding to the estates), who m. Mary, eldest dau. and heiress of
John Carew, and d. 13 Oct. 1842.   (B.L.G.)

6. All black background

On a lozenge   Arms: As 5.
Motto: J'espere bien   Supporters: As 2.
For Mary, widow of George Henry Carew, d. 18 Mar.
1852.   (Source, as 5.)

7. Dexter background black

Qly, 1st and 4th, Carew, 2nd, Barry of six or and azure, on a chief or
three pallets between two gyrons azure, over all an inescutcheon ermine
(Mortimer), 3rd, Gules a lion rampant within a bordure engrailed or
(Powell), impaling, Qly, 1st and 4th, Sable an eagle displayed or,
beaked and membered gules, on a chief azure bordered argent a chevron
between in chief two crescents argent and in base a cinquefoil or
(Mynors), 2nd and 3rd, Argent a chevron gules between three roundels
azure (Baskerville)
Crest and mantling: As 1.   Motto: J'espere bien   Supporters: As 2.

For George Henry Warrington Carew, who m. 1856, Mary Philippa, dau. of Peter Rickards Mynors, and d. 24 Jan. 1874.   (B.L.G. 1937 ed.)

8. Sinister background black
Argent a bear rampant sable muzzled or (Barnard), impaling, Carew
Mantling: Gules and argent   Cherub's head above
For Elizabeth, dau. of Thomas Carew, who m. James Barnard, of the Middle Temple, and d.s.p. 12 Dec. 1805, aged 74.   (B.L.G. 1937 ed.; M.I.)

9. All black background
Barnard arms only
Crest: A demi-bear sable muzzled or   Mantle: Gules and ermine
tasselled or   Winged skull in base
Probably for James Barnard, of the Middle Temple, who d. 29 Aug. 1811, aged 77.   (B.L.G. 1937 ed.; M.I.)

CURRY RIVEL

1. All black background
Two lozenges, the dexter overlapping the sinister
Dexter, surmounted by a countess's coronet, Sable a fess countercompony argent and azure between three bezants (Pitt), impaling, Vert on a cross argent five roundels gules (Grenville)   Sinister, surmounted by a baroness's coronet, Grenville
Supporters: Dexter, A lion rampant guardant charged on the breast with a slip of oak fructed proper   Sinister, A stag proper collared and lined or
For Hester, Baroness Chatham, only dau. of Richard Grenville, who m. William Pitt, 1st Earl of Chatham, and d. 3 Apr. 1803.   (B.E.P.)

DUNSTER

1. Dexter background black
Qly, 1st and 4th, Or a bend between six martlets sable (Luttrell), 2nd and 3rd, qly i. & iv. Gules on a chevron or three cross crosslets sable (Hadley), ii. & iii. Or on a bend cotised sable three bears' heads argent muzzled gules (Durborough), impaling, Argent a chevron gules between three water bougets sable (Yard)
Crest: An otter passant sable   Mantling: Gules and argent   Motto: Quaesita marte tuenda arte   Supporters: Two swans argent ducally gorged and chained or   Skull below
For Alexander Luttrell, who m. Dorothy (d. 19 Nov. 1723), dau. of Edward Yard, and d. 22 Sept. 1711.   (B.L.G. 1937 ed.)

2. Dexter background black
Luttrell, impaling, Gules a demi-horse argent issuing from the sea barry wavy argent and azure (Trevelyan)

Crest: From a ducal coronet or a plume of five ostrich feathers
argent   Mantling: Gules and argent   Motto: As
1.   Supporters: As 1.   Cherubs' heads to dexter and
sinister   Frame decorated with skulls and crossbones
For Alexander Luttrell, who m. 1726, Margaret, dau. of Sir John
Trevelyan, Bt., and d. 4 June 1737.   (B.L.G. 1937 ed.)

3. Sinister background black

Qly, 1st and 4th, Azure two eagles displayed and a molet in base argent
(Fownes), 2nd and 3rd, Luttrell   In pretence (over line of
impalement), and impaling, Luttrell
Shield surrounded with rococo shell design, swags of roses and cherubs'
heads   Frame decorated with skulls and crossbones
For Margaret, dau. of Alexander Luttrell, who m. 1747, as his 1st wife,
Henry Fownes-Luttrell, and d. 1766.   (B.L.G. 1937 ed.)

4. Dexter two-thirds background black

Qly, 1st and 4th, Luttrell, 2nd and 3rd, Fownes   In pretence (over
line of impalement): Luttrell   Also impaling two coats per pale,
Luttrell, and, Or a chevron between three boars' heads couped facing to
the sinister gules (Bradley)
Crest, mantling and motto: As 2.
For Henry Fownes-Luttrell, who m. 2nd, Frances, dau. of Samuel
Bradley, and d. 30 Oct. 1780.   (B.L.G. 1937 ed.)

5. Dexter background black

Qly, 1st and 4th, Luttrell, 2nd and 3rd, Fownes, impaling, Ermine a
lion passant gules (Drewe)
Crest and motto: As 2.   Supporters: As 1.
For John Fownes Luttrell, who m. 1782, Mary, dau. of Francis Drewe,
and d. 16 Feb. 1816.   (B.L.G. 1937 ed.)

6. All black background

On an asymmetric lozenge surmounted by a cherub's head
Arms: As 5.
Mantling: Gules and argent   Skull in base
For Mary, widow of John Fownes Luttrell, d. 20 Mar.
1830.   (B.L.G. 1937 ed.)

7. Dexter background black

Qly, 1st and 4th, Azure a bend between six martlets argent (Luttrell),
2nd and 3rd, Fownes, impaling, Drewe
Crest: As 2.   Motto and supporters: As 1.
For Francis Luttrell, who m. 1824, Emma Louisa, dau. of Samuel
Drewe, and d. 4 Jan. 1862.   (B.L.G. 1937 ed.)

8. All black background
Qly, 1st and 4th, Or a bend between six martlets sable (Luttrell), 2nd
and 3rd, Fownes
Crest: As 2.   Mantling: Azure and or   Motto and supporters:
As 1., but swans collared and chained or
Probably for John Fownes Luttrell, who d. unm. Jan. 1857, or Henry
Fownes Luttrell, who d. unm. 6 Oct. 1867.   (B.L.G. 1937 ed.)

9. All black background
Arms: As 8.
Crest: As 2.   Motto and supporters: As 1.
Probably for John or Henry Fownes Luttrell (see 8.)

EVERCREECH
1. Sinister background black
Or on a chevron between three bulls sable a pheon argent (Rodbard),
impaling, Azure a lion rampant argent (for Cozens)
Cherub's head above
For Mary, dau. of Harry and Elizabeth Cozens, who m. William
Rodbard, and d. 17 Aug. 1756, aged 37. He d. 30 Apr. 1784, aged
67.   (M.I.)

2. Dexter background black
Gules a lion rampant or within a bordure engrailed or ermined sable
(Talbot)   In pretence: Or on a chevron between three bulls sable a
pheon argent (Rodbard)
Baron's coronet   Crest: On a chapeau gules and ermine a lion
statant tail extended or ermined sable   Mantling: Gules and
or   Motto: Forte et fidele   Supporters: Dexter, A talbot
or   Sinister, A lion gules
For James, 3rd Lord Talbot de Malahide, who m. 1804, Anne Sarah,
2nd dau. and co-heir of Samuel Rodbard, of Evercreech House,
Somerset, and d. 20 Dec. 1850.   (B.P. 1875 ed.)
(There is another hatchment for him at Malahide, Dublin)

3. All black background
On a lozenge surmounted by a baroness's coronet
Arms: As 2.
Motto: Resurgam   Supporters: As 2.
For Sarah, widow of James, 3rd Lord Talbot de Malahide, d. 13 Mar.
1857.   (B.P. 1875 ed.)

FARLEIGH HUNGERFORD
1. Dexter background black
Qly, 1st and 4th, Argent on a fess wavy between three talbots' heads
erased azure three bezants (Houlton), 2nd and 3rd, Gules a bordure
sable charged with estoiles or, on a canton argent a lion rampant sable

an annulet or for difference (White)   In pretence: Or on a cross
sable five crescents or (Ellis)
Crest: A talbot's head erased azure, langued gules, gorged with a collar
or charged with three roundels gules   Mantling: Gules and
argent   Mottoes: (over crest) Semper fidelis   (below shield)
Resurgam
For John Houlton, of Farley Castle, who m. 1799, Mary Ann, only dau.
and heir of Thomas Ellis, of Rollestone, Devon, and d. 17 Feb.
1839.   (B.L.G. 7th ed.; M.I.)

GOATHURST

1. All black background

Qly, 1st and 4th, Gules a lion couchant guardant between six cross
crosslets argent (Tynte), 2nd and 3rd, Argent three bars wavy azure,
over all a bend gules (Halswell), over all the Badge of Ulster
Crest: A demi-griffin argent armed gules   Mantling: Gules and
argent   Frame decorated with skulls and crossbones
For the Rev. Sir John Tynte, 4th Bt., Rector of Goathurst, who d. unm.
15 Aug. 1740.   (B.P. 1949 ed.)

2. Dexter background black

Qly of six, 1st, Gules a lion couchant between six cross crosslets argent,
in dexter chief the Badge of Ulster (Tynte), 2nd, Vert on a chevron
argent three pheons sable (Kemeys), 3rd, Azure a bend engrailed argent
plain cotised or (Fortescue), 4th, Halswell, 5th, Tynte, 6th,
Kemeys   In pretence: Or three arrows in fess points downwards
sable feathered argent, on a chief sable three molets or (Busby)
Crest: A unicorn sejant argent   Mantling: Gules and
argent   Motto: Dvw dy ras   Frame decorated with skulls and
crossbones
For Sir Charles Kemeys Tynte, 5th Bt., who m. 1737/8, Anne, dau. and
co-heir of the Rev. Thomas Busby, and d.s.p. 25 Aug. 1785.   (B.P.
1949 ed.)

3. All black background

On a lozenge surmounted by a cherub's head
Qly, 1st, Gules a lion dormant between six cross crosslets argent
(Tynte), 2nd, Halswell, 3rd, Fortescue, 4th, Kemeys   In pretence:
Busby   Motto: Resurgam
For Anne, widow of Sir Charles Kemeys Tynte, 5th Bt., who d. 24 Mar.
1798.   (B.P. 1949 ed.)

4. All black background

On a lozenge surmounted by a cherub's head
Qly, 1st and 4th, Gules a lion couchant between six cross crosslets
argent (Tynte), 2nd and 3rd, Kemeys   In pretence: Qly of six, 1st,
Vert three adders erect argent (Hassell), 2nd, Tynte, 3rd, Kemeys, 4th,

Sable a bouget argent within a bordure or charged with eight pairs of
lions' gambs erased in saltire gules (Wharton), 5th, Per pale or and
gules a lion rampant between three fleurs-de-lys counterchanged
(Goodwin), 6th, Argent three bars azure a label of four points gules
(Grey)
For Jane, only dau. of Major Ruisshe Hassell, and niece of Sir Charles
Kemeys Tynte, 5th Bt., who m. 1765, John Kemeys-Tynte (formerly
Johnson), and d. 1825. He d. 1807.   (B.P. 1949 ed.)

5. Sinister background black

Qly, 1st, qly i. & iv. Tynte, as 4., ii. & iii. Kemeys, 2nd, Barry wavy of
ten azure and argent over all a bend gules (Halswell), 3rd, Wharton,
4th, Or a lion rampant within a double tressure flory counter-flory gules
(Stewart), impaling, Gules three chevrons or (Leyson)
Supporters: Dexter, A bull argent ducally gorged per pale or and
gules   Sinister, A lion rampant gules crowned and fretty
or   Motto: As 2. Cherub's head above shield
For Anne, dau. of the Rev. Thomas Leyson, who m. 1798, Charles
Kemeys Kemeys-Tynte, and d. 26 Apr. 1836. He d. 22 Nov.
1860.   (B.P. 1949 ed.)

6. Dexter background black

Qly, 1st, Tynte, as 4., 2nd, Kemeys, 3rd, Halswell, as 1., 4th, Fortescue,
impaling, Gules on a bend or three martlets sable, a crescent for
difference (Brabazon)
Crests: Dexter, A unicorn sejant argent   Sinister, A demi-griffin
or   Mantling and motto: As 2.
For Charles John Kemeys-Tynte, who m. 2nd, 1841, Vincentia (d. 14
Oct. 1894), dau. of Wallop Brabazon, and d. 16 Sept. 1882.   (B.P.
1949 ed.)

7. All black background

Qly, 1st, Tynte, as 4., 2nd, Kemeys, 3rd, Azure three bars wavy argent
over all a bend gules (Halswell), 4th, Fortescue
To dexter of main shield, Qly, as main shield   In pretence: Qly,
1st, Argent a fess between three griffins segreant gules (Frome), 2nd,
Azure a lion rampant and in chief three escallops argent (Clutterbuck),
3rd, Argent a bend gules between two choughs proper, a chief chequy or
and azure (Pleydell), 4th, Qly ermine and gules in the 2nd and 3rd
quarters a goat's head erased argent armed or (Morton) S.B1   To
sinister of main shield, Qly, as main shield, impaling, Vert a stag's head
couped within a bordure engrailed or (Fothergill) D.B1.
Crests: Dexter, A unicorn sejant argent maned and armed
or   Sinister, A demi-griffin or   Mantling and motto: As 2.
For Charles Kemeys Kemeys-Tynte, who m. 1st, 1848, Mary, dau. of the
Rev. George Frome, and 2nd, 1873, Hannah, widow of T. Lewis, and

3rd, 1879, Elizabeth, dau. of Richard Fothergill, and d. 10 Jan. 1891.
She d. 18 Mar. 1933.　　(B.P. 1949 ed.)

8. All black background

Qly, 1st, qly i. & iv. Tynte, as 4., ii. & iii. Kemeys, 2nd, Halswell, as 7., 3rd, Wharton, with maunch instead of bouget, 4th, Azure a wolf's head erased argent (Lupus)

Crests: Dexter, as 7. but unicorn azure　　　Sinister, A bull's head argent ducally gorged per pale gules and or　　Motto: As 2.　　Supporters: As 5.

Probably for Charles Kemeys Kemeys-Tynte, widower of 5. He d. 22 Nov. 1860.　　(B.P. 1949 ed.)

HARDINGTON

1. All black background

On a lozenge　　Argent on a bend gules three molets argent, in chief the Badge of Ulster (Bampfylde)　　In pretence: Azure on a chief indented or three molets sable (Moore)

For Catherine, dau. of Admiral Sir John Moore, Bt., who m. 1776, Sir Charles Warwick Bampfylde, 5th Bt., and d. 20 Mar. 1832.　　(B.P. 1949 ed.; L.C. Bampfylde)

HINTON CHARTERHOUSE

1. Dexter background black

Argent a lion rampant vert (Jones), impaling, Gules a lion rampant or within a bordure engrailed or ermined sable (Talbot)

Crest: A sun in splendour or　　Mantling: Gules and argent　　Motto: Propositi tenax

For Thomas Jones, of Stapleton and Hinton Charterhouse, who m. 1835, Margaret Nugent, dau. of James, 3rd Lord Talbot de Malahide, and d. 8 May 1848.　　(B.P. 1949 ed.)

HORSINGTON

1. Dexter background black

Two coats per fess, in chief, Azure three buglehorns argent stringed or (Dodington), in base, Sable three stirrups leathered or a bordure engrailed or charged with roundels gules (Gifford), impaling, Gules a bezant between three demi-lions rampant couped argent (Bennet)

Crest: A stag lodged to the sinister regardant argent antlered or, in the mouth an acorn or stalked and leaved vert　　Mantling: Gules and argent　　Motto: Mors via vitae

Unidentified

KELSTON

1. All black background

Gules fretty argent (Hudleston), impaling, Argent on a chief or three pallets gules (for Marshall)

Crest: Two arms embowed proper vested argent in the hands a scalp
proper   Mantling: Gules and argent   Motto: Soli Deo honor et
gloria
For John Hudleston, of Laura Place, Bath, who m. 1788, Honoria, dau.
of the Rev. Joseph Marshall, Recor of Maghera, Ireland, and d. 6 Mar.
1835. She d. 24 Sept. 1807.   (B.L.G. 1937 ed.; M.I.)
(Repainted by the Rev. E. J. Rowe, 1980)

KEYNSHAM
1. All black background
Ermine on a fess gules three bezants (Milward)
Crest: A lion's gamb sable grasping a sceptre or   Mantling: Gules
and argent   Motto: In coelo quies
Probably for Alfred Milward, who d. 12 Aug. 1854, aged
31.   (M.I.)

KINGSTON ST MARY
1. Dexter background black
Qly of 11, 1st, Gules crusilly fitchy a lion rampant argent, the Badge of
Ulster (Warre), 2nd, Or three leopards' faces gules (   ), 3rd, Barry
of eight or and sable a bend ermine (Meriet), 4th, Argent two wings
conjoined gules, over all a bend azure (Kentisbere), 5th, obscured by
inscutcheon, 6th, Per pale azure and gules three lions rampant argent
(   ), 7th, Or three door keys wards upwards two and one gules
(Claville), 8th, Argent a cross botonny gules (Percehay), 9th, Argent
two bendlets wavy sable (   ), 10th, Azure a chevron between three
stags' heads cabossed or (Chipleigh), 11th, Argent on a bend azure
three   argent (   )   In pretence: Argent on a bend dancetty
sable cotised azure bezanty three fleurs-de-lys argent (Cuffe), also
impaling, Azure a saltire voided between four spear heads erect or
(Harbin)
Crest: An ostrich's head argent in the beak a spur or   Mantling:
Gules and argent   Motto: Je trouve bien   Supporters: Dexter,
not discernible   Sinister, A wyvern sable
For Sir Francis Warre, Bt., who m. 1st, Ann, dau. of Robert Cuffe, and
2nd, Margaret, dau. of John Harbin, and d. 1 Dec. 1718.   (B.E.B.)

2. Dexter background black
Or on a bend gules three pierced molets argent (Bampfylde), impaling
two coats to the sinister, 1st, Barry wavy of six or and gules (Basset),
2nd, Gules crusilly fitchy a lion rampant argent (Warre)
Crest: A lion's head erased sable ducally crowned or   Mantling:
Gules and argent   Motto: Delectare in Domino   Frame
decorated with skulls and crossbones
For John Bampfylde, who m. 1st, Elizabeth, dau. of John Bassett, and
2nd, Margaret, dau. of Sir Francis Warre, Bt., and d. 17 Sept.
1750.   (B.E.B.)

3. Dexter background black
Qly, 1st and 4th, Or on a bend gules three molets argent (Bampfylde),
2nd and 3rd, Warre, impaling, Argent three pallets gules within a
bordure engrailed azure, on a canton gules a spur or (Knight)
Crest and mantling: As 2.   Motto: In coelo quies   Unframed
For Coplestone Warre Bampfylde, who m. Mary, dau. of Edmund
Knight, of Wolverley, and d. 29 Aug. 1791.   (B.P. 1949 ed.)

4. Dexter background black
Qly of six, 1st and 6th, qly i. & iv. Warre, ii. & iii. Bampfylde, as 2.,
2nd, Argent a fess gules between three garbs sable banded argent
(Tyndale), 3rd, Bampfylde, as 2., 4th, Warre, 5th, Or four bars azure a
bend ermine (Meriet)   In pretence: Gules a cross flory argent, over
all a bend azure (Farrell)
Gold bow above shield   Motto: Je trouve bien
For John Tyndale Warre, who m. 1789, Elizabeth, dau. and heir of
Joseph Farrell, and d. 1819.   (B.E.P.)

5. All black background
Gules three martlets argent betwen two bars and six billets or, on a
canton argent a mascle sable (for Beauchamp)
Crest: A tyger statant or ermined sable   Mantling: Gules and
argent   Motto: Veritas vincit
Probably for Robert Farthing Beauchamp, who d. 6 Jan. 1841, aged
64.   (M.I.)

LYMPSHAM
1. All black background (should be dexter black)
Or a mural coronet azure between three cross crosslets fitchy gules
(Stephenson), impaling, Sable three leopards' faces or (Gurdon)
Crest: A cross crosslet fitchy gules surmounted by a mural coronet
or   Mantling: Gules and argent   Motto: Tulit crucem ferat
coronam
For the Rev. Joseph Adam Stephenson, who m. Elizabeth (d. 12 Dec.
1857), dau. of Philip Gurdon, and d. 22 Apr. 1837.   (M.I.s)

MIDSOMER NORTON, R.C. Church
1. All black background
Argent on a saltire engrailed sable five escallops argent, in centre chief a
crescent gules for difference (Conolly), impaling two coats per fess, in
chief, Argent a chevron between three bucks courant sable collared gules
(Rogers), and in base, Vert a dexter hand apaumy couped in base and in
chief an arrow fessways argent (Loughnan)
Crest: A cubit arm erect vested azure cuffed argent charged with a
crescent argent, the hand proper grasping a chaplet of roses
or   Mantling: Sable and argent   Motto: En Dieu est tout

For Charles Conolly, who m. 1st, Dorothy Rogers, and 2nd, Teresa
Loughnan, and d. (B.L.G. 2nd ed.)

2. All black background
Conolly   In pretence: Or a cross gules charged with a cross crosslet
fitchy or, in the dexter chief quarter a lion rampant sable, in the sinister
chief quarter a sinister hand couped gules (Bourke)
Crest, mantling and motto: As 1.
For Charles Conolly, who m. Maria Rebecca, dau. and co-heir of
Thomas Bourke, and d. 1828.   (B.L.G. 2nd ed.)

3. All black background
Qly, 1st and 4th, Conolly, 2nd and 3rd, Bourke, impaling two coats per
fess, in chief, Sable on a bend argent three molets gules (Clifton), and in
base, Or on a chief indented azure three garbs or (Lawless)
Crest, mantling and motto: As 1.
For Charles Thomas Conolly, who m. 1st, 1814, Elizabeth, dau. of John
Clifton, of Lytham Hall, and 2nd, 1828, Jane Anne, dau. of Philip
Lawless, of Dublin, and d. 13 Feb. 1850.   (B.L.G. 5th ed.)

4. All black background
Qly, 1st and 4th, Conolly, 2nd and 3rd, Bourke   In pretence,
surmounted by a coronet or: Qly, 1st and 4th, Azure on a bend or
between four lions' gambs proper three eagles displayed (Brancaccio),
2nd and 3rd, Qly or and gules a bordure compony azure and sable
(Dotto di Dauli)
Crest, mantling and motto: As 1.
For Charles John Thomas Conolly, of Cottles, Wilts., and Midford
Castle, Somerset, who m. 1840, Louisa Lucy Margaret Catherine
Brancaccio, in her own right, Marchesa di S. Agata, only child of Nicola
Maria Brancaccio, Marquis of Rivello, Prince di Ruffano, by Margaret,
dau. of Gulielmo, Baron Dotto di Dauli, and d.s.p. 1871.   (B.L.G.
5th ed.; Ruvigny, Nobilities of Europe)
(These four hatchments, recorded since the Survey began, were sold and
their present whereabouts is unknown)

MILBORNE PORT
1. All black background
On a lozenge   Gules on a chevron argent between three lions' heads
erased or three barrulets gules and fourteen roundels azure (Coles),
impaling, Azure a fess dancetty or between three eagles displayed argent
(Walter)
For Jane Walter of Stalbridge, who m. William Coles, of the Close,
Salisbury, and d. 11 Apr. 1801.   (M.I. in cathedral)

2. All black background
On a lozenge surmounted by a cherub's head

Qly per fess indented gules and azure three lions rampant argent
(Medlycott), impaling, Coles, with five barrulets and fifteen roundels
For Jane, dau. of William Coles, who m. Thomas Medlycott, and d.
1824. He d. 15 May 1795.   (B.P. 1949 ed.)

3. All black background
On a lozenge   Qly per fess indented gules three lions rampant or,
the Badge of Ulster (Medlycott), impaling, Azure three garbs or tied
gules, on a chief argent a boar's head couped sable langued gules
(Tugwell)
For Elizabeth, dau. of William Tugwell, of Bradford, Wilts., who m.
1796, Sir William Coles Medlycott, 1st Bt., and d. 31 July 1847. He d.
25 May 1835.   (B.P. 1949 ed.)

4. Dexter background black
Medlycott, as 2., with Badge of Ulster
Crest: From a mural coronet gules a demi-eagle displayed
or   Mantling: Gules and argent   Motto: Dat cura quietem
Probably for William Coles Paget Medlycott, 3rd Bt., who d. unm. 8
Jan. 1887.   (B.P. 1949 ed.)

NAILSEA Court
1. Dexter background black
Qly, 1st and 4th, Argent on a chevron between three stags' heads
cabossed sable three crescents or (Whorwood), 2nd and 3rd, Sable on a
chevron between three griffins' heads erased or three molets sable
(Adeane)   In pretence: Qly, 1st and 4th, Argent three snakes
involved vert (   ), 2nd, Sable a lion rampant or (   ), 3rd, Gules
a chevron between in chief two fleurs-de-lys and in base a wolf rampant
argent (   )
Crest: A griffin's head erased or collared sable between two wings erect
or   Mantling: Gules and argent   Motto:
Resurgam   Crossed flags and cannons behind shield   Inscribed
on frame: Gen. James Whorwood Adeane, M.P. for Cambs of Chalgrove
Oxon & Babraham, b. 1740, d. 1802 son of Simon W. Adeane and Mary
Bridges, grand-daughter of 8th Earl Chandos
For General James Whorwood Adeane, who m. Anne, only child and
heiress of Robert Jones, of Babraham, co. Cambridge, and d.
1802.   (B.L.G. 1937 ed.; inscription on hatchment frame)

2. All black background
On a rococo lozenge surmounted by a cherub's head
Arms: As 1., but Adeane chevron argent
Inscribed around base of lozenge: Wm. Edkins   City
Painter   Bristol

Inscribed on frame: Anne, b. 1747, d. 1832, dau. and heir of Robert
Jones of Babraham M.P. for Huntingdon, m. 1763, Gen. James
Whorwood Adeane, of Chalgrove, Oxon, M.P. for Cambs.
For Anne, widow of General James Whorwood Adeane, d.
1832.   (Sources, as 1.)

3. Dexter background black
Gules on a pale or in chief a squirrel holding an acorn proper and in
base a moor's head couped proper (Des Voeux), impaling, Sable a fess
ermine between three crescents or (Coventry), over all in chief the Badge
of Ulster
Crest: A squirrel holding an acorn proper   Mantling: Gules and
or   Motto: In coelo quies
For Sir Henry William Des Voeux, 3rd Bt., who m. 1839, Sophia
Catherine, widow of Sir Roger Gresley, 8th Bt., and dau. of George
William, 7th Earl of Coventry, and d. 4 Jan. 1868.   (B.P. 1875 ed.)

4. Dexter background black
Qly, 1st and 4th, Argent a canton sable (Sutton), 2nd and 3rd, Or two
bars azure a chief qly azure and gules, on first and fourth two fleurs-de-
lys or, on second and third a lion passant guardant or (Manners),
impaling, Argent on a fess double cotised gules three griffins' heads
erased or (Dashwood)
Baron's coronet   Crest: On a chapeau gules and ermine a peacock in
pride proper   Motto: Pour y parvenir   Supporters: Dexter, A
unicorn proper charged on the shoulder with a cross flory
azure   Sinister, A unicorn proper charged on the shoulder with a
portcullis azure
For John Thomas, 2nd Baron Manners, who m. 1848, Lydia Sophia, 3rd
dau. of Vice-Admiral William Bateman Dashwood, and d. 14 Nov.
1864.   (B.P. 1949 d.)

5. All black background
On a lozenge surmounted by a countess's coronet
Qly, 1st and 4th, qly i. Argent a cross Calvary gules with the figure of
Christ thereon (   ), ii. Or on a chief indented azure a crescent for
difference (Butler), iii. Gules three covered cups or (Butler), iv. Ermine
a saltire engrailed gules (Fitzgerald), all within a bordure ermine, 2nd,
Per pale indented or and gules (Bermingham), 3rd, Argent a
doubleheaded eagle displayed sable between three crosses formy gules
(Morrys), impaling, Azure on a chevron argent between in chief two
swans argent and in base a dolphin embowed or three bees or (Mellish)
Supporters: Dexter, An eagle argent   Sinister, A wolf per fess sable
and or collared, chained and maned or   All on a mantle gules and
argent
For Margaret Lauretta, younger dau. and co-heir of William Mellish, of
Woodford, Essex, who m. 1834, Richard, 2nd Earl of Glengall, and d.
1863.   (B.E.P.)

6. All black background
Lozengy ermine and sable a canton or (   )
Crest: A demi-lion holding a crook in pale or   Mantling: Gules and
argent ending in tassels or
Unidentified
(These six hatchments are no longer at the Court, and their present
whereabouts is unknown)

NORTON FITZWARREN
1. Dexter background black
Per fess argent and sable a pale and three horses' heads erased
counterchanged, on a chief ermine two bombs fired proper (Slade),
impaling, Azure on a bend engrailed or three martlets gules (Dawson),
the Badge of Ulster over line of impalement
Crest: On a mount vert a horse's head erased sable encircled with a
chain in the form of an arch or   Mantling: Gules and argent,
tasselled or   Motto: Fidus et audax
For Sir John Slade, 1st Bt., who m. Matilda Ellen, dau of James
Dawson, of Fork Hill, Armagh, and d. 13 Aug. 1859.   (B.P. 1963
ed.)

2. Dexter background black
Argent on a bend gules between two roundels azure three molets or
(Welman), impaling, Argent on a saltire sable five fleurs-de-lys or
(Hawkins)
Crest: A demi-lion rampant argent holding a molet or   Mantling:
Gules and argent   Frame decorated with skulls and crossbones
For Simon Welman, of Poundisford Park, who m. 1709, Elizabeth, dau.
of Benjamin Hawkins, and d. 1716.   (B.L.. 1937 ed.)

3. All black background
Qly, 1st and 4th, Welman, 2nd and 3rd, Sable on the waves of the sea
proper a lion passant or in chief three bezants (Hawkins)   In
pretence: Qly, 1st and 4th, Argent three roundels and a chief gules, a
label of three points azure (Tristram), 2nd and 3rd, Argent two lions
passant azure (Hanmer)
Crest: As 2.   No mantling   Motto: Mors janua
vitae   Unusually decorative surround to shield   Frame
decorated with skull and crossbones
For Isaac Welman, of Poundisford Park, who m. 1737, Jane, dau. and
heir of Robert Tristram of Barnstaple, and d 9 Feb. 1782.   (B.L.G.
1937 ed.)

4. All black background
Qly, 1st and 4th, Welman, 2nd and 3rd, Tristram, impaling two coats
per fess, in chief, Per fess or and azure a pale counterchanged and three
hawks or (Locke), in base, Or fretty gules a canton ermine (Noel)

Crest: As 2.   Mantling: Gules and argent   Motto: The dead in
Christ shall rise first
For Thomas Welman, of Poundisford Park, who m. 1st, 1785, Elizabeth
(d. 16 Mar. 1788), dau. of John Locke, and 2nd, Charlotte, dau. of Sir
Gerard Noel, and d. 28 Jan. 1829.   (B.L.G. 1937 ed.)

NORTON MALREWARD
1. Dexter backgound black
Qly, 1st and 4th, Azure a pale between two griffins segreant or (Adams),
2nd and 3rd, Per chevron sable and or, in chief two eagles displayed or
(Shute), impaling, Qly, 1st and 4th, Azure three lozenges argent
(Freeman), 2nd and 3rd, Sable on a fess or between two lions passant
guardant argent three crescents gules (Tyler)   Also, in pretence:
Argent a chevron between three swans sable (   )
Crest: A demi-griffin or   Mantling: Gules and argent   Motto:
Resurgam
For Shute Adams, who m. 1st, Kevenhappuck, who d. Sept. 1744, and
2nd, 1751, Frances, dau. of Francis Freeman, of Bristol, and d. 10 Jan.
1766. She d. 20 Jan. 1755.   (B.L.G. 1937 ed.; M.I.)
(This hatchment has recently been restored by Lt.-Col. R. L. V. ffrench-
Blake)

PITMINSTER
1. All black background
Qly, 1st and 4th, Azure a cross vairy or and azure between four molets
or (Hawker), 2nd and 3rd, Argent a cross patonce gules between four
escallops azure (Sampson)
Crest: On the stump of a tree lying fessways a hawk
proper   Mantling: Gules and argent   Motto: Delectare in
Domino
For William Hawker, who m. Elizabeth, dau. and heir of Thomas
Welman, and was bur. 18 Feb. 1806.   (P.R.)

2. All black background
On a lozenge surmounted by a cherub's head
Qly, 1st and 4th, Or a cross vair between four molets of six points sable
(Hawker), 2nd and 3rd, Per pale ermine and or a cross patonce gules
between four escallops azure (Sampson)
For Ann Hawker, d. 13 Oct. 1834. (M.I.)

QUEEN CAMEL
1. All black background
Qly, 1st, Argent three lions rampant azure (Mildmay), 2nd, Azure on a
canton or a molet sable (   ), 3rd, Sable a chevron embattled or
between three roses argent (Cornish), 4th, Gules on a bend argent three
trefoils slipped vert (Hervey)   Two escutcheons of pretence: Dexter,
Sable two bars gemel between six martlets three, two and one argent

(Eastmount)   Sinister, Qly, 1st and 4th, Argent a chevron between
three roses gules (Phelips), 2nd, Or on a chevron azure three birds'
heads erased argent (   ), 3rd, Gules a chevron between three garbs
or (Blake)
Crests: Dexter, A lion rampant azure   Sinister, A leopard passant
collared and chained or holding in the dexter forepaw a trefoil slipped
azure   Mantling: Gules and argent   Motto: Allah ta
hara   Skull under helm   Frame originally decorated with skull
and crossbones, now plain
For Carew Hervey Mildmay, who m. 1st, 1718, Dorothy, dau. and heir
of John Eastmount, and 2nd, 1744, Edith, dau. of Sir Edward Phelips,
and d. 16 Jan. 1784.   (B.P. 1949 ed.)

2. All black background
On a lozenge surmounted by a cherub's head
Qly, 1st and 4th, Mildmay, 2nd, Hervey, 3rd, Eastmount
Unidentified

RODDEN
1. All black background
On a lozenge   Qly, 1st and 4th, Sable three lions rampant argent
langued gules (Prowse), 2nd and 3rd, Or three bendlents azure within a
bordure engrailed gules (Newborough), impaling, Gyronny of eight or
and ermine a tower triple-towered sable (Hooper)
For Abigail, dau. of the Rt. Rev. George Hooper, Bishop of Bath and
Wells, who m. as his 2nd wife, John Prowse of Axbridge, son of John
Prowse and Anne, dau. and co-heiress of Roger Newborough of Berkley,
and d. 15 Nov. 1763, aged 79.   (M.I. in Axbridge church)

SHAPWICK
1. Dexter background black
Sable two lions passant argent each charged with three pallets gemel
gules (Strangways), impaling, Argent a lion rampant tail nowed gules
collared or, in chief three falcons proper (Bewes)
Crest: A lion as in the arms   Motto: Resurgam
For Henry Bull Strangways, who m. Elizabeth, dau. of H. Bewes, of
Plymouth, and d. 22 May 1829, aged 52.   (M.I.)

SHEPTON MALLET
1. Dexter background black
Azure a chief argent (Provis), impaling, Ermine three lozenges conjoined
in fess sable (Pigott)
Crest: A pelican in her piety argent   Mantling: Gules and
argent   Motto: Resurgam
For William Provis, who m. 1762, Ann, dau. of John Pigott, of Brockley,
and d.   (B.L.G. 1937 ed. under Smyth-Pigott of Brockley)

2. Dexter background black

Qly, 1st and 4th, Or a griffin segreant sable (Morgan), 2nd and 3rd, Argent on a chevron gules between three buglehorns stringed sable three cross crosslets fitchy or (Burt)   In pretence: Argent five lozenges conjoined in fess sable between two bars gules (   )
Crest: From a ducal coronet a griffin's head argent   Mantling: Gules and argent   Motto: Resurgam
Unidentified

3. All black background

Sable a griffin passant or a crescent for difference (Brice)
Crest: A lion's head erased ermine transfixed with an arrow or   Mantling: Gules and argent   Inscribed in base: Mr. Worthington Brice departed this life the 14th day of July 1720 aged 69 years
For Worthington Brice, who d. 14 July 1720, aged 69.   (Inscr. on hatchment)

4. All black background

Argent on a chevron azure three garbs or (Newton)
Crest: A negro on one knee crowned or proferring a sword argent hilted or   Mantling: Gules and argent   Motto: Mors janua vitae
Unidentified

SOMERTON
1. Dexter background black

Qly, 1st and 4th, Gules three crescents or issuing from each a cross crosslet fitchy argent (Pinney), 2nd and 3rd, Or a double-headed eagle displayed vert, beaked and legged gules (Pretor), impaling, Ermine three battleaxes sable (Weekes)
Crest: An arm in armour embowed, the part above the elbow in fess proper, the hand proper holding a cross crosslet fitchy argent   Mantling: Gules and argent   Motto: Amor patriae
For John Pretor, who took the name and arms of Pinney, m. 1772, Jane, dau. of Major William Burt Weekes, of Nevis, and d. 23 Jan. 1818.   (B.L.G. 1937 ed.; M.I.)
(There is another hatchment for John Pinney in St George's, Bristol)

2. Dexter background black

Qly, as 1, impaling, Or a bend engrailed between two lions rampant gules (Dickinson)
Crest, mantling and motto: As 1.
For John Frederick Pinney, who m. 1801, Frances, dau. of William Dickinson, and d. 19 Sept. 1845.   (Sources, as 1.)

TAUNTON Museum
1. Sinister background black
Qly, 1st and 4th, qly i. & iv. Azure three bars wavy argent (Sanford), ii. & iii. Argent a chevron between three martlets sable (Sanford), 2nd and 3rd, Argent two ashkeys vert between two chevrons sable (Ayshford), impaling, Qly of six, 1st and 6th, Argent three bears' heads couped sable muzzled or (Langham), 2nd, Ermine a chevron gules a bordure engrailed sable (Revell), 3rd, Argent a fess wavy between three leopards' faces sable, on a canton azure two goats salient addorsed gules (Goodday, and canton for Samwell), 4th, Azure six annulets, three, two and one or (Musgrave), 5th, Azure three sinister gauntlets or (Vane) Cherub's head above
For Henrietta, dau. of Sir William Langham, Bt., who m. 1817, as his 1st wife, Edward Ayshford Sanford, and d. 24 Aug. 1836.   (B.L.G. 1937 ed.)

2. All black background
Qly, 1st and 4th, Azure three bars wavy argent (Sanford), 2nd, Argent a chevron between three martlets sable (Sanford), 3rd, Argent three ashkeys vert between two chevrons sable (Ayshford), impaling two coats per pale to sinister, 1st, Argent three bears' heads erased sable muzzled or (Langham), 2nd, Qly ermine and gules a crescent or (Stanhope)
Crest: A martlet sable   No mantling   Motto: Ferme en foy
For Edward Ayshford Sanford, who m. 1st, 1817, Henrietta, dau. of Sir William Langham, Bt., and 2nd, 1841, Caroline (d. Nov. 1856), dau. of Charles, 3rd Earl of Harrington, and d. 1 Dec. 1871.   (B.L.G. 1937 ed.)

THORNFALCON
1. Dexter background black
Gules a boar's head couped or langued azure (Chisholm), impaling, Azure a molet pierced or, on a chief or a branch with three leaves vert (   )
Crest: A dexter hand holding a dagger erect proper, on its point a boar's head couped gules   Mantling: Gules and or   Motto: Feros ferio
Unidentified

WESTON-SUPER-MARE
1. All black background
Qly, 1st and 4th, Ermine three fusils conjoined in fess azure (Pigott), 2nd and 3rd, Argent on a chevron gules three martlets or, on a chief gules a chamber piece or (Coward)
Crest: A wolf's head erased azure collared argent, charged with four roundels sable   Mantling: Gules and argent   Motto: Mors janua vitae   Inscribed around frame: Revd Wadham Pigott, died 25 Dec. 1823.
For the Rev. Wadham Pigott, son of John Bigg-Pigott and Ann, sister and co-heir of Thomas Coward. He d. 25 Dec. 1823.   (B.L.G. 1937 ed.)

WHITESTAUNTON

1. All black background (should be sinister black)
Paly of six or and gules on a bend sable three pierced molets or (Elton),
impaling, Argent three martlets sable between two chevrons gules
(Peach)
Crest: An arm in armour embowed the hand holding a scimitar
proper   Mantling: Gules and argent   Motto: Artibus et
armis   Date below motto: 1763
For Sarah, dau. of Samuel Peach, who m. 1763, as his first wife, Isaac
Elton, and d. 15 Dec. 1763.   (B.P. 1949 ed.)

2. All black background (should be dexter black)
Elton, impaling, Azure two lions rampant respectant or supporting a
sword in pale argent hilted or (Tierney)
Crest, mantling and motto: As 1.   Date below motto: 1790
For Isaac Elton, who m. 2nd, 1768, Ann, dau. of James Tierney, and d.
31 Mar. 1790. She d. 13 Aug. 1816.   (B.P. 1949 ed.)
(There is another hatchment for Isaac Elton in the church of SS Philip
and Jacob, Bristol)

3. All black background (should be dexter black)
Elton, impaling, Azure a chevron and in base a horse rampant argent
(Bayard)
Crest, mantling and motto: As 1. Date below motto: 1837
For Isaac Elton, who m. 1794, Catherine, dau. of Robert Bayard, and d.
19 Apr. 1837. She d. 10 Feb. 1853.   (B.P. 1949 ed.)

4. Sinister background black
Elton, impaling, Azure a chevron between three molets or
(Chetwynd)   On a shield suspended from a lover's knot with sprays
of leaves in saltire below; cherubs' heads on both sides and below; also
below shield 1866
For Mary Henrietta, dau. of Richard Walter, 6th Viscount Chetwynd,
who m. Robert James Elton, and d. 30 Nov. 1866. He d. 28 Feb.
1869.   (B.P. 1949 ed.)

5. Dexter background black
Elton, impaling, Chequy azure and argent on a fess argent three
escallops azure (   )
Crest, mantling and motto: As 1.   Cherub's head below
Unidentified

6. All brown background
Argent a lion rampant between five cross crosslets fitchy gules (Brett)
Crest: On a chapeau gules and argent a lion statant tail extended
gules   Mantling: Gules and argent ending in tassels or

Frame decorated with skulls, leaves and roundels   A 17th century
hatchment
Unidentified

WOOLLEY
1. Sinister background black
Or three roundels gules (Courtney), impaling, Sable three conies
courant argent (Cunliffe)
For Elizabeth, dau. of Sir Robert Cunliffe, 2nd Bt., who m. 1782,
Clement Stafford Courtney, and was bur. 30 June 1835. (B.P. 1949 ed.;
P.R.)

2. All black background
Arms: As 1.
Crest: From a ducal coronet or a dolphin embowed
argent   Mantling: Gules and argent   Motto: Tout en Dieu
For Clement Stafford Courtney, who was bur. 17 May
1836.   (Sources, as 1.)

3. Sinister background black
Per fess gules and azure three bezants (Cabanel), impaling, Or on a
chief embattled sable three bezants (Lee)
For Margaret Ann, dau. of Robert Lee, of Louth, Lincolnshire, who m.
Daniel Cabanel (d. 22 Aug. 1857), and d. 2 June 1846, aged
79.   (Sources, as 1.; M.I.)

YEOVIL
1. All black background
Qly, 1st and 4th, Or a fess engrailed azure between three escallops
gules (Prynne), 2nd and 3rd, Azure two chevronels ermine between three
martlets argent (Hunt)
Crests: Dexter, From an Eastern coronet or a demi-eagle rising proper,
winged argent   Sinister, A dexter arm embowed vested gules cuffed
argent the hand holding a pink rose slipped and leaved
proper   Mantling: Gules and argent   Motto: Resurgam
Perhaps for George Bragge Prinn, of Charlton Park, Glos., and of
Yeovil, who d. 1839, aged 72.   (M.I.)

2. All black background
Azure a chevron ermine between three anchors erect or (Batten),
impaling, Or a saltire sable, on a chief sable three escallops argent
(Copeland)
Helm, but no discernible crest   Mantling: Gules and
argent   Motto: Resurgam
For John Batten, who m. 1813, Sarah, dau. and co-heiress of John
Copeland, and d. 27 June 1854.   (B.L.G. 1937 ed.; M.I.)

3. Dexter background black

Azure a saltire voided between four spearheads erect or (Harbin)
Crest: A cubit arm sable holding a spur or   Mantling: Gules and
argent   Motto: Resurgam
Unidentified

SELECT BIBLIOGRAPHY

P. G. Summers, *How to read a Coat of Arms* (National Council of Social Service, 1967), 17-20.

P. G. Summers, *The Genealogists' Magazine*, vol. 12, No. 13 (1958), 443-446.

T. D. S. Bayley and F. W. Steer, 'Painted Heraldic Panels', in *Antiquaries Journal*, vol. 35 (1955), 68-87.

L. B. Ellis, 'Royal Hatchments in City Churches', in *London and Middlesex Arch. Soc. Transactions* (New Series, vol. 10, 1948), 24-30 (contains extracts from a herald-painter's work-book relating to hatchments and 18th-century funerals).

C. A. Markham, 'Hatchments', in *Northampton & Oakham Architectural Soc. Proceedings*, vol. 20, Pt. 2 (1912), 673-687.

INDEX

180

Digby, Jane Elizabeth, 83
Dillon, Luke, 124
Dirdoe, Frances, 47
Dive, Beatrix, 53
Dodington, 160
Doughty, Sir Edward (9th Bt.), 123
Doughty-Tichborne, Sir James (10th
 Bt.), 123
Drake, Charlotte Elizabeth, 86
Draper, Mary, 109
Drax, Sarah Frances, 53
Drewe, Emma Louisa, 156
Drewe, Mary, 154, 156
Dyer, Gen. Sir Thomas (7th Bt.),
 117
Dysart, Wilbraham, 6th Earl of, 137

Eastmount, Dorothy, 168
Edwards, Elizabeth, 108
Edwards, Mary, 33
Edwards, Mary Ann, 105
Elcho, Francis, Lord, 84
Eliot, Elizabeth, 75
Eliot, William (2nd Earl of St
 Germans), 11
Eliott, Francis (2nd Baron
 Heathfield), 38
Ellenborough, Edward, 1st Earl of,
 83
Ellis, Mary Ann, 158
Elton, 171
Elton, Isaac, 70, 171
Elton, Robert James, 171
Erington, Mary, 115
Erle-Drax, Richard Edward, 53
Erle-Drax-Grosvenor, Jane, 44
Erle-Drax-Grosvenor, Richard, 53
Evans, Catherine Brandreth, 153
Eversley, Charles, 1st Viscount, 111
Eyre, George, 99

Fairbridge, Mary, 140
Fane, Rear-Adm. Francis William,
 50
Farrell, Elizabeth, 162
Fenwick, Susan, 149
Fielder, Mary, 141
Filiol, Lieut., 52

Fitzgerald, Eleanor, 120
Fitzroy, Georgiana Frederica, 67
Fleming, Dorothy, 137
Fletcher, Sarah, 80
Flint, Anne, 50
Floyer, Anthony, 59
Fortescue, Lady Elizabeth, 32
Fortescue, Hugh, 1st Earl, 36
Forward, Agnes, 45
Fothergill, Elizabeth, 160
Fownes-Luttrell, Henry, 156
Fox, Jane, 138
Foxcroft, Frances, 69
Fox-Strangways, Henry (3rd Earl of
 Ilchester), 43
Fox-Strangways, William (4th Earl
 of Ilchester), 43
Frampton, 115
Fraunceis, Amy, 46
Freeman, Frances, 167
Freke, Susannah, 29
Frome, Mary, 159
Fuller-Eliott-Drake, Sir Thomas
 (1st Bt.), 38
Furse, 26
Furse, Philip, 27

Gamon, Anne Eliza, 94
Garrard, Emily, 125
Gascoyne, Frances Mary, 45
Gaulis, Albertina Marianna, 8
Gennys, Mary, 32
Gibbs, 71
Gibbs, James, 71
Gifford, 160
Gist, Samuel Gist, 88
Glengall, Richard, 2nd Earl of, 165
Glisson, Gilbert, 52
Gollop, Elizabeth, 52
Goodden, Elizabeth, 55
Goodden, Robert, 54
Goodden, Wyndham, 55
Goodlake, John Hughes, 87
Gordon, 70
Gore, Rev. Charles, 150
Gould, Mary, 45
Gould, Sarah, 59
Graves, Elizabeth Anne, 81

Graves, Morgan, 80
Graves, Rev. Richard Morgan, 81
Graves, Walwyn, 80
Greathed, Edward, 47
Grenville, Hester (Baroness
 Chatham), 155
Grenville, Hester, 36
Grenville, Richard (1st Duke of
 Buckingham and Chandos), 93
Grose, Capt. Edward, 141
Grose, Sir Nash, 141
Grose-Smith, Edward, 141
Grove, Elizabeth, 103
Grove, Harriet, 152
Guise, Sir John (1st Bt.), 77
Guise, Gen. Sir John (4th Bt.), 78
Guise, Sir William (4th Bt.), 78
Guitton, Elizabeth, 121
Guitton, Mary Anne, 121
Gulston, Elizabeth, 103
Gurdon, Elizabeth, 162
Gurnell, Mary Anne, 6
Gwillim, Elizabeth Posthuma, 37
Gwillim, Thomas, 37
Gwyn, Francis, 46, 47

Hale, 66
Hale, Robert Hale Blagden, 66
Halford, Eleanor, 38
Hall, Elizabeth, 33
Hall, Humphrey, 32
Halsey, Sophia, 44
Hambrough, John, 142, 143
Hamilton, Katherine Jane, 101
Hammond, Ursula Mary, 35
Harbin, 172
Harbin, Abigail, 54
Harbin, Margaret, 161
Harris, 29
Harris, Christopher, 29
Harris, Lady Frances, 112
Harris, Jane, 107
Harvey, John, 135
Hassell, Jane, 159
Hastings, Hans (12th Earl of
 Huntingdon), 97
Hawker, Ann, 167
Hawker, William, 167

Hawkins, Elizabeth, 166
Hawkins, Grace, 11
Hawkins, John, 9
Hawley, Henry William, 110, 111
Hay, Lady Elizabeth, 122
Hayes, Anna Maria, 99
Hayne, Charles, 20
Hayne, Sarah, 22
Hearle, Harriet, 11
Heathfield, Francis, 2nd Baron, 38
Hedges, Thomas, 152
Hele, 27
Helyar, William, 152
Henn-Gennys, Edmund, 32
Henning, Dorothy, 46
Herbert, Charles, 102
Herbert, Henry (2nd Earl of
 Carnarvon), 102
Herbert, Henry (3rd Earl of
 Carnarvon), 102
Hereford, Edward, 12th Viscount,
 84
Herring, Harriet, 116
Hervey, Louisa, 12
Hickes, Jane, 87
Hickman, Martha, 23
Hicks, 85
Hill, 69
Hill, Vice-Adm. Henry, 133
Hinxman, 104
Hinxman, Joseph, 103
Hodge, Mary, 10
Holden, Catherine, 142
Holdsworth, Arthur, 21
Holford, 73
Holland, Swinton Colthurst, 75
Holmes, Hon. Catherine, 144
Holmes, Hon. Elizabeth, 135
Holmes, Henry, 143
Holmes, Martha, 108
Holmes, Mary, 143
Holmes, Thomas, Baron, 144
Home, 113
Honywood, Annabella Christiana,
 72
Hooper, Abigail, 168
Horne, Mary, 154
Horsley, Margaret Jane, 79